A History of

A History of London

ROBERT GRAY

Taplinger Publishing Company | New York

First published in 1979 by
TAPLINGER PUBLISHING CO., Inc.
New York, New York

LIBRARY OF CONGRESS CATALOGING IN PUBLICATION DATA

Gray, Robert.
    A history of London.

    Bibliography: p.
    1.   London—History.   I.   Title.
DA677.G66   1979   942.1'2   78-22605
ISBN 0-8008-3884-X (cloth)
ISBN 0-8008-3885-8 (pbk.)

Printed in the United States of America

9 8 7 6 5 4 3 2

'If it was esteemed an honour among the
Greeks to be born in Athens, if among
the Italians to be a Roman, if among
the Spaniards to be a Toledano, why
should it be a lesse honour for an
Englishman to be born in London?'

JAMES HOWELL, *Londinopolis*, 1657

Contents

List of maps and diagrams

Introduction

'Have I not enough without your mountains?'

Nothing fosters a love of London so effectively as familiarity and knowledge. Without them the visitor (or indeed the Londoner) may well find entertainments to enjoy but he is hardly likely to form any strong attachment to the capital. Such places as museums, art galleries, theatres, concert halls and night clubs do not convey any distinct impression of London; no more do international hotels. But let anyone turn from the town's amusements to the town itself and his understanding and appreciation immediately become dependent on a sure sense of context.

Of course that is true of all cities, but especially so of London. There are certainly other capitals which make a more immediate impact – New York with its skyscrapers and vitality, Rome with its antiquities and its beauty, Paris with its spacious grandeur and romantic reputation. London, by contrast, is an acquired pleasure, a town that invites discovery rather than demands admiration. If there is little splendour to compel instant respect, neither is there much stately formality to discourage more intimate association. At first it may seem a problem to find one's bearings amidst such an apparently shapeless urban mass, but a day or two can suffice to break the circle of bewilderment and to kindle an inexhaustible fascination. For just learning to get about the town provokes a host of enquiries – why, how, when did these hundreds of miles of street appear? – and questions straightway bring the asker within the ambit of London's spell. By answering some of them this book aims to contribute to the process of bewitchment.

Obviously the manner in which the town grew must be the prime theme. London began when the Roman legions bridged the Thames (sixty or so yards downstream from the present London Bridge) shortly after their arrival in AD 43. They thereby concentrated land and sea communications at that one point, and turned an unpromising looking site into the main British port for Continental traffic. The easy access to Europe by way of the Thames across the North Sea was always the basis of London's prosperity. But a thousand years after the Roman conquest there was another beginning, when Edward the Confessor (1042–66) abandoned the town which had sided with his enemies and established a royal palace a mile and a half away to the south-west on the Isle of Thorney, 'that terrible place', where he was rebuilding Westminster Abbey.

For six more centuries London and Westminster remained entirely distinct, except for the bishops' and nobles' palaces which came to line the river between the two places. By 1600 the westward expansion of London had proceeded no further than Holborn; beyond was pasture-land. During the Civil War (1642–6) the city wall which had first been built by the Romans still formed the inner ring of London's defences, while the gates therein – Aldgate, Bishopsgate, Moorgate, Cripplegate, Aldersgate, Newgate and Ludgate were not demolished until the second half of the eighteenth century. Even today the area of medieval London, with boundaries not greatly altered from those agreed in the thirteenth century, is still known simply as 'the City', in proud defiance of the vast metropolis which now surrounds it.

The City and Westminster, moreover, each retain something of the different character conferred by their origins. Although the port has now moved further down the Thames in order to accommodate modern shipping, the City's prestige as a financial centre is a direct offshoot of its former trading activities. And although Henry VIII was the last king to live in the palace between the river and the Abbey, Westminster is still the centre of the country's government.

Wealth and power, though, are apt to make jealous neighbours. Throughout the Middle Ages kings who were desperate for money continually wrangled with merchants who were not inclined to lend it without extracting privileges for themselves and their City. The consequent struggle was fierce and no monarch chose to remain for any length of time in the City unless at the Tower, which had been specially built as a security against the citizen's hostility, and which was in any case strictly speaking outside the town's limits. By the early thirteenth century the City had gained royal recognition of its right to order its own affairs through an elected mayor, and the privilege has been so zealously maintained that even today the City still governs itself independently of the rest of the capital. Yet what now appears as a quaint survival was once a matter of momentous import. Time and time again the drift of national events was determined by the Crown's failure to control the City. Indeed the prized liberties of the English may be in considerable degree attributed to the persistent avarice of London's merchant class.

But for all their antagonism the fortunes of Westminster and the City were indissolubly linked. Eventually, like a squabbling couple doomed to proximity, and anyway too dependent on each other to make a final break, they gave birth to the urban monster that now encompasses them. In the sixteenth century began a steady building expansion which has pushed the limits of the town further and further out, always tending to carry the weight of population away from the centre to the fringes of the town. Even before the Great Fire of 1666 devastated the medieval City, there were probably more people living outside than inside its limits. Thereafter 'London', which had for so long been synonymous with the City, came to embrace not only Westminster and the nearby villages such as Marylebone, Kensington and Chelsea, but also huge tracts of the surrounding counties. The pace of building became ever faster until the town actually quadrupled its area in the twenty-one years between the World Wars. The Second World War helped to establish a 'green belt' of countryside twenty to twenty-five miles from the centre of London, but this barrier has in no wise contained the centrifugal force. Over the last thirty years population within the ring formed by the 'green belt' has been drawn off to the areas beyond, so that the London region may now be reckoned to have a forty-mile radius.

Yet 'London' is officially taken to mean only about an eighth of that area, the six-hundred-odd square miles which come under the jurisdiction of the Greater London Council (see map on page 296). It is not surprising to discover that the administrative framework has always lagged behind the phenomenal explosion of the town, but it *does* seem astonishing that right up to 1889 London scarcely possessed a government at all. The City doggedly refused to acknowledge responsibility for the town beyond its limits, yet no ministry dared to antagonize so powerful an interest by creating another London authority. So, and this is possibly the single most important point about London's development, the metropolis grew according to the whims of private capital, relatively untrammelled by the restraints and plans of monarchs or bureaucrats. That is why a closer knowledge of London forever reveals new quirks, oddities and delights that reflect the avarice, ideals, competence and taste of those who have owned the land.

But of course individualism is not confined to landlords, nor is London's history only concerned with the town's physical development. It is also about the Londoners and how they lived. The challenge is not just to explain what happened (any account will be unavoidably selective in the face of such teeming complexity), but also to make it seem real, to bring the reader properly back to date. This is not always easy, for the passing centuries can completely change an area's character. It needs a powerful imagination, for instance, to conjure up a monastic precinct on ground off Fleet Street now occupied by the *News of the World* newspaper. Yet even there a clue exists in the name Whitefriars; and almost everywhere in London the ingenious explorer will be able to find such leads, which, whether they be street names, building styles, boundary lines of parishes, underground rivers or whatever, will help him to piece together a mental image of what the area must have been like in former times.

And always, when the imagination begins to juggle with time and space, there will be shades crowding forward to people its creations, even as they haunt existing buildings. St Margaret Westminster, for example, a beautiful six-teenth-century church in the shadow of the Abbey, is a popular choice for society weddings – yet what contem-porary match, however dazzling, can charge the atmosphere so dramatically as the knowledge that three hundred years and more ago both John Milton and Samuel Pepys were married in the selfsame spot? (Pepys at least never allowed the memory of this event to prevent him from casting an appraising eye over other female worshippers on his subsequent visits to the church.) Again, however elegant the steeple of Wren's St Bride's by Fleet Street, readers of Boswell's *London Journal* may find themselves smiling at the ring of the bells, and remembering how in 1763 they sounded in that amorist's ear as, once more in search of 'the melting and transporting rites of love', he drove towards the nearby Black Lion Inn with the doubtfully refined Louisa. His somewhat ill-received remark that 'this night the bells in Cupid's court would be set a-ringing at our union' was triumphantly proved by the 'luscious feast' which she afforded, inspiring Boswell to write in unabashed admiration of his own prowess and (later) to seek medical assistance for a seemingly inexplicable malady. Or, to take another building at random, the presence of the French Protestant church in Soho Square might put the passer-by in mind of the Huguenots who settled in the area (and in Spitalfields) after the Revocation of the Edict of Nantes (1685). As a great port London has always been a cosmopolitan town, though in the past, at least, it was certainly not a hospitable one. A French Catholic who in 1765 found himself roundly abused at every street corner – 'notwithstanding the simplicity of my dress' – was quick to conclude that the Huguenots must have given his country a bad name. But his self-assured Gallic reasoning had failed to take the full measure of a xenophobia that will constantly recur throughout these pages. For the truth was that the Huguenots were hardworking and sober craftsmen whose Protestantism partially mitigated in Londoners' eyes the irredeemable iniquity of being French.

Only the genius of the dead can leap out of the darkness as vividly as their foibles and prejudices. Anyone seeking loftier company than that so far encountered can think of the eight-year-old Mozart writing his first symphony at 180

Ebury Street: or of Handel being visited at 25 Brook Street by that blaze of inspiration that produced the *Messiah* in three weeks; or of Wagner walking across Kensington Gardens from a friend's house at Number 12 Orme Square to conduct his own works at the Albert Hall. Voltaire once lodged in Maiden Lane and, on the other side of the Strand, his arch enemy Rousseau quarrelled with the philosopher Hume in Buckingham Street. Tolstoy pronounced that London inspired him with a profound disgust for modern life, but very likely even heaven is producing a similar impression in that angry mind. An easier man was Benjamin Franklin, whose Duke Street landlady reduced the rent by more than half to retain the pleasure of his company; and no doubt another transatlantic visitor, Mark Twain, added considerably to the merriment at Brown's Hotel. Van Gogh spent the happiest year (1873-4) of his unhappy life in London, with a job at a gallery in Southampton Street off the Strand and lodgings at 87 Hackford Road, Lambeth, until, alas, he discovered that the landlady's daughter was already betrothed to another. A far harsher character once lived at 18 Dean Street, Soho: there Karl Marx further complicated his struggles against capitalism by making his servant pregnant. And further north, in St Pancras, Lenin was astonished in 1902 by the sudden arrival of Trotsky, until then only a name to him, at his rooms in 30 Holford Square (now demolished and the site of a school between the Pentonville Road and Percy Circus).

Such a list could be multiplied almost at will, and it contains only foreigners. In central London there is hardly a street without a blue plaque recalling some famous inhabitant. More sobering reflections on the frailty of the worldly great are available at St Peter-ad-Vincula in the Tower where lie any number of distinguished men and women who fell victim to the Tudor monarchs' (and particularly to

Henry VIII's) penchant for truncating the persons as well as the careers of those who incurred their ire. Before the high altar Henry's two beheaded queens (Anne Boleyn and Catherine Howard) flank two dukes (Somerset and Northumberland) who suffered in the succeeding reigns. Nearby lies a third beheaded queen whose 'reign' only lasted nine days), Northumberland's beautiful and talented daughter-in-law Lady Jane Grey, who in 1554 at the age of sixteen shared the inevitable consequences of his attempt to wrest the throne from the Tudors. The church might also be deemed a likely spot for miracles as no fewer than three Catholic saints (Thomas More, John Fisher and Philip Howard) are buried there, by courtesy of Henry VIII and Elizabeth I.

But to populate the past exclusively with the great is to risk missing the infinite variety of London's story. It is, after all, the vast mass of anonymous Londoners who have borne the great pageant towards us over nineteen centuries. At the beginning the scenery and plot seem entirely foreign; then gradually the familiar props appear and the outline becomes more distinct; then suddenly here we are, speaking our lines, living out our parts . . . and making our exits as the show rumbles on to someone else's present. Truly in remembering the millions of obscure we are pleading for ourselves.

So, if we allow our imagination to simper after the strumpets of fortune who littered Charles II's St James's, let us not eschew less highly rewarded practitioners like Joan Jolybody, common bawd, who plied her trade in fifteenth-century London. If we picture ourselves conversing brilliantly with Macaulay and company at Holland House let us not deny ourselves the rowdier pleasures of Vauxhall Gardens. If we follow Shakespeare's great bald dome of a head across London Bridge to the

Globe Theatre let us mingle also with the reeking ground-lings for whom he wrote. If we hurry after Charles Dickens as he prowls through the slums by night let us be sure to peer as keenly as he into the filthy crowded courts. If we watch Dr Johnson springing away 'with a kind of pathetick briskness' into Bolt Court after his last farewell to Boswell, let us also stand under the arches in front of Victoria Station where the troops are spending their last moments with their wives before returning to the trenches of the First World War. If we gasp at the beheading of Charles I in Whitehall let us also jostle among the mob gathered to crow over the obscenely barbarous executions at Tyburn (Marble Arch). And if we follow the Duke of Wellington's catafalque into St Paul's let us also witness the plague victims being shovelled unceremoniously into the pits.

'Have I not enough without your mountains?' Charles Lamb once enquired of Wordsworth. He was referring to the buzz, excitement and activity of London, which gave him such joy. And for many, even the still, sad music of humanity will echo more loudly in the press of the town than among the meadows and the woods and the mountains.

Acknowledgements

My greatest debt is to Julian Watson, who not only gave me the chance to write this book but also, as editor, supplied the immense amount of enthusiasm, encouragement, advice, kindness, severity and psychiatric counselling required to make me finish by about the third deadline. Though he may often work less hard for greater results, he will assuredly never earn more heartfelt gratitude from an author.

The commission would hardly have come my way without the intermediacy of Harriet Waugh, whose notion of friendship extended even unto urging the transcendent merits of my prose. So I render all thanks to her, and to Emily Wheeler, who subjected that same prose to her eagle gaze and even prevailed on me to remove some of its infelicities. The maps and diagrams are the fruit of Rodney Paull's patient and skilful labours.

I would also like to record my appreciation of the unfailing courtesy and helpfulness of the staff at the Museum of London, which should be the first port of call (via Barbican station) for anyone interested in London's history.

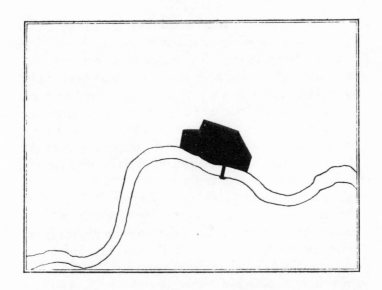

1. 'Famed for commerce and crowded with traders'
[Beginnings to 410]

A CITY BUILT ON GRAVELS

Throughout the Middle Ages, and even later, it was widely believed that London had once been inhabited by giants, a legend which derived from the massive bones which were occasionally unearthed in and around the City. Sometimes these finds were put on display in City churches: during the sixteenth century, for instance, St Mary Aldermary exhibited a huge thigh-bone, 'more than after the proportion of five shank bones of any man now living', together with a twelve-foot drawing of a Goliath-like figure to assist the ignorant public in the work of reconstruction.

As the bonds of credulity began to loosen after the Reformation, however, a more sceptical strain appeared in the reports of antiquaries. John Stow, who lived between 1525 and 1605, described an immense thigh-bone of a man '(as it is taken)', which he had seen as a boy in St Lawrence's Jewry, adding a footnote with the suggestion that it 'might be that of an Oliphant'. This inspired guess received support at the end of the seventeenth century when an amateur archaeologist named John Conyers dug up 'the body of an elephant' from a site now covered by King's Cross Road, near Granville Square. In fact it was a mammoth, but as the discovery included a pair of tusks there could at least be no mistaking the skeleton for that of a giant.

But how on earth had 'elephants' come to be in London? For a while this puzzle seemed satisfactorily answered by the timely remembrance that the Emperor Claudius had brought elephants to Britain on his triumphal visit in AD 43. This explanation, however, carried less and less conviction as further finds made the soil of London seem like a veritable zoo burial ground. The Emperor Claudius could hardly have brought the woolly rhinoceros uncovered in Leadenhall Street, the hippopotamus that had once languished on the ground under Waterloo Place, or the lions that had breathed their last on the site of Trafalgar Square.

Actually these (and many other) discoveries did offer certain clues towards solving the mystery of the animals' presence. For instance, the various bones belonged to species divisible into two distinct groups, one consisting of creatures like hippopotami and lions naturally adapted to warm climates, the other of animals such as mammoths and musk oxen at home in arctic temperatures. Further, the remains were found at different levels in the gravel patches overlying the London clay, indicating that gravels and skeletons dated from the same period. It was also noticeable that the creatures preferring hot conditions were found at the top, and those insulated against the cold at the bottom, of the gravel layers. But the significance of these observations could not be appreciated as long as the book of Genesis was accepted as an authoritative account of the earth's origin.

On the immense geological time-scale which replaced that of the Bible, London's ground is relatively young. The thick clay that can still frustrate gardeners was laid down between seventy to forty million years ago, at the bottom of a muddy sea which filled the declivity in the earlier chalk now known as the London basin. Over the succeeding aeons, right up to about two million years ago, the sea continued to advance and retreat over the area, although few of its deposits from this era remain. Yet if clay had remained the only surface soil London could never have existed. In its natural state clay supported dense oak forest like that still found at Epping, twelve miles to the north-east of the City. But clay does not drain well, so that where it forms the riverside terrain, or is covered only by alluvial muds, the ground is naturally swampy, a more fitting habitat for marsh birds than for men. The unembanked Thames was continually flooding, and was in any case both shallower and wider, as the boat-rings on the eighteenth-century Somerset House, which now stands back from the river, still testify.

It was the gravels that made London possible. Not only did these sections drain better; they were also covered with lighter woodland than the clay, and were therefore easier to move across and to clear. But the importance of the gravel was by no means confined to the prehistoric period.

Its presence is indicated in place names like Putney, Battersea, Chelsea and Hackney: in Anglo-Saxon the '–ea' and '–ey' endings signify 'islands' above the surrounding marsh. Westminster Abbey and Palace once stood in isolation on what was then called the Isle of Thorney, this particular 'island' being a patch of gravel hemmed in by the Thames and the twin streams of the river Tyburn. The swampy ground to the south and west of Westminster – Pimlico and Victoria – was not built on until the nineteenth century. Moorfields, one of the few parts of the City without gravel, was not effectively drained until the seventeenth century, although it lay only just to the north of the Roman wall. Even today the district contains most of the City's green spaces: Finsbury Circus and Square, Bunhill Fields and the Artillery Ground. Over most of London, however, the gravels are so widespread (see the diagram below) that it was scarcely necessary to build on clay before the nineteenth century.

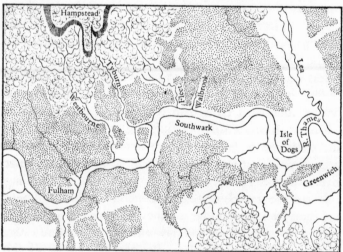

The London area before the houses, enclosed by forest. The dots show the presence of the Thames gravels.

ARRIVAL OF THE GRAVELS, AND OF MAN

Like so many subsequent benefits enjoyed by the capital, the favourable terrain was conferred by the river Thames. What was arguably the most important event in London's history occurred roughly three-quarters of a million years before any building appeared on the site, when the Thames began to flow on its present course through the area. Previously its line had been ten miles to the north, through Finchley, but this route became blocked during the Ice Ages. That was as far south as the ice sheets ever reached in Britain, but very far from being the limit of their influence either on the Thames or on the future town.

As the plural suggests, the Ice Ages were not one prolonged million-year freeze-up, but a series of cold periods interspersed with warm intervals, one of which actually lasted more than 200 000 years. It was the effect of these alternating climatic eras on rivers that caused the deposition of gravel. During the cold millennia, the rain that fell on land was not returned to the sea by rivers, but was piled up as ice; as a result, the sea level went down. The Thames, too far south to be frozen permanently, thus had to make a steeper descent to reach the sea. Following the laws of gravity it flowed faster and eventually eroded a deeper channel corresponding to the lower sea level. But when the ice melted with the return of milder conditions, the sea rose – though never in fact quite regaining its former height – and the Thames began to flow sluggishly, flooding over wide areas. Pebbles and other particles which had been rolled along the river bed when the current had been swift now came to rest on the flood-plain.

The repetition of this process has left gravels at four levels in the central London area – at one hundred, fifty, twenty-

five and ten feet above present sea level – these heights being
those of the river's flood-plain in the warm periods between
glaciations (see the diagram below). Most of the slopes in
central London are between one gravel 'terrace' and another:
for instance, to walk up St James's Street, or up Exhibition

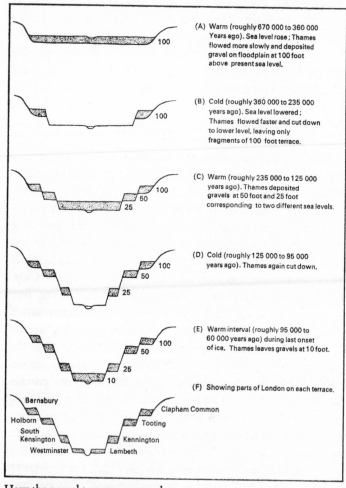

(A) Warm (roughly 670 000 to 360 000 Years ago). Sea level rose; Thames flowed more slowly and deposited gravel on floodplain at 100 foot above present sea level.

(B) Cold (roughly 360 000 to 235 000 years ago). Sea level lowered; Thames flowed faster and cut down to lower level, leaving only fragments of 100 foot terrace.

(C) Warm (roughly 235 000 to 125 000 years ago). Thames deposited gravels at 50 foot and 25 foot corresponding to two different sea levels.

(D) Cold (roughly 125 000 to 95 000 years ago). Thames again cut down.

(E) Warm interval (roughly 95 000 to 60 000 years ago) during last onset of ice. Thames leaves gravels at 10 foot.

(F) Showing parts of London on each terrace.

How the gravel terraces appeared.

Road from South Kensington station to Kensington Gardens (past the Geological Museum which contains an excellent wall-map showing the precise position of the various London gravels), is to move from the twenty-five foot to the fifty-foot terrace.

It is entirely logical, then, that the sun-loving animals should have been found at the bottom and middle of the gravel layers, whereas the position of the mammoths nearer the surface reflects the end of deposition with the onset of another cold period. As Britain was joined to the Continent until 8000 years ago, the various animals were able to come and go as the changes in temperature dictated. It was around half a million years ago that a strange new two-legged species began to wander into the London region.

Man, or ape-man, soon found that the Thames gravels provided both flints from which to fashion primitive weapons and prey on which to use them. The earliest quasi-human skull discovered in Britain, with a brain capacity equal to that of a modern man, was unearthed from the river gravels at Swanscombe in Kent, while in London itself a flint hand-axe was found close to the King's Cross mammoth and another under Leadenhall Street in the City. The original owners of these tools did not, of course, live in any one place: for hundreds of thousands of years man's predecessors were a rare species in the area, struggling to keep alive by hunting across the gravels. Around 50 000 years ago appeared a new variety of the breed named *Homo sapiens*; and only over the last 6000 years in Britain has this creature learnt to produce enough food with sufficient certainty to make fixed communities possible. Even then, there is no evidence of London – that is, a permanent settlement on the site of the City – having existed before the second Roman invasion of AD 43. By contrast, the gravels at Barnes, Hammersmith, Fulham, Wandsworth, Chelsea and

Battersea have all yielded signs of pre-Roman occupation, and there was a sizable Celtic village on the site of Heathrow airport.

THE THAMES: A LINK WITH EUROPE

Of course the absence of any remains from a pre-Roman London may simply mean that they have perished in the course of the innumerable upheavals of the ground for building purposes. The name 'London' is certainly of pre-Roman origin and has been connected with a word meaning 'wild' or 'bold' in the language of the Celtic tribes that lived in Britain: conceivably the adjective described someone associated with the area. But there would have been no *compelling* attraction about a site which was, as a name like St John's Wood still reminds us, hemmed in by forest. The gravels made London possible but then did not of themselves ordain its appearance in any particular place. Indeed, if it is difficult for us to imagine the desolate scrubland on which the town rose, an ancient Briton would have needed prophetic genius to envisage its destiny.

With a map of Europe to hand, however, he would only have needed common sense to predict a port somewhere along the Thames. Although in remote prehistoric times such trade as existed had been along routes to the west of Britain, well before the Romans arrived the island's commerce was mainly directed towards northern Europe. As the Thames estuary faced that of the Rhine (into which river the Thames in fact once flowed across the North Sea land), it provided unrivalled access to the Continent, and especially to the Low Countries, which would become the richest part of Europe in the Middle Ages. Moreover the Thames's position halfway between the Baltic and the Mediterranean, two natural spheres of trade, meant that a port on its banks would be ideally placed to become the point of exchange between them.

These excellent sea communications were the more valuable because, right up to the age of the railway, water transport was really the sole means of moving bulky goods over long distances. After the Great Fire of 1666, for example, building wood was cheaper and easier to obtain from the Baltic than from Britain's forests. Nearly all England's ancient towns were on navigable streams: exceptions like Shaftesbury, Malvern and Old Sarum are not notable examples of urban vigour. It was almost inevitable that the Thames, which offered the best water transport, should have the biggest town on its banks. Yet people talk of 'London's river' as though the Thames owed its fame to the happy chance of running through the capital. The truth is that for centuries London owed its wealth to each ebb and flow of the tide. 'The river's London' would more accurately describe a relationship that was clearer before 1800, when Londoners were accustomed to seeing a forest of masts in the very heart of the City. When, in the sixteenth century, Bloody Mary vented her fury with the capital by threatening to move Parliament and the Law Courts ('Terme') to Oxford, an alderman countered with the innocent query 'whether she meant also to divert the River of Thames from London, or no?' Being satisfied on this point he roundly declared: 'Then by God's grace we shall do well enough at London, whatsoever become of the Terme and Parliament.'

But this is to run ahead. The key question has yet to be answered – why was the Thames's port established so far upstream?

THE FIRST BRIDGE

It was the construction of a bridge across the Thames by

the Roman invaders shortly after their arrival in AD 43 which, by concentrating land and sea communications at one point, fixed the precise position of the port. Yet even the Romans can scarcely be said to have *chosen* the site. They had landed at Richborough, on the east coast of Kent, and the main centre of British resistance was at Colchester, in eastern Essex. Between the two forces lay the barrier of the Thames estuary. Clearly, if the Romans were to sustain effective pressure on the British stronghold, a secure and easy crossing of the Thames was a first necessity – and the further downstream the better, as this would shorten the march of the legions coming from the south on their way to Colchester.

The rest was dictated by the facts of geography. The site for a bridge must have firm ground, sufficiently raised to be safe from floods, on both sides of the river. Such conditions were common enough along the northern bank but far less so to the south. The land of the lower Thames remained a malarial swamp throughout the Middle Ages, and was not in the main reclaimed for industry until the last century. The Romans built their bridge a little to the east of the present London Bridge, as near as practicable to the sea. To the south of the bridge the land on which Southwark subsequently rose has always been liable to flooding, but a thin strip of gravel running towards the Thames ensured a passable approach. Today, though the Roman ground level is thirty feet below the surface, Duke Street Hill still rises on to this strip from the east. As a road it is unremarkable enough, but there is no more significant incline in London.

There was another consideration in favour of this site. The Romans were skilled bridge-builders: Caesar reports that their engineers once spanned the Rhine in ten days. But as their techniques had been learnt in Italy, where the rivers flow into the tideless Mediterranean, they did not want to risk contending with a tide. On the other hand, they needed to cross as far downstream as possible and thus favoured a site just beyond the tidal limit, which was then, by a happy coincidence, very near the gravel spit at South-wark.

Had it remained there London would have been spared countless flooding disasters. Since Roman times, south-east England has gradually subsided, while the sea, due to ice melting in the Arctic Circle, has risen considerably. At Tilbury, twenty-five miles downstream from London Bridge, some Romano-British wattle huts built on dry land sixteen centuries ago now lie thirteen feet below high-water mark, which means that the sea has been encroaching at an average rate of nine inches a century. It is not yet clear whether or not the Ice Ages have ended; the matter is of some significance, though, since it has been alarmingly calculated that if all the ice at the earth's poles were to melt, the sea would top Nelson's column in Trafalgar Square.

Beside such reckoning, the thirteen feet which now separate low and high water at London Bridge may not seem much, but the effects have certainly not been negligible. Although the flood defences have risen from century to century they have never succeeded in containing the Thames for long. In reality the river's variations have been enormous. As late as 1114 there was 'so great an ebb tide everywhere in one day . . . so that men went riding and walking over the Thames eastward of London Bridge'. Yet from 1236, when watermen were rowing their boats inside Westminster Hall, to 1953, when the Thames flooded huge areas of Essex and lapped the very top of the Victoria Embankment, Londoners have rarely been long without some destructive evidence of the sea's rise. Medieval churchmen added insult to injury by attributing the flooding to the Almighty's wrath with the evil lives of Londoners. Gradually, though, more scientific attitudes prevailed. On 7 December 1663, the diarist Samuel Pepys recorded 'the greatest tide that was ever remembered in England to have been seen in this river, all of Whitehall having been drowned'. Very likely the general memory did not deceive. Today the tidal limit is nineteen miles from London Bridge, and would be even further upstream but for the weir at Teddington. A tidal barrier is now being built at Woolwich which may or may not be completed in time to spare London another flooding disaster.

About the first bridge, the structure which created London, extraordinarily little is known. The earliest reference to London Bridge is from the tenth century, when some unfortunate woman was drowned there for being a witch. No definite remains of the Roman bridge have been discovered and even our knowledge of its existence depends chiefly on deduction from the subsequent growth of the City, and from the alignment of Roman roads towards that crossing place. Further confirmation came in the nineteenth century when a large number of coins and other objects, including a magnificent bronze head of Hadrian, were dredged up from the Thames while the river was being deepened after the construction of a later bridge. But very few certain statements can be made about the Roman bridge. It was wooden, though possibly built on stone piers which also served for its Saxon successors. There must have been a drawbridge, since Roman boats of sixty tons and more have been discovered upstream. And, since London had become a substantial town by AD 60, the bridge was certainly built very early in Roman rule, perhaps even while the legions, after their initial successes, were waiting for the Emperor Claudius to arrive and lead them in triumph to Colchester.

There is, however, one awkward statement which seems to undermine this account of London's origins. The historian of the Roman invasion, Cassio Dio, describes how the Britons, after initial reverses in Kent, fell back on to the Thames 'near where it empties into the ocean and forms a lake', which must certainly mean within the tidal area. The Britons apparently crossed the river without difficulty 'since they knew where the firm ground and the fords were; the Romans, pressing after them, were brought to a halt'. Some of the legionaries swam across, while others '*got over by a bridge* a little further upstream'. If true, Dio's story supports the notion of a pre-Roman London, for it is difficult to imagine a bridge without some kind of settlement at either end. But Dio was writing over 150 years after the event and may easily have got his facts garbled. One would not take a modern Englishman's account of Waterloo, based on hearsay, very seriously. Would the Britons, using fords themselves, really have left their bridge undefended? Or does Dio mean that the Romans themselves threw a temporary military bridge across the river?

The leading British tribe, the Catuvellauni, certainly had every reason to bridge the Thames before the Romans arrived. Their sway extended over both sides of the river and they maintained a steady trade with the continent, importing fine pottery and other luxuries and exporting food, slaves and, so a Roman historian tells us, 'clever hunting dogs'. But probably they lacked the resources, organization and skills to build a permanent bridge; and without it Colchester made as good a capital as London.

The number of weapons and other finds in the Thames between Battersea and Kew shows that the Britons regularly forded the river there and provides another indication that they had no bridge. Brentford, as the name suggests, was an important crossing-place, and there may have been a ford

as far downstream as Westminster. It is interesting that
Watling Street, probably the earliest Roman road, points
towards a Westminster crossing from both north (where its
line is now followed by the Edgware Road) and south (the
A2 from Canterbury to Greenwich) of the river, whereas the
other Roman roads lead to the City and London Bridge.
Perhaps in constructing Watling Street the Romans developed a pre-existing track which used the Westminster
ford. Despite the rising sea level the Thames has been forded
there even in this century. It is curious, though, that no
Roman road leading south from Marble Arch to Westminster has ever been discovered, while the line of Watling
Street from Greenwich to Lambeth is not certain.

THE PORT BY THE BRIDGE

Once the Romans had built their bridge, London immediately became the leading British port. How much easier to
ship goods into the heart of the country than to lug them
all the way from the Channel ports. London's natural
geographical advantages were soon underscored by the
Romans, who made the City the centre of a spider's web of
roads reaching out to all parts of the country. Watling
Street, running south-east to the Channel ports of Richborough and Dover and north-west to St Albans and
eventually to Chester, was only the first. Others soon
followed, and their ancient line is often represented by
present-day London streets (see the map opposite). The
main Roman routes from London were the Colchester
Road, now followed by Aldgate and Whitechapel High
Streets; Ermine Street leading north to Lincoln (Bishopsgate,
Kingsland Road, Stoke Newington High Street, Stamford
Hill); and Stane Street running south to Chichester (Kennington Park Road, Clapham Road, Tooting High Street).

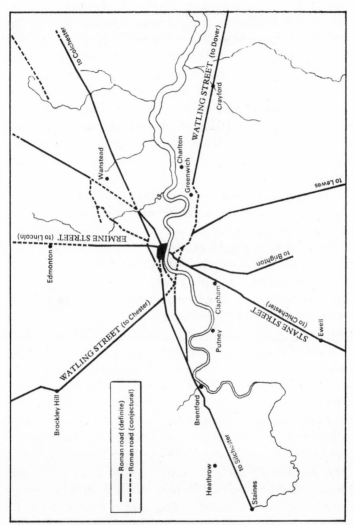

London at the centre of the Roman road system.

To the west there were two roads. The most important ran along the line of Newgate, New Oxford Street, Oxford Street and the Bayswater Road to Notting Hill Gate; there the ground dropping away to the west offered an excellent vantage point for a change of alignment to a slightly more southerly direction, down Holland Park Avenue and the Goldhawk Road, carrying straight on to skirt the Thames at Brentford on its way to Silchester and Bath. The other Roman road west followed the line of Fleet Street, the Strand, Kensington Road, Kensington High Street and King Street, Hammersmith, before joining the Silchester Road at Chiswick.

The Romans built these roads primarily for military reasons, although the pack-horse soon followed the legions along their courses. In no sense, however, did the roads 'make' London: indeed, except for the western routes, their lines cannot be traced within the City for the simple reason that London was established before they were laid down. The roads had to stop where the streets, which were in the usual Roman grid-pattern of straight lines intersecting at right angles, already existed. The two western roads, though, were undeniably important within the City, one running roughly on the line of Cannon Street, and the other 150 yards or so to the north (for these and other Roman remains in the City, see the map on p. 43). This last proved useful to Sir Christopher Wren during the rebuilding of St Mary-le-Bow. As the Roman streets had been formed from gravel pounded into a rock-hard surface, Wren was able to solve the problem of finding an adequate foundation for the tower by deliberately building it on the Roman metalling.

Already by AD 60, according to the Roman historian Tacitus, London was 'famed for commerce and crowded with traders'. The centre of all this activity, to judge by the number of early coins found there, was just to the east of the stream which ran down to the Thames between two flat-topped gravel slopes (later Ludgate Hill and Cornhill) and which entered the river about a quarter of a mile above London Bridge. Today's 'Walbrook' is a narrow lane overshadowed by unlovely office blocks, scarcely what fancy demands of the nucleus around which the first London grew. And what has happened to the 'brook'?

It has not been seen these last 500 years. As the Thames's level rose the tributaries flowed more slowly and became increasingly prone to flood. From the second century onwards tolerable living conditions could only be maintained on the banks of the Walbrook by dumping clay in order to raise the ground level. In this way a valley which had once been thirty feet deep was, over the centuries, almost entirely filled in. Like the far bigger Fleet and other 'lost rivers of London' shown in the map on p. 22, the Walbrook, at best only fourteen feet wide, deteriorated from a stream into a ditch and from a ditch into a sewer, until in the fifteenth century it was finally covered over completely. Whereas the river Westbourne, which was dammed in the eighteenth century to form the Hyde Park Serpentine, still appears in less spectacular guise crossing the line at Sloane Square station by overhead conduit, the Walbrook is committed to pipes buried well underground. In places, though, its valley is still visible. Standing outside Cannon Street station and looking west, it is easy to see the dip along the bottom of which, rather to the west of Walbrook Lane, the stream once flowed. From there its course has been traced more or less due north under the Bank of England, and thence, joined by several tributaries and taking a rather more wayward line, beneath the Roman wall, where two culverts have been found, to its source at springs in Shoreditch and Hoxton.

BOUDICA'S REVOLT

The Walbrook retained its importance throughout the Roman period and even today its presence is discernible in the boundary lines of the wards, administrative divisions of the City first fixed in Saxon times. The fortunes of the young City, however, received an early and terrible check from a British revolt. The trouble began with the death of Prasutagus, king of the Iceni, a British tribe occupying East Anglia. Lacking male heirs, Prasutagus sought to protect his daughters' inheritance from confiscation by leaving half of his considerable wealth to the Emperor. The Roman tax gatherers, though, were not impressed by this gesture and insisted on seizing the entire legacy. During the ensuing row the king's daughters were, in the language of the more chaste historians, 'insulted', an outrage in no way mitigated by the loss of their inheritance. It was, to say the least, rash of the Roman officials to behave in this manner while the main legionary force under the governor Suetonius Paulinus was away in the west; rasher still to scourge the widowed queen Boudica, whose character exemplified the maxim that the female is deadlier than the male.

When, under her leadership, the Iceni rose in revolt, soon to be joined by other tribes, the Romans possessed no immediate means of combating them. Colchester fell to the rebels, then St Albans, and the inhabitants of both places were promptly butchered. Suetonius, leaving the main body of his army to follow, rushed back to save London, but, once there, decided that the small band which he had brought with him was not a sufficient force with which to face the native horde. So he withdrew to fight another day, abandoning London to Boudica's mercy, not a quality to be counted on. Boudica, who has been admired as a prototype of

dauntless British womanhood, burnt the town to the
ground and her rabble ran amok burning, hanging and
crucifying all those Londoners who had been rash enough
to remain. Tacitus reckoned (probably exaggeratedly) that
70 000 were massacred in the three towns that fell to
Boudica, an achievement for which she is honoured by a
statue on Westminster Bridge.

A more fitting memorial lies in the ground alongside the
Walbrook. The decapitated heads which have been found
there may or may not have been Boudica's victims. But the
earth still bears the scars of her fury in a layer of burnt
debris which stretches from King Street to Gracechurch
Street, giving some idea of the first London's extent. The
charred remains show how easily the town would have
burnt, for the main building materials were simply inter-
woven wooden stakes (wattle) smeared with clay plaster
(daub). There are no quarries near London so stone has
always been sparingly used there, and in the Roman period
was restricted to important public building. It is not
surprising, therefore, that so little remains of ancient
London: the City had been devastated by fire many times
before the great conflagration of 1666. Within seventy
years of Boudica's revolt, for instance, another fire destroyed
a London which had not merely recovered from the earlier
holocaust but had grown well beyond its former bounds.
The buildings might be combustible but the town was
clearly indestructible.

Boudica herself did not long survive the sack of London
because the well-disciplined legions, although heavily
outnumbered, soon made mincemeat of her straggling army.
According to tradition the queen herself took poison,
certainly a wise decision for, as ever, the forces of civilization
did not prove notably more humane than the barbarians.
Not content with slaughtering Boudica's followers,

Suetonius proceeded to ravage the territory of the rebellious tribes. Fortunately for the Britons, though, help was at hand, and from an unexpected source – the Roman Procurator of Britain, Julius Classicianus, whose very grand tomb was found built into the City wall on Tower Hill, near where his (modern) statue now stands. The Procurator was responsible for the province s finances and, although below the military governor in status, was answerable to the Emperor alone. Classicianus, perhaps worried by the economic consequences of Suetonius' retributive raids, appealed to Rome against them. Astonishingly the Emperor Nero, not a man known to history for compassion, recalled Suetonius, whose successor initiated a gentler regime.

PRINCIPAL TOWN OF ROMAN BRITAIN: THE FORT AND BASILICA

The presence of the Procurator in the City suggests that London had already become the province's financial centre. Yet undoubtedly the original pre-invasion plan had been to set up the capital at Colchester, which was accordingly designated a 'colonia', the highest category of Roman town. There also, in the first years of Roman rule, was erected a great temple dedicated to Emperor worship, the state religion used to Romanize natives, involving all manner of games, spectacles and other festivities for which the provincial capital was the natural focus. London, by contrast, was not a 'colonia', but its rapid growth and prosperity soon undermined the earlier plan. It seems that London became the centre for Emperor worship soon after Boudica's revolt. An early stone inscription, the lettering of which in size and content suggested a large temple connected with this cult, has been discovered in the City, although the site of the temple itself has never been determined.

Obviously a town which had attained such importance needed defending, though the Romans may have ruefully reflected that this lesson would have been better learnt *before* Boudica's rebellion. Still, around the turn of the first and second centuries they built a stone fort to the north-west of London, covering twelve acres and providing quarters for 1000 or more men. It conformed to the conventional Roman pattern, being rectangular with two roads running straight across the inside to gates in the middle of all four walls. The fort's position is easy to find since the north–south road within coincides almost exactly with the northern part of Wood Street (arguably, therefore, the oldest street in London), while remains of the west wall can be seen from Noble Street.

With hindsight the fort seems badly sited, because the main threat to Roman London was eventually to come from the east, from raiders crossing the North Sea. But the possibility of the Empire's collapse had no part in the defensive calculations of AD 100. Rather, with Boudica's revolt still a living memory, another native rising must have been the chief worry. As Roman rule became more securely established, however, there cannot have been much for the legionaries to do in London. They would more likely have been required for guard or ceremonial duties than for actual fighting. This is borne out by the tomb of one Celsus, on which he is described as a 'speculator', a title well suited to the modern City, but which in fact signified a member of the governor's staff responsible for law enforcement. The governor himself, incidentally, was probably lodged in the palace which now lies under Cannon Street station.

At roughly the same period as the fort was being constructed, one of the largest buildings in the whole empire was taking shape on Cornhill. This was the basilica, a kind of town hall including law courts, offices and a great administrative chamber. Its scale – for the length was about the same as St Paul's Cathedral today – leaves no doubt that London had become the effective capital of Britain. The main part of this gigantic showpiece was a huge nave, with vaulted stone roof and apses at either end. The nave was flanked by aisles and the southern aisle opened on to the forum, the chief market and meeting place in London. This information is owed entirely to the archaeologist. A visitor can walk up Cornhill and Leadenhall Street from St Michael's Alley to Whittington Avenue in order to measure the length of the building, and diving down an alley to St Peter's Cornhill he will discover a churchyard, the width of which nearly matches that of the basilica's nave. But the remains of the basilica itself, the grandiloquent centrepiece of Roman London, lie fifteen feet in the earth. Anyone objecting to the City's modern architecture can take heart from this.

THE CITY WALL

Only one structure of Roman London is still visible, and that only in small sections, to the casual wanderer: the City wall. This is fitting enough, because, with medieval patching and additions, it served its purpose for fourteen centuries. As late as the 1640s Londoners redug the ditch on the outside in order to guard against the possibility of royalist attack. The effects of the wall's former presence still persist today. For 1000 years it was the City's boundary, and although the limits were later extended, the City retains something of the shape which its defences dictated. And no wonder, for the wall was a formidable barrier by any standards, two miles of Kentish ragstone rising to at least twenty feet. At the base it was eight feet across, though tapering a little on the inside at courses of bonding tiles which ran through the fabric every three feet or so. The ditch without was as deep as a man's height and the earth therefrom was piled up against the inside of the wall. As a feat of sheer labour and organization the work compares with the building of the medieval cathedrals, and the question immediately forms: why on earth did the Romans ever undertake such a massive task?

The wall has been dated, on the evidence of pottery and coins, to the end of the second century, by which time south-east Britain had long been subdued. But the province was ruled by Claudius Albinus, who saw it principally as a base from which to pursue his imperial ambitions. By 193 he must have known that a showdown in Gaul with his chief rival for the Empire, Septimius Severus, was inevitable; and he may have been concerned for Britain's defences during his absence abroad with the legions. That is conjecture, but it *is* certain that several British towns were given additional defences at this time. Generally these were earthworks only, but London clearly qualified for special treatment. The City was not merely provided with a wall, but with one so long that it must have left several patches of green within the enclosed space, even allowing for a population of 30 000 or more. There is no better way of getting the 'feel' of Roman London than to walk over the wall's line (see the map on p. 43).

Tower Hill, where a fine specimen of wall and the ground-plan of an internal turret survive in Wakefield Gardens, in front of the Tube station, makes a convenient starting point. Thanks to a sunken area in these gardens, the Roman wall is visible here from its base up to eleven feet, at the modern ground level, above which the remains are medieval. A little to the north, behind Cooper's Row, another piece of wall still stands, but thereafter the remains on this side of the City, though traceable in cellars and basements, are less easily viewable. Evidence of the wall's presence is not lacking on the surface, however, for Jewry Street and Duke Place faithfully follow its line. To pass from the first to the second, it is necessary today, as it was seventeen centuries ago when the wall was being built, to cross the Roman road to Colchester. Here, as the name of the street still testifies, stood Aldgate. The name is Saxon, a reminder that the gate outlasted the Romans: indeed the last Aldgate was only demolished in the eighteenth century.

The gate, being also something of a fortress, made an obvious point at which to change the wall's direction. Hitherto this had run due north, except for a slight kink near the river. From Aldgate the line bent north-west and soon reached another great Roman road, Ermine Street, which left the City at Bishopsgate. Another realignment took the wall across the north of the City, just inside the marsh of Moorfields. In Roman times there was no gate in this section: Moorgate belongs to the fifteenth century. As the road rather misleadingly called London Wall only keeps to the old line in its eastern section, up to Moorgate, the continuing straightness of the wall itself is best followed from above, on the modern highwalk to St Alphage's churchyard, where another substantial chunk survives. By this point the City wall has become one with that of the fort, because the Roman engineers, with commendable laziness, integrated the two defences, thus saving much labour to the detriment only of the wall's symmetry on the map. But because the fort's wall was thinner than the width prescribed for the City wall, a thickening was added on the inside in order to bring it to the required standard. The resulting 'double' wall can be seen in section from the east end of St Alphage's churchyard, and again from Noble Street where the remains are less high but no less interesting, particularly those

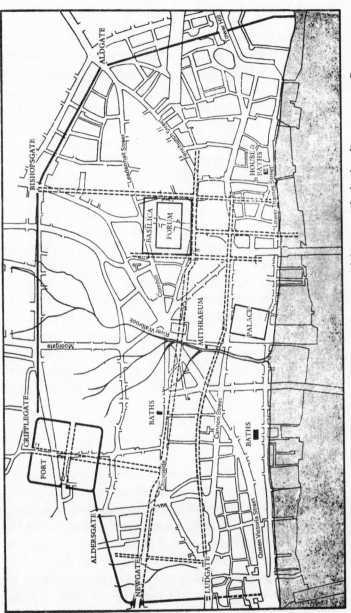

Some buildings of Roman London superimposed on a modern map of the City. The broken lines represent Roman streets.

opposite Oat Lane, at the south-west corner of the fort. Here the thickening ends, and it is easy to see why: the fort wall curves round to the east, enclosing a turret, while the City wall, a separate entity once more, makes off in a new direction, pretty well due west towards Aldersgate.

Although this gate was Roman it was probably added after the wall was built. Certainly it did not straddle any major Roman highway, unlike Newgate which was constructed in an imposing manner befitting the main road to the west. Towers on either side were joined across the road by an upper storey supported on a central pier which created a dual carriageway through the gate. In the early days of the wall there must have been considerably more traffic through Newgate than its neighbour Ludgate, the other western gate, although, as the route along the Strand was developed, the gap between the relative importance of the two narrowed. So today the sites of all four original gates in the wall – Aldgate, Bishopsgate, Newgate and Ludgate – are still traversed by main roads to and from the City, while the gates of the fort, which were not built to fit into any road system, have vanished and left not a route behind.

From Ludgate south the wall has never been certainly traced: probably it reached the Thames just to the east of the river Fleet which, being then perhaps 100 or more yards across at its mouth, would have prevented anyone attacking along the north bank of the Thames. Many experts discount the idea of a riverside wall and no continuous line has ever been traced there. It seems inconceivable, though, that the Romans should have made such enormous efforts to defend London from land attack, only to ignore the danger from the river. Of course, they may have reckoned that no invader could penetrate further upriver than London Bridge and that a British naval attack downstream was impossible. But the Roman temperament did not usually accept such let-outs and in any case the stretch of riverbank east of the bridge would still need to be defended. A tradition first recorded in the twelfth century maintained that the Thames had 'in a long space of time ... undermined and subverted the walls on the south side of the City' and excavations at the Tower have shown that in one place at least exactly this had occurred. Further, massive fragments of wall have been unearthed in both Lower and Upper Thames Street, roads which may conceal further evidence. It is already clear, however, that some kind of defensive system existed on this side of the City.

TRADE AND PIRACY

If Claudius Albinus was responsible for building the wall, he did not live to profit by his forethought for he was killed in Gaul in 197. The victorious Septimius Severus, clearly determined that Britain should not again serve as a stepping-stone for imperial ambitions, divided the island into two separately administered provinces, and although London was the capital of one of them, this change must have entailed some loss of status. A more serious threat to the town's prosperity, however, was the decay of the Empire in Gaul during the third century. Britain was isolated from the worst trouble, but on the Continent political chaos, with fifty-five pretended Caesars in forty years, presented barbarian invaders with such opportunities that town life in Gaul was virtually destroyed. London's growth was checked by the decay of its trading partners.

The hitherto flourishing commerce between Roman Britain and the Continent had involved much the same kind of articles as the pre-Conquest trade. Luxuries – beautifully ornamented pottery, delicate glass, silver and bronze ware, wine in huge jars and olive oil for lamps and cooking – were imported to bring some degree of sophistication to life in this outpost of civilization, while the outpost of civilization exported more basic products – cloth, hides, furs, gold, lead, corn and, at least in the period of conquest, slaves – from the defeated British tribes. But London's rise and the closer connections established with the Continent meant that the scale of this traffic increased beyond all recognition after the Conquest. The Museum of London's collection only contains objects which were lost or thrown away, yet the number of imports on display there shows how trade prospered.

The great Roman quay recently excavated at the Custom House was clearly designed to serve a lot of shipping: it seems to have stretched a quarter of a mile along the river-front to the east of the bridge. There were also quays upstream of the bridge. In 1962, during construction of the Blackfriars underpass, a Roman boat was discovered, complete with cargo of Kentish ragstone, in what had once been the mouth of the Fleet. It was flat-bottomed, a typical Thames barge in fact, and a reminder that by no means all the port's traffic was overseas trade. The coin placed in the mast hole for luck had failed in its function, for the vessel had been wrecked at the end of the second century. So the stone may well have been intended for the wall, one of 1300 such cargoes which would have been required for the complete work.

It was not just the political and economic malaise which threatened the port in the middle of the third century. Attacks by Pictish and Saxon pirates on shipping in the North Sea were an increasing menace, to which the Romans reacted with characteristic vigour. An admiral named Carausius was especially successful in suppressing piracy, but he amassed so much plunder at the expense of the plunderers that he became officially suspected of colluding with them. Preferring a non-judicial death, Carausius, who had strong support amongst the legions, set himself up in Britain as the Emperor Augustus. He defeated the imperial fleet sent to chastise him and proved a capable ruler for six years, during which period he established the first official London mint. He also organized an efficient coastal defensive system against raiders before being murdered by his finance minister, Allectus. But imperial vengeance soon closed in upon the usurper's usurper and Constantius Chlorus, the true Caesar of Britain, entered London in triumph in 296. This victory was the occasion for the first surviving picture of London, on a medal struck in honour of the event. Constantius is shown on his horse prancing in front of the town's towers, while a grateful female labelled 'Lon' kneels to welcome the conquering hero with open arms. But since the medal was struck at Trier, any accuracy in the portrayal of Roman London would be purely coincidental.

LIFE IN ROMAN LONDON

In any case, the life of the town is not to be rediscovered in a public parade of the great. History is a snob to catch such empty performances in its net, while allowing the day-to-day activities of the multitude to slip through the meshes into oblivion. But the revenge of the commonplace is sweet. The marvellous and eventful happenings so carefully recorded end up as dry facts to plague schoolboys. The routine and the ordinary, should they miraculously survive history's screening, acquire increasing value as the centuries heap over them, until they become prized as gems illuminating the blackness of the past.

So, eighteen centuries ago a child ran across some still soft tiles when the baths in Cheapside were being built, and today, looking at the footprint, it is easy to imagine (if not in Latin) the angry remonstrations at this folly. Another tile bears the graffiti, 'Australis has been running off on his own for the past fortnight.' Was Australis the love-sick victim of a fellow-worker's joke, or simply a shirker? We shall never know, but his wanderings are imperishably preserved. Better documented wanderings are those of Aulus Alfidius Olussa, born in Athens but with a tombstone on Tower Hill, to remind us that London was peopled with officials and merchants from all parts of the Empire. Whither the master went the slaves too had to follow, but their condition was not necessarily abject. Anencletus was a London slave who somehow scraped together enough money to set up an impressive tombstone to his nineteen-year-old wife, Claudia Martina. He might have bought his freedom for the same sum no doubt, but he obtained immortality for them both instead.

Another extraordinary survival, however, brings home the callousness of slavery. Sometimes the stylus used for writing on wax tablets penetrated to the wood underneath, leaving the message inscribed there. 'Rufus, son of Callisunus, sends greetings to Epillicus and all his fellow-servants. I think you know that I am well. If you have made a list, please send it. Look after everything carefully, and see that you turn that slave-girl into cash. . . .' Even 'that slave-girl', though, could have been luckier than the owner of the leather 'bikini' trunks which were rather ominously discovered in a first-century well. And what kind of foul deed provoked this determinedly comprehensive curse? 'I curse Tretia Maria and her life and mind and memory and liver and lungs mixed up together, and her words, thoughts and memory; thus may she be unable to speak what things are concealed, nor be able . . .' It looks as though blackmail was not unknown in Roman London.

These, and many other objects in the Museum of London, possess a power far greater than a recital of facts to jerk the visitor back into the reality of the Roman town. However fragmentary the ruins of buildings, something of the lives passed within them, on surfaces now buried twelve feet and more underground, can be pieced together from the small change of civilization – the buckles, hooks, rings, hairpins, brooches, knives and countless other accessories. But the way into the *minds* of these first Londoners is not so much through their means of living as through their attitude to the death which overtook them all so long ago.

RELIGION IN ROMAN LONDON

The Romans practised a tolerance in religious affairs that subsequently took more than a thousand years to regain from the Christians. Only those refusing lip-service to the state cult of Emperor worship were persecuted and, as a consequence, innumerable cults proliferated, especially in a town as cosmopolitan as London. Several figures representing traditional Roman gods – Apollo, Diana, Mercury, Venus and the like – have been found there, although sometimes these appear more like local British deities thinly disguised in Roman garb. Such gods gave no moral guidance for this world, and no hope of happiness in the next: none the less a steady stream of offerings was required to propitiate their fickle fancy. For this purpose coins, tools, weapons and other valuables were cast into the river, eventually to gladden the hearts of archaeologists, if not their intended recipients.

There were, however, more optimistic religions, deriving from the Middle East and Asia Minor, and introducing at least the possibility of eternal bliss. Secrecy was the keynote in many of these cults, the rituals and mysteries of which were revealed only to initiates. From the Thames at London Bridge has been dredged a delightful statuette of Harpocrates, son of the Egyptian goddess Isis, who still emphasizes the need for silence with fingers pointing towards his lips. London certainly possessed a temple to Isis herself because a pottery jug found in Southwark has an inscription referring to it. A rather more demanding mother goddess figure was Cybele, whose predilections, a trifle illogically for a deity especially associated with the renewal of life each year, included the castration of her priests. Clearly the symbolism of autumn was not forgotten in the enthusiasm for spring. Cybele's worship tended to degenerate into scenes of debauchery which, it was perhaps over-confidently predicted in 1955, 'would make a modern Englishman blench'. Blenching, however, is still common practice at the sight, in the Museum of London, of the bronze forceps which may have been used to render Cybele's priests fit for her exclusive service.

The most renowned of all pagan cults followed in Roman London was Mithraism, the teachings of which resembled those of Christianity in several respects. Life was deemed to be a constant struggle between good and evil, and Mithras, the god of light, would judge men (and only men, for women were excluded) according to their combat record. The just were awarded happiness without end; the unjust a similar period of roasting. Qualities of personal honour, such as integrity, truthfulness and conscientiousness, being demanded of devotees, Mithraism appealed especially to soldiers and merchants, professions well represented in London.

The Christians, however, were quick to sniff a rival in a creed which appeared to them as a blasphemous parody of their own, and as soon as they gained official favour, instituted a bitter persecution of Mithraism. Around the beginning of the fourth century the priests at the Mithraic temple on the Walbrook were forced to take the precaution of burying their valuable statuary, including marbles imported from Italy, under the floor pending safer times. The figures and other Mithraic objects did not see the light of day again until 1954, when the temple was discovered between the old Walbrook and the modern lane during the building of Bucklersbury House after the Second World War. These statues are in the Museum of London, while a reconstruction of the temple's ground-plan, made from the original stone, can be seen from Queen Victoria Street, on the opposite side of Bucklersbury House to its former site.

There are no comparable Christian remains from Roman London: ironically, the best archaeological evidence of the Christian presence, apart from a monograph on one pewter bowl, is the concealment of the Mithraic statues. Probably this dearth reflects only that early Christianity was the religion of the poorer classes, without much to spend on elaborate works of art. There is, however, a record of the bishop of London having attended a council at Arles in 314. Moreover, a tradition persists that St Peter's Cornhill was a very early foundation. Certainly its clergy were accorded precedence over those of all other parishes in the Middle Ages; and as this church is on the site of the Roman basilica, the first of its predecessors, perhaps adapted from a pagan temple after the Emperor Constantine's conversion (324), could well have been part of that vast complex.

ROMAN DECLINE

To the historian Gibbon, the influence of Christianity, with its elevation of personal morality above the necessities of state, was one of the causes of the Empire's decline. Whatever Rome's troubles, however, the fourth century does not present an unrelentingly bleak record in London, the fifth largest town north of the Alps. Indeed at some stage it attained new honour, being granted the title of Augusta in recognition of its services. This distinction may well stem from 367-8, when the Picts (from North Britain) and the Scots (from Ireland) and the Saxons (from North Germany) succeeded, whether by luck or good management, in concerting their attack. A dire crisis resulted and London's defences were tested to the full. But the town held out behind its walls until reinforcements arrived; later it was the base of the campaign to restore order.

The name Augusta, though, came too late in the Roman period to stick permanently. Henceforth the legions were gradually withdrawn to confront the increasing chaos on the Continent. Matters were not improved when yet another soldier, Magnus Maximus, proclaimed himself Emperor from Britain and marched off to defeat in Gaul with valuable troops (388). By 410 the Emperor Honorius could only respond to a British plea for help by telling them to look after their own defences. London had probably already done so: the wall's bastions, from which catapults could rain down heavy rocks on attackers, were added in late Roman times.

Left alone to face the Picts and the Scots, the British found even the Saxons acceptable allies, and paid these mercenaries off with grants of land. Perhaps the very early Saxon settlements at Croydon and Mitcham, in south London, originated in this way. The temporary ally, though, was to prove the permanent conqueror. The soldiers of fortune were soon joined by their Germanic kith. Pagan, illiterate and savage, the future English began to insinuate and force themselves into Britain.

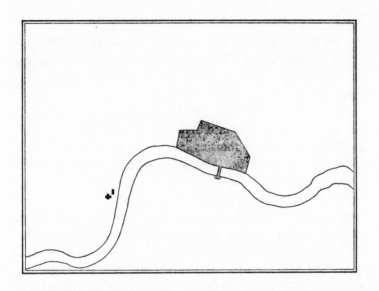

2. 'Richer in treasure than the rest of the kingdom'
[410-1066]

A BRITISH ENCLAVE?

For 200 years after the Roman legions left, nothing certain is known of London. Perhaps this is not surprising. The City's *raison d'être* had been trade with the Continent; the Anglo-Saxon invaders were simply land-grabbing farmers, initially too preoccupied with conquest and subsistence to maintain regular links with their homelands across the North Sea. They had never lived in towns and regarded Roman ruins with superstitious awe. 'Cities are visible from afar,' one of their poets relates, 'the cunning work of giants. . . .' So the walls of London must have appeared to peoples with no knowledge of stone building. As late as the seventh century the Anglo-Saxons had to import foreign masons.

It is possible, then, that the invaders were content to skirt London on their way into the country. Certainly very few early Anglo-Saxon remains have been discovered in the City or its environs. The settlements at Mitcham and Croydon are eight miles and more from London Bridge. (And what became of the Roman bridge?) The only Saxon cemetery which has been unearthed any nearer the City than Mitcham was at Greenwich, five miles downstream. The Thames was a natural route into the country and invaders who reached Greenwich must have been familiar with London. They do not, however, seem to have settled there: the bridge, in whatever state of repair, was neither a final destination nor, apparently, a hindrance to their continued passage. Even some way upstream, the gravels alongside the river at Barnes and Hammersmith, which had proved such attractive ground for prehistoric men, failed to entice the Anglo-Saxons. The historian Ammianus describes how Germanic tribesmen, having taken Roman towns on the Rhine, 'established themselves in the suburbs, for the barbarians shunned fixing themselves in the actual towns, looking upon them as graves surrounded with nets'. At London they were apparently wary even of the suburbs.

Was it really just superstition, though, that kept them away? Is it not conceivable that London, secure behind its walls, remained an outpost of native British resistance as the invaders swept on to the west? Such a notion cannot be proved. Its opponents point out that the medieval street plan bears little resemblance to the Roman grid-system, and deduce that London must have been an uninhabited ruin at some intervening period. On the other hand in Rome itself the modern streets hardly correspond at all to their ancient predecessors, and for a certainty *that* city has been continuously occupied. And after all, no one would conclude that life halted in the City of London during the nineteenth century because King William Street and Queen Victoria Street, entirely new thoroughfares, were cut at that time.

The Anglo-Saxon Chronicle records that in 456, after defeat at Crayford in Kent, 'the British fled with great haste to London'. That entry was written down more than 400 years after the event but at least it shows that the *tradition* of a British London was extant in the ninth century. Tantalizingly insubstantial wisps of evidence have been invoked in support of this tradition. For example the tiny coins called *sceattas* which were minted in London during the eighth century were modelled on Roman coins produced in the same place – but then Roman influence is equally evident on indisputably Anglo-Saxon coins. A similar objection can be advanced against the argument that aspects of London's legal code were inconsistent with normal Anglo-Saxon practice. It is true that the traditional system of inheritance in medieval London followed Roman law in allowing a man to bequeath property away from his family, whereas Anglo-Saxon custom precluded the simple pleasure of disappointing one's natural heirs. But Roman rules of inheritance were not unique to London, being found in York and other places where no claims of British survival can be upheld.

Still, there is no doubt that London's law was independent. A ninth-century charter refers to the 'ordinances which the bishops and reeves belonging to London had ordained'. That phrasing opens up a whole new line of enquiry.

'Bishops and reeves *belonging to London* . . .': did the City's authority then extend over a wider area than the town itself? The same question is posed by the hunting privileges which Londoners enjoyed in the Anglo-Saxon period. These rights stretched over several shires, from the Chiltern Hills, through Hertfordshire and Middlesex to Kent 'as far as the river Cray', and some scholars have indulged the temptation of associating them with the hypothetical British enclave based on London in the years of the Saxon invasions. In this connection the fragments of dyke called Grim's Ditches are suggestive. They are found near Wallingford (by the Chilterns), Berkhamsted (in Hertfordshire), Pinner (in Middlesex) and Bexley (by the river Cray). These sections, very likely constructed in the sixth century, consist of a bank with an exterior ditch facing towards London, and could have been built to contain expansion therefrom. Certainly their coincidence with London's traditional hunting grounds is thought-provoking.

There is little sign that the Anglo-Saxons were settled in London before the sixth century. Moreover the early evidence of their presence has nearly all come from the west side of the City, that is from Ludgate Hill rather than Cornhill, which had been the hub of the Roman town. It is interesting that the newcomers should have called the stream running between the two hills the Wal-brook, meaning 'stream of the British'. (The same root is found in 'Wales'.) Taken together the river name and the distribution of archaeological finds support the conjecture that when the Anglo-Saxons first began to live in London the British were still on Cornhill, perhaps camping within the ruined basilica, although there cannot have been many of them if corn was indeed growing on the hill. Throughout the Middle Ages, London continued to bear traces of a split between its west and east sides. Each half possessed its own market centre (or 'cheap') and its own shipping centre (Billingsgate and Queenhythe); and the town was sometimes divided into two parts for administrative purposes, with the Walbrook as the line between them.

LONDON BECOMES CHRISTIAN: THE CHURCHES

It was on Ludgate Hill that the Anglo-Saxons built their first London churches after conversion to Christianity. Whereas the only early church on Cornhill was St Peter's (which, as we have noted, may have existed in Roman times), there were two churches on Ludgate Hill with dedications, one to St Gregory and the other to St Augustine, which were associated with Rome's first effort to convert the Anglo-Saxons. St Gregory was the pope who sent the mission to Britain and St Augustine was the man who led it, somewhat reluctantly journeying across Europe to land in Kent in 597. Gregory, very likely drawing on memories of Roman Britain, had originally intended that Augustine should be bishop of London, which was therefore, together with York, to have authority over all other sees. Political necessity altered this plan. The first notable convert was Ethelbert of Kent (560–616) who claimed overlordship of much of England; and in order to preserve this powerful support Augustine established himself in Ethelbert's capital at Canterbury, which has kept its primacy ever since.

For once political necessity may have dictated the better choice. Throughout London's history the affairs of this life have generally claimed precedence over those of the next, and when Londoners have spared time from their businesses to take account of their souls they have tended to bring the ethos of the market-place to their spiritual transactions. So the rich and successful have cashed in their worldly chips for a share in some paradisal commerce; and so London has gained many churches and monasteries without ever becoming a religious centre.

The City still seems crowded with churches today, although there are only thirty-one (besides St Paul's) within the old area of the walls, compared with about 100, or one for every three acres, in the twelfth century. Many of these tiny parishes originated in late Saxon times (the ninth to the eleventh centuries), often through the generosity of rich merchants. Sometimes the church's name, like that of St Mary Woolnoth in Lombard Street or of St Benet Algar (now the Welsh Church) Paul's Wharf in Upper Thames Street, has preserved the memory of the founders (Wulfnoth and Aelfgar) long after the first buildings have disappeared. Almost no Anglo-Saxon fabric survives within the walls; the majority of their churches, indeed, do not even have any modern successor. But in All Hallows Barking, near to the Tower, there is a seventh-century arch, the oldest in London, which serves as a reminder that many City churches, whatever date their present building, have histories which stretch back before the Norman Conquest. Doubtless the original Saxon churches would appear to us as no more than tiny chapels, but their sheer number represents an astonishing investment in terms of the resources of their age.

Yet the predominately secular tenor of London life in Saxon times is suggested by the fact that the monastic revival of the ninth century produced no foundations there, although plenty of space must have been available within the walls. Indeed, there was only one religious house in London before the Norman Conquest (unless one counts the canons at St Paul's) and that, St Martin's-le-Grand, where the General Post Office building now stands, was founded in 1056 more to provide royal officials with an adequate supply of this world's goods than to enable the zealous to shun them.

Even back in Augustine's time London had shown no extraordinary devotion to Christianity. The town then came under the aegis of King Sibert of the East Saxons; and as he was the nephew of Augustine's convert, Ethelbert of Kent, the most powerful man in the country, neither Sibert nor the citizens were slow to appreciate the attractions of the new religion. Mellitus, the bishop of London appointed by Augustine, acquired a diocese with the same boundaries as the East Saxon kingdom, and King Ethelbert was responsible for building the first St Paul's Cathedral over a Roman burial ground on Ludgate Hill. Although built of wood, this St Paul's was doubtless, like its successors, the largest church in the City.

It did not, however, prove a symbol potent enough to overawe the Londoners. When Ethelbert and Sibert died, their successors rejected Christianity and the citizens once more followed their rulers' example, maintaining their apostasy even after Ethelbert's son was finally converted. The trouble was that Sibert's three sons, who ruled the East Saxons jointly, were impressed by the magic properties of holy bread but could see no cause to become Christian in order to obtain it. Somehow Mellitus failed to get across the finer points of the doctrine of transubstantiation, and was unceremoniously booted out of the town for wilfully withholding his magic powers. It was another fifty years or so before London was permanently reconciled to the faith.

The main reason for this prolonged apostasy was that there was no political power capable of supporting the missionary efforts of the church in London. England was split into kingdoms which constantly disputed the leadership. The East Saxon kings were a feeble line, unable to impose themselves on a town which was, in any case, largely cut off from them by a ring of forest. King Ethelbert of Kent possessed some authority in London, for there is a tradition that, besides building St Paul's, he had a royal palace in the Aldermanbury district. Another source ascribes this palace to King Offa (757–796), the ruler of the midland kingdom of Mercia and the first man to achieve effective and lasting sway over the whole of the midlands and south together. Between Ethelbert and Offa, however, there could rarely have been any outside power capable of enforcing its will on London; indeed the chief impression left by this period is one of political muddle. For example, Bishop (later Saint) Erkenwald, the most distinguished man in early London church history, who finally established Christianity there in the late seventh century, was appointed by the East Saxon kings, but was called 'my bishop' by Ine of Wessex. Out of such confusion the tradition of independence was born: London was left free to pursue its own destiny.

A MARKET-PLACE FOR MANY PEOPLES

That destiny, by dint of the same geographical facts which had brought London into being, was to be a great commercial centre, and not even political weakness could prevent its fulfilment. In the second half of the ninth century, and again 100 years later, England was subjected to constant attack from Scandinavia. London's position and wealth rendered it especially vulnerable, and more than once the town fell to the Vikings. But the Viking plunderers could no more destroy the natural advantages concentrated at the bridge than the fires which frequently consumed the buildings. As long as there was traffic with the Continent, London was bound to flourish. And as the Anglo-Saxons, invaders no more, began, from the seventh century on, to create England out of Britain, so trade gradually revived. By the early eighth century the Venerable Bede, a monk writing in distant Northumbria, had heard enough of London to call it 'a market-place for many peoples, who come by land and by sea'. The extent to which London continued to prosper despite all the disturbances of the late Anglo-Saxon period can be gauged by the amount of wealth put into the founding of churches. When the Viking King Canute (1016–35) took a tribute from his new kingdom, London was required to provide an eighth of the total for the whole country.

Only an occasional record survives to document the trade of these centuries. Thus Bede tells a story about a Northumbrian nobleman captured in battle and sold as a slave in London to a Frisian, one of the merchants hailing from the country on the borders of present-day Holland and Germany. The Frisians dominated North European commerce from the sixth to the ninth century, but the slave trade, being peculiarly well-suited to the talents of the Vikings, survived their decline. Then we know of a commercial treaty between King Offa and the Emperor Charlemagne, from which London, connected to Offa's Mercia by Watling Street, must have benefited. The Emperor, however, found cause for complaint in the shortness of English cloaks and in the way merchants from England avoided tolls by pretending to be pilgrims. Tolls are the inevitable accompaniment of trade and English kings claimed their share of London's prosperity. A law code of King Ethelred (978–1016) shows the Crown charging tolls on cargo at London Bridge, and otherwise regulating trade with merchants from the Rhineland, Normandy and Flanders. Clearly the City had regained the cosmopolitan tinge of its Roman past.

The cargo being shipped would have occasioned no

surprise to a Roman merchant. The English economy remained in its 'colonial' phase until the fourteenth century, exporting raw materials such as tin, lead, corn, hides and, above all, wool; and importing luxuries like pottery, jewellery, wine and spices. After the Norman Conquest the wool trade became the basis of England's wealth, but King Ethelred's law code shows that the vital connection with Flanders, where the cloth industry increasingly depended on English wool, had been established before 1066. London was assured an important part in the wool trade on two counts. Its position between the chalk ranges of the Chilterns and the Downs, on which sheep were pastured, made it a natural outlet for wool producers. At the same time, its port, just across the North Sea from Flanders, was thoroughly convenient for Flemish buyers. But this is really to anticipate. The Flemish connection and other links across the narrow seas were much strengthened by the Norman Conquest, not least because William the Conqueror had married a Flemish princess.

LONDON AND THE VIKINGS

For centuries before 1066 London's fortunes – and mis-fortunes – depended on Scandinavia. The popular image of Vikings is of savage and heathen warriors in horned helmets disembarking from their ships bent on rape, loot and devastation, very likely in that order. The sight of their battle-axes and other weapons in the Museum of London makes one grateful for humane inventions like the gun. The Tower possesses a decorated iron stirrup which shows that the Vikings even shipped cavalry across to England. They were, however, traders as well as pirates, although it is not always easy to disentangle the two activities. Moreover London, like England, on which the Viking threat forced a unity the squabbling Anglo-Saxon kingdoms might never have achieved otherwise, showed profit as well as loss from their incursions. No trading outpost could suffer from being integrated into the vast crescent of Viking commerce, which stretched from Russia round the coastline of northern and western Europe to the Mediterranean, with offshoots to Greenland and North America.

These benefits, however, could hardly have been obvious to Londoners when, in the ninth century, the first raiders began to appear in the Thames; still less in 841, under which year the Anglo-Saxon Chronicle records 'a great slaughter in London'. Twelve years later, the Vikings 'took London by storm' and wintered in England for the first time. Doubtless they expected as little resistance as they encountered in the rest of Europe, but England was to be saved by the rare abilities of King Alfred of Wessex (871–99), the only English monarch to earn the sobriquet, 'Great'. Nevertheless, London suffered many tribulations before Alfred's victory was won. For several years after 871 it remained in Viking hands, and the invaders were sufficiently well settled there to mint coins. Alfred's recapture of London in 886 was a decisive moment in the town's history: for the first time since Roman rule it was effectively integrated into an English kingdom. Alfred certainly appreciated London's importance and potential, for he strengthened the fortifications and issued trade regulations. For all its international commerce, however, London was still a rural town. When the Danes once again hovered near in 896, Alfred had to send a force to ensure that the harvest could be safely gathered outside the walls.

By the end of the ninth century the main force of the first Viking onslaught had been exhausted. During the next hundred years London was left to prosper in peace, with the result that it hardly appears at all in contemporary records, which were almost exclusively concerned with warfare. By the time the second wave of Scandinavian (this time principally Danish) invasions broke in the late tenth century, London was strong enough to give a good account of itself. In 984 an attack was repulsed and, according to the Anglo-Saxon Chronicle, the invaders 'suffered more harm and injury than they even thought any citizens could do to them'. England, though, was no longer led by an Alfred; and King Ethelred (978–1016) resorted to the policy which Alfred had abandoned – paying the Danes off. To be fair, Ethelred's hand was sometimes forced: in 1011, for instance, the Danes had seized Archbishop Aelfheah of Canterbury. All the same, the payment of a vast sum in the next year did not prevent the archbishop being murdered at Greenwich by a drunken Viking horde, who employed the original means of pelting him with bones from their feast. Aelfheah's body was buried in St Paul's, where several miracles duly ensued, too many in fact for London's interests, as eleven years later the corpse graduated to the higher ecclesiastical dignity of Canterbury. The archbishop's memory lingers on in London as St Alphage, and the ruins of a church dedicated to his memory are still visible from the London Wall highwalk.

In the struggle against the Danes, London proved tougher than King Ethelred. In 1013 the city stoutly resisted a siege and only submitted after the king had fled. Ethelred then formed an alliance with Olaf, later king of Norway and later still St Olaf, who in 1014 regained control of London from the Danes in dramatic fashion. Coming up the Thames, his fleet was stopped at the well-fortified bridge. The resourceful Olaf covered his ships with wicker-work in order to protect them from weapons hurled from above, sailed boldly up to the bridge, attached ropes to the piles and rowed off downstream. The bridge, which must have been an exceedingly fragile structure, collapsed, leaving its defenders floundering in the river. This exploit was celebrated in a Norse saga of the twelfth century which became the basis of the nursery rhyme 'London Bridge is Falling Down'. Olaf was honoured by the dedication of no less than five City churches and his name survives in corrupted form in Tooley Street, to the south of the bridge which he once destroyed.

His fame is deserved, for no invader since has managed to take the City by storm. Maybe he was able to count on support from the citizens since London was conspicuously loyal to the English kings at this time and in the tenth and eleventh centuries its fortifications never proved inadequate against Danish attacks. Evidently the prolonged threat from Scandinavia had produced a well-organized defensive system, which was probably associated with the contemporary division of the City into twenty-four districts called wards. These areas are still the basic units of the City's administration and their jagged outline suggests that they were originally defined by holdings or property, the owners of which would have been obliged in emergencies to provide specified amounts of men and materials. The wards vary greatly in size, showing how unevenly settled the city must have been in the eleventh century. The largest are naturally on the sparsely populated edges of the old walled area, and, as the maintenance of the defences was part of their purpose, their boundaries do not, like those of the parishes, follow the line of the City wall, but take in land on the outer side.

Perhaps it was these arrangements which enabled London to resist the Danes so effectively during the last campaign which the English fought against them. When King Ethelred died, much of the country acknowledged the Danish Canute, but the Chronicle records that 'all the

councillors who were in London and the citizens chose
Edmund Ironside [Ethelred's son] as king. . . .' So, in 1016,
Canute 'turned against London with all his ships'. There is a
tradition, which seems unlikely granted that the siege only
lasted a month, that Canute met the problem of London
Bridge by constructing a canal which circumvented it on
the south bank. Anyway, London held out, although,
somewhat unfairly after such loyalty, Edmund gave the
city to Canute in the partition of the country which they
made later in 1016. A few days after, Edmund's death left
Canute in control of the whole of England.

Straightway he showed why London was worth fighting
for by granting Norwegian and Danish merchants the right
to stay there for a year at a time, instead of the forty days
normally allotted to aliens. But the Danish presence in
London is an enigma. If, before Canute, the Danes were
outsiders, it is hard to understand why, in the tenth century,
the main court for trade disputes was called the Husting,
certainly a Viking word. Far from having been expelled
from London after Alfred's victories, Danish traders must
have remained an active force in City life if such an important institution bore their mark. Nor, if a thirteenth-
century chronicle is to be believed, did they confine their
attention to legal matters. Apparently Londoners bitterly
resented their success with Anglo-Saxon women, based as it
was on the unmanly habit of combing their hair daily and
bathing every Saturday.

One might have expected a people with such comprehensive notions of conquest to have left more evidence of their
presence. Yet few street names betray Viking origin, and
not many Viking remains have been discovered in London.
The most impressive is the tombstone of one Tosti, found in
St Paul's churchyard, and now in the Museum of London.
There are more Danish survivals outside the City's walls. In

the Strand the name of St Clement Danes speaks for itself, the first church having been built on a Danish burial ground. St Bride, Fleet Street, is probably another Danish dedication, although a church had undoubtedly existed here in early Saxon times and the site had once been a pagan Roman cemetery. 'Bride' is a corruption of 'Bridget', an Irish saint popular with the Vikings. It looks as though there may have been something of a Danish settlement to the west of the City, but by no means only there: Greenwich and Woolwich are both Viking names.

EDWARD THE CONFESSOR AND WESTMINSTER

Danish rule in England was destined to be short-lived. Despite Canute's relaxed attitude to monogamy none of his sons long survived him. When the last one, Harthacnut, died at a wedding celebration at Lambeth in 1042, London once more showed its partiality for the Old English monarchy by supporting Ethelred's son Edward. Even before Harthacnut was buried, according to the Anglo-Saxon Chronicle, 'all the people chose Edward as king in London'. It was a choice which London, at least, apparently came to regret. Edward had spent a quarter of a century as an exile in Normandy and his instinctive preference for a Norman alliance, Norman ministers and perhaps even a Norman successor, antagonized the powerful and ambitious Earl Godwin of Wessex, whose hopes had been raised by Edward's marriage to his daughter, only to be dashed by the king's childlessness. In 1051 Edward succeeded in forcing Godwin into exile, but thanks largely to London's backing the earl was able to regain his position the next year. When Godwin appeared with a fleet in the Thames he was allowed to pass through London Bridge unmolested, whereupon he encircled the royal fleet and forced Edward to terms before the king was able to bring up reinforcements. Exactly why London supported Godwin in this crisis is not clear, but the decision was crucial for England's future. The restoration of Godwin's family meant that William of Normandy could only attain the throne as a conqueror, instead of peaceably as Edward's appointed successor. Meanwhile, for the remainder of Edward's reign, effective power increasingly passed to Godwin's son Harold.

The king himself was left free to concentrate on his favourite project of rebuilding Westminster Abbey. Three centuries previously King Offa had founded a monastery 'in that terrible place', the isle of Thorney, but the first Abbey never achieved much importance. (The 'isle' was created by the Tyburn, another river that has since gone underground, splitting roughly where St James's Park station now stands, so that it reached the Thames in two streams. Edward's plans were on an altogether grander scale.) The Bayeux tapestry gives an idea of what his Abbey looked like, its romanesque style reflecting the king's Norman taste. Edward's building has now disappeared but the foundations, underneath the present nave, show that it was as long as today's Abbey. In terms of London's history, however, the main significance of Edward's massive undertaking was that, in order to oversee the project, he built a palace between it and the river. This was the first step in a long process whereby, over the next centuries, the king's government was to become permanently fixed at Westminster, thus creating a powerful magnet drawing the City's expansion westwards.

Edward seems to have envisaged that his Abbey should be both a burial place and a coronation church for English kings; and his death in January 1066, a few days after the consecration of the chancel, meant that it was immediately used for both purposes. The new king was Godwin's son

Harold, who needed all the acclamations which London bestowed upon him, for he had precious little claim by inheritance. Nevertheless, his crowning at Westminster set a precedent which has been recognized by all his successors as an essential accompaniment of true kingship. Since Harold, the ill-fated Edward V and the uncrowned Edward VIII are the only monarchs not to have been publicly anointed in Westminster Abbey. But 1066 is still the only year in which two coronations have taken place.

THE NORMAN CONQUEST

The Norman victory at Hastings, where Harold was killed, is the best-known event in English history, but the notion that the battle by itself accomplished the conquest would not have gained the Conqueror's support. A realist if ever there was one, William was too good a soldier to imagine that one victory is enough to win a campaign. He immediately perceived that the key to ultimate success was London, 'a great city', as a contemporary wrote, 'overflowing with froward inhabitants and richer in treasure than the rest of the kingdom'. Thither the surviving English leaders had fled after Hastings, and there one of them, named Ansgar, was organizing resistance from the litter to which his wounds had confined him. There, too, was Edgar, the son of Edmund Ironside and the heir of the Anglo-Saxon kings.

When, in early December, William reached Southwark, on the south side of London Bridge, a force immediately sallied across the bridge to attack him. The Normans beat off this challenge, but William realized that he could not take the City by direct assault. He was not, however, a man to have his will thwarted: if London could not be stormed, London must be isolated. So Southwark was fired, and the Normans began a terrible march, ravaging and devastating as they went, first to Hampshire, then north to Wallingford, where the Thames was easy to cross, and finally completing the circle of destruction by turning back towards London. By the time he reached Berkhamsted, in Hertfordshire, the City knew that it had to deal with a man who would shrink from no atrocity to get his way. The English leaders 'with all the best men in London' went out to submit. With that surrender perished the Anglo-Saxon kingdom. The achievement of six centuries, during which scattered heathen groups had been forged by adversity and tribulation into one of Europe's most sophisticated states, had been crushed in three months by the Norman juggernaut.

THE ANGLO-SAXON LEGACY

A visitor might well conclude that London had suffered the same fate as the Anglo-Saxon kingdom. The Museum of London contains countless objects illustrating everyday life in the Saxon town, but almost no building of the period remains. Saxon London seems to have vanished without trace.

Nothing could be further from the truth. Even in purely physical terms the Saxon influence persists, for not only the parish and ward boundaries but the very street plan of the City derive from before the Norman Conquest. And in all other senses, any notion that Saxon London bequeathed nothing to the future would be utterly misleading. By 1066 the City was too important to be crushed, even by William the Conqueror.

Some idea of the sheer wealth of Saxon London can be gauged from the huge number of Saxon coins that have been found there. Sometimes they had been buried in hoards which it is possible to associate with a particular event. The panic that must have seized London at William's approach is conveyed by the discovery of a hoard of no less than six thousand coins which had been buried in the Walbrook in 1066, and which the unlucky owner never managed to recover. Anglo-Saxon currency was the most advanced in Europe, and London was the unrivalled centre of its control. From the ninth century the English kings issued coins stamped with the City's name, and by the Norman Conquest every mint in the country was obliged to obtain its dies from the London goldsmiths appointed to administer the currency.

Long before 1066 this financial supremacy had produced universal appreciation of the prime strategical and political importance of the City. Alfred, Ethelred, Edmund, Canute and Godwin, no less than William the Conqueror, had all made the capture and holding of London a vital objective of their campaigns. Nor was the City itself diffident in asserting its importance. London was at once remote from and involved with the emerging nation. On the one hand, the absence of effective political control over the town before Alfred's reign, and the distinguished part played by the City in the struggle against the Danes, had fostered a tradition of independence and self-reliance. On the other hand, by the eleventh century London was making its voice heard in the most fundamental of all political decisions, the choice of a new king. In theory this was not in the least the City's concern: in practice no king could afford to despise its acclaim. Henceforward, with the coronation service taking place in Westminster Abbey, the City's support would become a necessity. Not that Anglo-Saxon London, or rather Westminster, can truly be called a capital. It was the West Saxon kings who had achieved supremacy and, in so far as the peripatetic royal court had a capital at all, theirs was at Winchester. But how could Winchester, on an insignificant rivulet called the Itchen, ever compete with

London on the Thames? Whatever conquest might change in England the facts of geography were unalterable. Whoever ruled, the quays of Billingsgate and Queenhythe would always be busy.

Perhaps there were fewer people in the London of 1066 than there had been in the City's Roman heyday. Nevertheless the Anglo-Saxon period has as much claim to be considered London's determining era; and its influence, moreover, was transmitted without a break. In many respects, the rest of the City's story – and, however little advanced in this book, 1066 was, on London's time-scale, more than halfway to our present perspective – may be regarded as the fruiting of seeds sown well before the Norman Conquest.

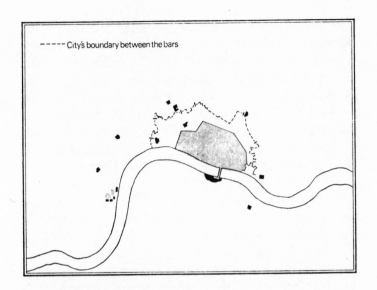

- - - - - City's boundary between the bars

3. 'No king but their mayor'
[1066-1222]

THE TOWER OF LONDON AND ITS GUARDIANS

London had pledged its loyalty to the new regime in 1066, but William the Conqueror was never a man to trust in words alone, least of all where the security of the most important town in his new kingdom was at stake. He readily conceived that nothing was likely to emphasize the sacred nature of an oath of allegiance more effectively than a permanent display of force. Immediately after his coronation, therefore, work began on a great fortress in the east of the City. As a temporary expedient a wooden castle was built by the river just inside the east wall, but massive stone walls were soon rising on adjacent ground. It took twenty years to complete the White Tower (so called because the walls were once whitewashed), but over the next centuries several of the Conqueror's successors, sheltering therein from the fury of the London mob, were to have cause to be thankful for the thoroughness of the work. The Tower has changed hands several times through guile, treachery or incompetence, but it has never been taken by storm.

Although extensive later defences now surround the White Tower, it remains the heart of the Crown's fortress within the City, still, after nine centuries, proclaiming in unmistakable terms the chill, uncompromising strength of the Normans. With how much force the building's message must have struck the Conqueror's London contemporaries, huddled together in their rickety houses of wood and wattle. To them the White Tower must have seemed what William intended, an impregnable symbol of an irreversible conquest. In the twelfth century a monk wrote that the mortar had been mixed with dragons' blood, but the facts of the keep's construction offer a more apposite and scarcely less potent symbol of its might. For the stone, like that used at Westminster Abbey and old St Paul's, came from Caen in Normandy.

Even building the Tower did not satisfy Norman anxiety about London. A day's march away, at Windsor, William raised another castle, from which reinforcements could be rushed to the City in case of trouble. And within London, just inside the west wall, were two further strongholds, Baynard's and Montfichet castles, named after the great barons to whom they were first entrusted.

But there lay a problem. It was one thing to construct impregnable fortresses: quite another to be sure of their keepers' loyalties. The Conqueror had no choice but to give such posts to the adventurers who had followed him from Normandy – they had to be rewarded and, anyway, whom else could an invader trust? But whereas William I was quite capable of keeping his lieutenants in check, his successors found that the guardians of the great castles were sometimes more inclined to defend them against the king than against the king's enemies.

In the Temple church, among several other fine medieval effigies (unfortunately damaged in the 1941 blitz) on the floor of the circular nave, lies that of Sir Geoffrey de Mandeville, a baron whose career (he died in 1144) typifies the threat of the over-mighty subject. A chronicler describes him rushing forth from the presence of the king on one occasion 'like a vicious and riderless horse, kicking and biting' in his rage. That was not the way in which great lords had behaved to the Conqueror. But Mandeville's family had provided Constables of the Tower for three generations, so that they had begun to think of the fortress as theirs by right of inheritance, independent of the royal will. Sir Geoffrey exploited to the uttermost the political chaos which existed after 1135, when the throne was contested by Henry I's daughter Matilda and her cousin Stephen of Blois. Using his control of the Tower as his main bargaining counter, he simply sold his loyalty to the highest bidder at any particular moment, accumulating more authority over London and its surrounding counties with every change of allegiance. Mandeville made the most of the power which he acquired in this way, so that Londoners came to loathe him with the venom traders always feel for those who disrupt their business and extort their profits. In fact Mandeville became frightened enough of the City's hostility to extract a promise, when negotiating with Matilda, that she would make no separate peace with the Londoners, since they were his 'mortal enemies'.

In the event he died before the citizens could be revenged. They had to be content with leaving his body unburied for twenty years, for which omission they themselves must have been the chief sufferers.

THE CITY WINS INDEPENDENCE

Ironically, London's own attitude to the Crown was strikingly similar to that of Mandeville. As long as the monarch was strong enough to secure peace and stability, the City was content to mind its own thoroughly profitable business. But if the Crown proved weak, or was threatened, there was opportunity for profit of another kind. The more uncertain a king's authority, the greater concessions he was compelled to make in order to gain London's valuable support. The prize which the City sought before all others was the freedom to conduct its own affairs according to its own interests, a quest which was pursued so consistently and successfully through periods of national division in the twelfth century that by 1215 King John found himself forced to recognize an elected mayor as the embodiment of London's independent status.

Even William the Conqueror had thought it as well to issue a charter, still in the Guildhall's possession, expressing his goodwill to 'all the citizens, French and English' and confirming the City's 'laws and customs as they were in King Edward's time'. London's wealth, in fact, secured the City greater immunity than any other part of the country from Norman domination. The survival of English surnames amongst influential Londoners of the twelfth century is striking, although it is also true that several citizens discovered a sudden affection for Norman first names like Thomas or William.

The restraint which the Conqueror had deemed it politic

to practise in his dealings with the City, his successors, faced with baronial revolts and rival claims to the throne, found absolutely necessary. Henry I (1100–35) granted London the right to collect its own tax and to choose its own sheriffs, an astonishing concession since the sheriff was the local representative of royal authority. During the turmoil of the next reign London supported Stephen against Matilda with such consistency that it seems as though he too must have bestowed some major privilege, although no charter has survived. On one occasion when Matilda had gained the ascendancy, the Londoners, 'like thronging swarms from bee-hives', chased her from the City, thus ruining her hopes of the Westminster coronation she needed to confirm her claim to the throne. Subsequently the City contributed generously to the army which restored Stephen.

Henry II (1154–89) was too powerful a king to have to make concessions, but he issued a charter acknowledging the citizens' rights and reaped the reward of London's support at a critical point in his son's rebellion of 1181. The next king, Richard I (1189–99) once more undermined the Crown's strength. For him England's wealth only existed to serve his crusading ambitions. 'If I could have found a buyer,' he bragged, 'I would have sold London itself.' But, the same chronicler remarks, 'not for a million silver marks' would Richard have sanctioned the events which followed his departure for Jerusalem.

For once more the City succeeded in exploiting the difficulties of national government to its own advantage. Richard had left his Justiciar, William Longchamp, in charge of the country, restricting himself to the glamour of crusading hero while forfeiting to his deputy the odium of his financial extortions. Almost as though determined to test Longchamp's mettle to the uttermost, Richard gave no power at all to his ambitious and ruthless brother John, an arrangement which at least had the merit of persuading Longchamp to undertake some pretty sharp work strengthening the Tower's defences. Seizing land to the east of the White Tower from St Katharine's Hospital, he built an outer stone wall and began work on a ditch, forerunner of the great moat created by Henry III and Edward I. It was to the Tower that Longchamp retreated when John, who had previously cultivated support in London, appeared in the City at the head of a large army. The Justiciar was safe enough behind his defences but powerless to control events. All depended on which side London would support.

A great meeting of citizens, nobles and ecclesiastics in St Paul's decided to throw in their lot with John. Longchamp was deposed as Justiciar and John accepted as Richard's successor should the king die without children. But there was a price to be paid for London's help. In return John granted that the citizens – or the 'commune' as he called them in the mass – should themselves be responsible for governing the City during the king's pleasure. On his return from the Crusade Richard tactfully avoided mention of whether he pleased or no.

About this time a new official, the mayor, began to appear in the records, acting as the City's representative in dealings with the Crown. There is no evidence that the first mayor was elected: he was called Henry FitzAilwin (Ailwin, interestingly, is an English name) and he held office for some twenty years. FitzAilwin was a prosperous City merchant who lived where the hideous St Swithin's House now stands, just north of Cannon Street beside Walbrook. All the same, he seems to have been the king's man as much as London's and in 1193 he was to the fore in collecting the money required to ransom Richard, then a prisoner in Germany.

But if John thought that he could keep control of the City through the mayor he was soon proved to be mistaken. When he became king (1199–1215) he found the baronial opposition as unscrupulous as he had been in angling for London's support against the Crown, while his disastrous campaigns in Normandy necessitated antagonizing the merchants with heavy taxes. The climax came in 1215. With rebellion threatening to overpower him, John made a last ditch attempt to regain London's loyalty by granting the citizens the right to elect the mayor annually. This bribe was gratefully swallowed but it was too late for any reconciliation. When the barons marched on London the citizens made no attempt to resist them. Significantly, the barons' leader, Robert Fitzwalter, was lord of Baynard's Castle, a post which traditionally carried with it leadership of the City's militia; and it is not surprising to find a Mandeville, perhaps intent on recovering his family's command of the Tower, among his associates. This alliance between London and the barons was crucial in forcing John to sign Magna Carta (1215), which set definite limits on the king's power and which has for that reason been regarded as the foundation of English liberty. But London, of course, cared only for its own freedom.

Nevertheless, the citizens were now fully committed to the baronial cause. The mayor, already a figure of national importance, was a member of the committee appointed to make sure that the king stood by the Charter, while as a further security the barons retained control of the Tower. When John did renege, the mayor and four other citizens backed the decision to invite Prince Louis of France to replace him. When Louis arrived in May 1216 the mayor and barons did public homage to him in St Paul's churchyard. It seemed that civil war was inevitable, but the crisis was defused by John's death. The problem then was to get rid of Louis, who required £7000 to be convinced of the superior attractions of his homeland. His cause evidently lingered on in London because five years after he left some poor wretch was executed for shouting a slogan in his support.

THE MAYOR AND THE RULE OF THE ÉLITE

Louis's departure certainly did not mean that London yielded its constitutional gains. Conservatives were appalled by how much King John had conceded. 'A commune', thundered one chronicler, 'is the puffing-up of the people, the terror of the realm and the emasculation of the priesthood.' In fact he could have spared his outrage: *within* the City the consequences of independence were thoroughly reactionary. The word 'commune' acquired a radical tinge in the nineteenth century, but conveyed no ideas of shared property or power to the rulers of thirteenth-century London. On the contrary, the system of City government which emerged from John's reign represented one more stage in the contraction of leadership.

In Saxon times the whole male population, at least theoretically, had had a say in City affairs. Three times a year the great bell of St Paul's had summoned every Londoner to a meeting in the north-east corner of the medieval churchyard, where they could signify assent to or dissent from whatever proposal was put to them. Tradition has it that these gatherings – known as folkmoots – actually pre-dated the Saxon cathedral, having originated in Romano-British London. At any rate the folkmoot was obviously an impractical means of grappling with the affairs of a great trading city, and inevitably more exclusive and specialized courts took over the day-to-day running of London. Thus the Husting (see p. 66) sat weekly to decide commercial disputes, while each ward was administered by its own court.

At the same time a narrower, legal, concept of 'citizenship' began to emerge. This no longer comprehended every Londoner but denoted a superior caste which could only be attained by inheritance, purchase or a seven-year apprenticeship to another citizen. By the thirteenth century only about one in three Londoners qualified for the privileges, such as exemption from tolls throughout the country and not being answerable to courts outside the City, which the king had been obliged to bestow on 'citizens'. The remaining two-thirds – foreigners, small tradesmen, apprentices, labourers, servants – were entirely excluded from these rights.

Even fully fledged citizens, though, gained no part in the government as a result of the events of 1215. John provided that the mayor should be elected by the folkmoot, but the City's leaders, having wrested the appointment of the mayor from royal control, had no intention of putting their proposals at risk by submitting them to popular approval. Instead, to the disgust of the citizens, they perpetuated their own power by narrowing down the electorate to the aldermen, as the heads of the twenty-four wards were called. The aldermen still select the mayor today, although now they have to choose from two candidates nominated by the City's Livery Companies (see p. 119). There was no such concession to democracy in the thirteenth century. The aldermen themselves were a privileged clique. Theoretically they were elected, but if a ward chose an alderman deemed unsuitable by his peers, the selection was promptly set aside.

So the City's government became a closed shop, dominated by a few closely interrelated families whose wealth and overseas connections made them masters of the key wool, cloth and wine trades. With their riches ostentatiously displayed in town houses and country estates these families naturally aroused popular resentment, and in the 1190s an adventurer called William FitzOsbert, or Longbeard, tried to exploit the bitter murmurs against the City's rulers. But he was up against ruthless men: when he fled into St Mary-le-Bow his enemies smoked him out by setting the church on fire. Longbeard was only spared for the gallows, and for more than half a century after his death the authority of the ruling families remained unchallenged.

One might have expected these men, great merchants as they were, to make common cause with the Crown which was, after all, their best customer, especially as the royal court became more regularly established at Westminster after John's loss of Normandy. But the aldermen loved power as well as money and were rarely prepared to act as mere lackeys of the king. They zealously maintained the City's independence in the face of the inevitable attempts of the Crown, always short of money, to regain control of its richest possession. John himself had tried to maintain royal authority by insisting that the mayor should come to Westminster immediately after his election in order to swear loyalty to the king in person: such was the origin of Lord Mayor's Day, when, on the second Saturday in November, the new mayor proceeds with much pomp to the Law Courts in the Strand, where he swears allegiance. No ritual, however, could prevent the medieval Londoner from regarding the mayor as the personification of the City's independence. 'Come what may,' a citizen had shouted in 1193, 'Londoners shall have no king but their Mayor.' That was constitutional rubbish, and treason to boot, but it expressed the spirit of the times. The mayor's office was laden with regal trappings: he had a personal sword-bearer and a guard of honour, and inside the

City everyone in the country, including all members of the royal family, apart from the king, ranked below him.

The mayor's place at the head of processions only reflected his position in City government. The sheriff, through whom the Crown had once ruled London, so dwindled in importance before the new star that he became nothing more than 'the eyes of the Mayor'. At the end of the Middle Ages a sheriff who was rash enough to kneel beside the mayor in St Paul's was relieved of £50 for his presumption. Early in the thirteenth century, the Mayor's Court had ousted the Husting as the chief commercial tribunal, and rules affecting every detail of London life – from the price of bread to precautions against fire, from the disposal of sewage to the repair of the bridge – were issued by the mayor and his council of aldermen responsible for enforcing laws in their wards.

But the true value of independence to the City was evident in the way that regulations were designed to channel profit into the hands of citizens. Foreign and provincial merchants were only allowed to remain forty days in the City (there were special hostels where they had to stay) and were forced to sell exclusively to citizens, who alone possessed the right to open a shop. Foreigners were not even permitted to deal with each other except through a citizen intermediary. If they ever gained exemption from these rules they were usually made to pay for it. Thus merchants from the Somme bought the privilege of long residence with annual contributions to the upkeep of the conduit which brought water to the City from a spring where Stratford Place now runs off Oxford Street. German traders were granted similar rights when they agreed to take over the maintenance of Bishopsgate. Maybe the delights of freedom are not to be measured in cash, but the leaders of medieval London certainly cannot be accused of funking the attempt.

The City's prosperity would have been obvious enough in the thirteenth century. Two sights in particular, London Bridge and old St Paul's, caught the eye before all others.

THE FIRST STONE BRIDGE

The new stone bridge, one of the most remarkable engineering achievements in medieval Europe, was undertaken because its predecessors, timber constructions built on the original Roman foundations, had quite literally disappeared in smoke every ten years or so. The number of fires in medieval London remains astonishing even after the obvious points about combustible materials and densely packed housing have been made. In the seventy-odd years following the Norman Conquest there were ten major fires and every one destroyed or damaged the bridge. (Interestingly, several counties provided labour for repairs, which shows that London Bridge was deemed a national asset.) The new bridge needed continual patching and repair, but at least the stone did not burn. Begun in 1176, it remained the only bridge downstream from Kingston until the eighteenth century and only narrowly failed to survive into the reign of Queen Victoria and the era of photography. Doubtless it would still be standing had not Progress demanded a wider roadway and fewer arches; and even Progress took two years (1831–2) to demolish the massive stonework. Today all that remains of old London Bridge, for centuries the first home of hubbub and bustle, are a few blocks of stone in the deserted churchyard of St Magnus, reminders that the crossing lay between its Roman predecessor further downstream and the present bridge. The alcoves from the bridge in Victoria Park, Hackney, were eighteenth-century additions.

During the demolition of the medieval bridge the bones of its creator, Peter of Colechurch, were found under the chapel. As the head of the Fraternity of St Thomas, an order which specialized in bridge-building, Peter had already been responsible for the last timber crossing. It was perfectly normal for engineers to operate under the wing of the church in the Middle Ages: after all, there were few other sources of education. The architect of the Tower, for instance, had been the bishop of Rochester. Church patronage was also useful when it came to raising money. Among the contributors towards the cost of London Bridge were the papal legate and the archbishop of Canterbury, which must have helped to establish the project as a worthy outlet for Londoners' charity. Where charity failed the state compelled, for the bridge also benefited from a tax on wool.

The total cost must have been enormous because the work took thirty-three years to complete (Peter of Colechurch died after thirty). Yet seventy years after it was finished the bridge was a ruin. Henry III had granted its revenues to his Queen Eleanor, who was never inclined to reinvest the income in repairs which were continually necessary. For the bridge had to withstand tremendous pressure at top and bottom alike. No sooner was it built than houses sprouted up along the roadway crossing, reducing it to a narrow lane which was so invariably clogged with traffic that the watermen were kept in flourishing business ferrying passengers across the river. Before long both sides of the bridge, except for the drawbridge in the centre, were entirely lined with buildings: thus the piers were supporting not just a crossing but a jumble of workshops and homes.

At the same time the bases of the structure were under continuous attack. Nineteen arches, of varying width according to the availability of firm foundations in the inconsistent river bed, were needed to span the Thames, and all that stone set across the stream impeded the river's flow. The bridge, in fact, acted as a partial dam: at high and low tides the water level dropped by several inches through the arches and the river rushed down the narrow channels with a roar. It was difficult to sleep in the houses above, although bridge dwellers gained the compensation of being less vulnerable to the plague. In order to protect the piers against the Thames's force they were surrounded by great wooden platforms which further narrowed the passages, so that the total breadth of flow through the arches was only a quarter that of the whole river. As a result it became still more dangerous to pass under the arches when the tide was flowing. In the course of the bridge's history there were many who, like Dr Johnson, looked on the cascading torrent from their boats, felt the force of the adage that 'London Bridge was made for wise men to go over and fools to go under', and disembarked to rejoin their waterman on the other side of the crossing. The worst single accident occurred in 1428, when a barge overturned, drowning the Duke of Norfolk and several of his cronies, but never a year went by without deaths under the bridge.

Inevitably such a spot was popular with suicides, not always easily distinguishable from the young bucks who vied with each other in 'shooting the bridge'. Pride of place must go to Sir Dudley North, who managed to swim through unscathed. Others brought less conviction to their daredevilry. In 1661 the diarist Samuel Pepys watched a Frenchman approaching the bridge. 'When he saw the great fall he began to cross himself and say his prayers in the greatest fear in the world, and as soon as it was over he swore *"Morbleu, c'est le plus grand plaisir du monde"*, being the most like a French humour in the world.'

The obstruction of flow at the bridge created something of a pond upstream, which tended to freeze over more quickly than the rest of the river. Occasionally it was possible to drive a coach and horses along the Thames from Westminster to the City; and, especially in the seventeenth century, England's 'little ice age', there were 'frost fairs', when oxen were roasted and stalls, including even printing presses, were set up on the ice. But the thaw could be dangerous, not least to the bridge. In 1282, for instance, the weight of ice grinding against the piers brought down five of the arches. This disaster at least had the good effect of impelling the mayor to set the bridge's finances on a proper basis. The ground where Mansion House now stands was cleared and a market set up, the rents from which were reserved for the bridge's upkeep. What with this provision, more rents from the houses on the crossing, tolls (in 1281 a penny for a horseman and a farthing for a pedestrian), and countless bequests, there was generally enough to keep the bridge in shape. Indeed over the centuries a handsome surplus built up so that when the present London Bridge opened in 1973 it was entirely paid for out of its predecessors' funds.

OLD ST PAUL'S

The other marvel of medieval London, old St Paul's, never attained such a healthy financial position. Like the bridge, its building had been occasioned by fire, which entirely destroyed the wooden Saxon cathedral in 1087. The Norman replacement was constructed on a colossal scale, apparently in a deliberate effort to emulate and excel the slightly earlier cathedral at Winchester. Despite offers of indulgences to contributors in various parts of Europe, the money supply never kept pace with the grandiose plans: it was two centuries before old St Paul's finally stood in the form which survived until the seventeenth century, when Inigo Jones dressed it in a classical casing shortly before its destruction in the Great Fire.

The cathedral was the largest building in the land and, at 585 feet, considerably longer than the present St Paul's. By sheer bulk it dominated medieval London as insistently as its outline still claims first attention from the eye on old maps of the City. The wooden spire, soaring up to 450 feet, must have provided many travellers with their first glimpse of London. In comparison the cross on top of the present St Paul's is a mere 365 feet high, and even the famous spire at Salisbury is only 404 feet, so perhaps we should spare a thought for Robert Godwin who fell from the very top of old St Paul's when fixing a weathercock in 1462. 'The rope broke and he was destroyed upon the pinnacles, and the cock was sore bruised, but Brickwood the king's plumber set it up again,' John Stow somewhat callously records. In 1561 the spire was burnt down during a storm, an event which the godly were quick as ever to attribute to divine vengeance.

In truth, old St Paul's had little enough to boast about in matters spiritual. The cathedral was governed by a dean and thirty canons who, increasingly as the Middle Ages wore on, tended to be royal officials, with notions of religion which rarely extended beyond the obligation of drawing their incomes from the St Paul's estates. These lands also supplied a bakehouse and brewery within the precinct: in 1286 St Paul's produced 67 814 gallons of beer. The world intruded rowdily into the cathedral itself. In 1385 the bishop, Robert de Braybroke, railed against those who 'expose their wares as it were in a public market, [and] buy and sell without reverence for the holy place. Others too by the instigation of the Devil do not scruple with stones and arrows to bring down birds, pigeons and jackdaws which nestle in the walls and crevices of the building; others play at ball and at other unseemly games, both within and without the church, breaking the beautiful and costly painted windows to the amazement of the spectators.'

If the bishop's admonitions had any effect it was short-lived: a generation later there was a proclamation against wrestling in the sanctuary. By 1554 it had become necessary to issue ordinances against leading horses through the building and against pistol shooting therein. Of course St Paul's was a gift of a target for playwrights. In *Arden of Feversham* (1592), an apprentice declares that it is time to shut his stall in order to avoid pilfering by the crowds coming out of St Paul's, while one of Ben Jonson's characters explains that he had been smoking and had only come inside the cathedral in order to spit.

Outside, in the churchyard, the flesh and the devil were more than adequately represented. Edward I (1272–1307) had strengthened the wall surrounding the cathedral on account of the 'robberies, homicides and adulteries' (a fairly comprehensive list) committed there. This wall enclosed twelve and a half acres and there were bitter complaints from Londoners that the chapter was denying them their traditional assembly place for folkmoots by keeping the gates shut. Indeed, until the seventeenth century, public meetings were held in the north-east angle of the cathedral, where stood St Paul's Cross, an outdoor pulpit used for proclamations as well as sermons.

ECCLESIASTICAL FOUNDATIONS

There was no avoiding the church in medieval London.

When old St Paul's was completed the entire population of
the City, perhaps 35000 in 1300, might have crammed into
the cathedral. Yet over a century before a monk named
William Fitzstephen had counted 126 parish churches
within and without the wall. Their physical presence must
have been as pervasive as the clangour of their bells, but
their contribution was vital as well as inescapable. It was
not that the churches made much impression on London's
worldliness, although, in an age when death was constantly
at every shoulder, Londoners were as committed as anyone
else to belief in the after life.

Pending the resurrection, however, the church was also
the one institution at all concerned to soften the rigours of
this world. As the parish churches and monasteries were
centres of communal as well as spiritual life, they accordingly
assumed social as well as religious responsibilities. For the
needy and infirm they represented the only hope of relief
from the afflictions of poverty, sickness and age; for the
rich and successful they provided a focus for many activities
and societies, professional and convivial, which flourished
amongst Londoners in times when house interiors were
sordid enough to spare their inhabitants the joys of domestic
life. In this context the number of churches in the Middle
Ages appears no more remarkable than their diminution
since. Due mainly to the Great Fire of 1666, none of the
actual buildings in Fitzwilliam's total survive, unless he
included the chapel in the Tower, which was not really a
parish church. Otherwise the most impressive relic of a
Norman parish church in today's City is the crypt of St
Mary-le-Bow in Cheapside, though this church was too
large to be typical. The church of St Ethelburga, in Bishopsgate, albeit fifteenth-century and restored beyond retrieval,
gives a better idea of the tiny size of most of London's
medieval churches.

On a much grander scale, and often set in correspondingly large precincts, were the churches of the monks and friars (see the map on p. 93). Yet today they are so little remembered in the City that the name Blackfriars, for instance, rarely suggests anything more than a bridge, station, or underpass. The virtual extinction of the monasteries is a measure of how thoroughly Henry VIII's government pressed home its attack on them during the Reformation of the 1530s. Buildings can always be reconstructed but Henry VIII annihilated the very institutions themselves. Some of London's monastic buildings escaped by becoming parish churches; a few still exist, in whole or part, at St Helen's Bishopsgate, Southwark Cathedral and St Bartholomew the Great. Generally, however, the royal policy was to sell the monasteries lock, stock and barrel to the highest bidder or else to pay off courtiers and favourites with their gift. As preservationists the new owners compared unfavourably with today's property speculators. The result is that nowhere in the City save at the Charterhouse, founded by a Hundred-Years-War veteran named Sir Walter Manny in 1371, has the atmosphere of the cloister survived, a pleasing irony since the Carthusian monks heroically endured the most revolting of Henry VIII's savageries. For the rest, drivers swear, businessmen repine and secretaries gossip, totally oblivious of their cowled predecessors who sought salvation from the very same ground.

Not that London was ever an obvious choice for monastic seclusion. In the century after the Norman Conquest about 400 houses were founded in England, but only one of any note within the City wall. Nor was that one, the priory of Holy Trinity at Aldgate (all that remains is a plaque in Mitre Square), remarkable for any austerities practised by the inmates. Some were scholars, some were occupied with good works, while the priors were always ready to count hospitality amongst the attributes of godliness.

The world pressed still more insistently into the second major house within the wall, the convent of St Helen's Bishopsgate, which was founded by a rich goldsmith in 1212. In some records this convent seems little better than a boarding house for smart girls who had been seduced from the call of matrimony by a less taxing vocation. More than once the nuns were reprimanded for dancing and revelry and in 1385 it was necessary to warn them to 'abstain from kissing secular persons, a custom to which they have become too prone'. Their partiality for attractive veils also gave the ecclesiastical authorities cause for concern. But since so many of the nuns were daughters of City merchants there was never a shortage of rich patrons: at its dissolution in 1538 the convent was one of the wealthiest in the country. The church fortunately escaped Henry VIII's destructive grasp and still exists, complete with the 'nuns' squints' which enabled the weaker sisters to view proceedings at the altar without being obliged to endure the rigours of attendance. The survival was due to the nuns' church having been built on to the north side of St Helen's parish church, which had itself been remodelled at the same time. At the Reformation the two naves were sufficiently well integrated – for the arcade between them is fifteenth century – to pass as a single parish church. The building's age is evident from the several steps, cutting through seven centuries of London detritus, down which it is necessary to pass in order to reach floor level. Inside, the many and splendid tombs justify St Helen's title of the 'Westminster Abbey of the City'.

There were no parish requirements compelling enough to save the churches of two other nunneries, the twelfth-century priories of St John's Haliwell ('Holy-well') in Shoreditch and St Mary's in Clerkenwell. Similarly, across

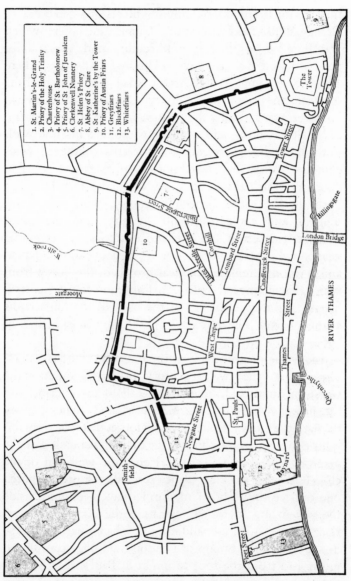

Medieval London, showing some of the monastic precincts.

the river in Bermondsey, only fragments of a gatehouse in Grange Walk stand witness to a Cluniac monastery which was founded in the eleventh century and which once possessed a huge church, over a hundred yards long, where Abbey Street joins Tower Bridge Road. The church of the Augustinian priory of St Mary Overie at Southwark, however, was saved by the creation in 1540 of a new parish called St Saviour's, and is now incorporated in Southwark Cathedral, which presents a conspectus of the previous churches on the site. In the north wall there is a Norman doorway which belonged to the original priory building, burnt in the early thirteenth century, while the north transept and choir (thirteenth century) and the south transept (fourteenth and fifteenth centuries) represent the next church. In the fifteenth century the stone roof collapsed and a wooden replacement was provided, the bosses from which, fascinating examples of macabre and comic medieval fantasy, are now displayed at the back of the nineteenth-century nave. The church only became a cathedral in 1905.

Today the magnificence of the monastic churches is best displayed at the twelfth-century St Bartholomew's the Great, in Smithfield. Indeed, the scale of the interior, and the power which the Norman piers and arches convey through the gloom, make it easy to forget that what remains is little more than the choir of the monastic church. For the gateway to the churchyard was once the west end of the church, so that walking thence towards the present porch one can see the stubs of the former nave's columns beside the pavement. At the Reformation the choir alone was reserved for parish use, and even that had a narrow escape in 1563 when the bishop of London tried unsuccessfully to pinch lead from the roof to use at St Paul's. 'For St Bartholomew's', the bishop somewhat disingenuously declared, 'I mean not to pull it down, but to change it into a churche more conveniente . . . unless some strange opinion should arise that prayer were more acceptable to God under leade than under sclate.'

The founder of St Bartholomew's was a courtier of Henry I called Rahere who, being seized with fever while on a pilgrimage to Rome, vowed to found a hospital in the event of his recovery. But convalescence was slow, so that Rahere inclined a receptive ear when St Bartholomew appeared in a vision with instructions of compelling clarity: 'I . . . have chosen a spot in the suburb of London at Smoothfield where, in my name, thou shalt found a church.' Certainly nothing but authentic religious zeal could have inspired the selection of such an impractical site, so wet and muddy that Rahere needed the help of a vast volunteer labour force of Londoners to clear it. Hospital and priory duly rose side by side, by no means an unlikely juxtaposition, because in the Middle Ages hospitals were themselves religious communities. Indeed, some originated as resting places for pilgrims, and as travellers spread disease so these 'hospices' became centres of treatment. The early records of St Bartholomew's make it clear that prayers to the patron saint were the principal panacea on offer, and indeed they could hardly have failed to be more efficacious than the prescriptions of John of Gaddesdon (1280–1361), one of the priory canons and a celebrated physician, who included beetles and crickets amongst his armoury of medicines. Still, the hospital, if not the patients, survived its treatments. Even the Reformation caused only a five-year break in its history, and the present St Bartholomew's Hospital stands on the same site as Rahere's foundation. It is only fair to add that since the seventeenth century the hospital's medical record has been immensely distinguished.

The hospital of St Katharine by the Tower, set up by

King Stephen's Queen Matilda as an old people's home, also survived the Reformation, though not the dock-building speculators of the nineteenth century (see p. 239). Another twelfth-century hospital, St Thomas's, which was originally associated with the priory of St Mary in Southwark, has been more fortunate, although it was transferred to a new site in Lambeth in 1871. Its patron, St Thomas à Becket, had been born and bred in London, and throughout the Middle Ages his name evoked amongst Londoners an especial devotion, which the saint himself may not have entirely reciprocated. There are hints that he was a shade touchy about his origins. His friend and biographer, William Fitzstephen, whose book opens with an encomium on London – the first full account of life in the City – is perhaps over-anxious to rebut any idea that his hero's father, a merchant from Normandy who had prospered greatly in London before his properties were burnt, was a rentier. Still, Becket's sister certainly put her money to unexceptionable use, founding a hospital in Cheapside, very possibly actually in the family home. There were many other charitable foundations in medieval London. If the leper hospital of St Giles in Holborn, set in large grounds which occupied the triangle now formed by the Charing Cross Road, St Giles High Street and Shaftes-bury Avenue, is singled out for mention, it is as a reminder of one of the curses of medieval existence. By the fifteenth century, when leprosy was almost extinguished, there were ten lazar houses around the City.

MILITARY ORDERS – AND LAWYERS

The name 'Knights of the Hospital of St James of Jerusalem', whose English headquarters were at Clerkenwell just north of Smithfield, might suggest another medical establishment: in fact this was an international order, part military, part monastic, which existed to protect the rights of Christians in Jerusalem. Another, similar, order founded in the twelfth century, the Knights Templar, whose former London precinct to the west of the river Fleet is still called 'Temple', had the allied purpose of protecting pilgrims to the Holy Land. The two orders had much else in common. Both possessed round churches modelled on the Holy Sepulchre at Jerusalem; both grew rich through gifts from the many people who preferred to discharge their crusading zeal through payments in cash or land rather than through the long tramp to the Holy Land and back; and both, on account of this wealth, attracted even greater hostility from other sources than they felt for each other.

The Templars' wealth and financial expertise, together with their extensive overseas connections on the way to Jerusalem, soon made them vital props of royal finance: in Henry II's reign the royal treasury was actually kept at the Temple. But in the Middle Ages there was no more risky status than king's creditor. When Philip IV of France, determined to free himself from Templar finance, pressed the Pope to dissolve the order, the Templars of London found the monarchy indifferent to their fate. Their suppression was a portent of Henry VIII's Reformation of 200 years later. The difference was that in the fourteenth century the pope's authority still remained to force the reluctant Edward II to hand over Templar property to their great rivals, the Hospitallers. Ironically, though, the Temple Church still survives, albeit much restored after the bombing of 1941, whereas that of the Hospitallers, who had become more offensively wealthy than ever as a result of their inheritance, was burnt down in the Peasants' Revolt of 1381. The only physical remains of the Hospitallers' ancient magnificence in Clerkenwell are the Gatehouse (reconstructed in 1504), and the church crypt, which, having been

built in two stages (the west end in the 1140s, the east end
in the 1180s), perfectly illustrates the manner in which the
rounded Norman arch gave way to its pointed Gothic
successor. The same stylistic development is evident at the
Temple church, which, quite apart from its outstanding
architectural interest, would be worth visiting just for its
effigies, or for the carved stone faces that ring the circular
nave with expressions hovering between the grotesque and
the real, all alive with the vitality of the Middle Ages. Very
likely many of them were modelled from the builders of the
church.

Notwithstanding the destruction of the Hospitallers'
church, it might be claimed that their order's spirit is better
reflected today by its distant descendant, the St John
Ambulance Brigade, than is that of the Templars by the
lawyers who now creep about their ground. Yet even
while the Templars flourished, they must have employed
legal advisers for their financial dealings with the king.
After the dissolution of the order the lawyers moved into
the Temple as the first tenants of the Hospitallers, and ever
since then they have proved far too canny to be evicted.
There could scarcely have been a more likely spot for the
profession. The Temple, after all, lies between the City and
Westminster, that is, between two parties in continuous and
permanent conflict.

One of the sources of dispute in the period following the
Norman Conquest had concerned the precise geographical
limits of the City, which had increasingly been spilling
further and further outside the walls. The cause of this
expansion was not yet one of over-population as there had
been no dramatic leap in numbers by the beginning of the
thirteenth century. It was rather that since the Church
owned so much land there were large patches within the
walls which were not available for houses. Green spaces

remained within the City's original area even while buildings were springing up along the main roads leading from
it. The resulting boundary dispute with Westminster was
resolved in 1222 when the final position of the bars, which
were boundary posts set in the routes issuing from the gates,
was agreed (see the map on p. 93) The size of the City
almost doubled to the present square mile. Today the bars
have disappeared from London but the City's heraldic lions
greet visitors at the same places. The lasting settlement of
that particular dispute, however, in no way inaugurated an
era of harmony between Westminster and the City.

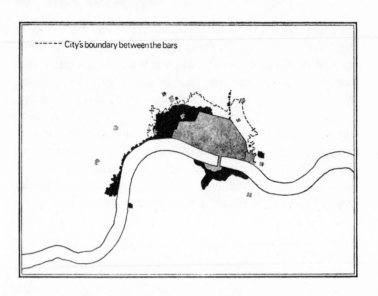

----- City's boundary between the bars

4. 'The most dangerous branch of a proud and dangerous people'
[1222–1485]

HENRY III (1216–1272) AND WESTMINSTER ABBEY

'Nauseously rich,' snorted Henry III in 1248, overflowing with resentful fury against the Londoners to whom he had just been compelled to pawn his jewels. Certainly he always contrived to keep himself quit of the corruptions of accumulated capital. He laboured under the dual handicap of being both artistic and extravagant, either of which characteristics might by itself have proved fatal to a medieval monarch. Henry combined them with a passion that became increasingly concentrated, as his disastrous reign proceeded, on his plans for rebuilding Westminster Abbey.

For the king was not just aesthetic, he was religious as well, with a special devotion to the Abbey's founder, King Edward the Confessor. For a century or so after the Confessor's death the world had remained ignorant of his extraordinary – and highly dubious – chastity, the happy tidings of which were first propagated in the middle of the twelfth century by a Westminster monk named Osbert de Clare. At that time the monastery was badly in need of an attractive cult, for since 1066 the Crown had shown precious little interest in the foundation. If the king was around London he would very likely stay at Westminster – conveniently near yet prudently removed from the City – but the palace was only one of several places where he lodged on his progress round the country, apparently no more favoured than other English bases like Winchester, Gloucester or Abingdon.

The Westminster monks might have drawn encouragement from the coronation services in the Abbey but these were not yet a long-established tradition. The only other sign of Norman preference for Westminster had been secular: William II (1087–1100) had added a magnificent hall to the palace. (The Westminster Hall which stands today is fourteenth century, but the walls incorporate eleventh-century stonework and the dimensions are original.) Westminster Hall, though, brought scant comfort to the monks who, disconcerted to discover their flight from the world no longer hampered by royal patronage, took to forging the charters which the Crown failed to produce in defence of their lands and privileges. Then, in 1161, their trump turned up: Edward the Confessor was canonized.

The new saint did not immediately speed to the rescue of the Abbey's finances, but in the next century he suddenly captured the biggest card in the pack.

Perhaps it was consciousness of their mutual ineffectiveness which attracted Henry III to the Confessor. At any rate he decided to pay Edward the doubtful compliment of knocking down his Abbey (already, if a papal bull is to be believed, 'consumed with excessive age') in order to build a yet more splendid setting for his shrine. Demolition began in 1245 and by 1269 the east end of Henry III's building was complete, including the transepts and the choir which, with great ceremonies like the coronation in mind, was set further into the nave than usual in order to provide a 'theatre' at the transept crossing. Work on the nave ceased after Henry's death, to be taken up again more than a hundred years later by Richard II, and finally completed, fortunately all in the same thirteenth-century style, in 1517. The early sixteenth century also saw the building of what is perhaps the Abbey's greatest glory, the Henry VII Chapel at the east end, in the exclusively English Perpendicular style. (One of the houses pulled down to make this addition possible, incidentally, had belonged to Geoffrey Chaucer, the first entrant to Poets' Corner.)

The main part of the Abbey has been called 'a great French thought, expressed in excellent English', a combination which naturally achieves complete success. Henry's English craftsmen had obviously studied Amiens and Rheims cathedrals, and this influence is evident in the soaring nave (at 103 feet the highest in England), the rose windows in the transepts, the apsed east end and the flying buttresses. Henry seems to have taken another French church, La Sainte Chapelle in Paris, as a model for wealth and variety of internal decoration. Even today, notwithstanding the efforts of Reformation vandals who, in the name of God, smashed the medieval glass and hacked off much of the ornamentation (the shrine of Edward the Confessor being stripped of Henry's most priceless treasures), the Abbey's overwhelming impact owes as much to the accumulation of details as to the grandeur of the whole. Often overlooked are the old monastic buildings, some of which remain as part of Westminster School.

PERSECUTION OF THE JEWS

If Henry III, despite being constantly broke, managed to find enough money to keep work at the Abbey in progress, that was at least partly because he was a devout enough Catholic to be able to rob the Jews with a good conscience. Indeed, in the thirteenth century Rome regarded such behaviour as a display of religious virtue.

Jewish financiers had come to England in the wake of William the Conqueror, and from the first their main community was in London, where their former quarters to the north of Cheapside are still called Old Jewry. Initially, under the Conqueror and his sons, the Jews prospered, so that in the twelfth century they were among the few Londoners to possess stone houses. But their position was always insecure, because as mere 'chattels of the king' they possessed no legal rights and were entirely dependent on royal protection. That was forthcoming under a king like William II, who enjoyed baiting Christian opinion with his tolerance; but even in such comparatively good times the Jews were harassed with tiresome regulations, like that which demanded that every Jew dying in England, be he so far from London as Exeter or York, should be buried in the special cemetery outside Cripplegate. That law, though, was just a crude device for raising money by taking tolls on the way to London. More fundamental was the rule which barred Jews from farming, manufacture and trade, so that they could only survive by lending money at interest, a practice which the medieval church condemned as the heinous sin of usury.

This meant that a king like Henry III, at once impecunious and pious, could satisfy his financial needs by borrowing from the Jews, and his religious scruples by failing to pay the money back. The Crusades had helped to make anti-Semitism respectable. At the coronation of Richard I, the Great Crusading Hero, there had been a riot when some Jews, eager to placate the king with rich gifts, had dared to slip inside Westminster Abbey. The disturbance spread to the City, where the mob surrounded Jewry and set the thatched roofs ablaze. Thirty Jews died, either burnt in their houses or butchered as they fled them, but only three culprits were brought to justice: one had taken advantage of the chaos to rob a Christian; the other two had accidentally fired a Christian house.

By 1215 Rome was demanding that all Jews should wear a badge and, as a loyal son of the church, Henry III insisted that it should be placed in an especially prominent position. But Henry was too religious (and too poor) to rest content with that. One of his favourite devices was to allege, with or without evidence, that the Jews had committed some horrific crime (the ritual murder of children was a favourite choice), torture a few into confession, hang them, and then levy an expiatory fine on the entire Jewish community. In 1239 this procedure resulted in the London Jews being relieved of a third of their property; and in 1244 the discovery of a child's body in a City churchyard, allegedly with an incriminating Hebrew inscription cut into the flesh, cost the whole country's Jews £40,000. These were not isolated incidents: altogether Henry III managed to extract over £160000 (more than six years' total Crown revenue) from English Jewry, which was utterly bankrupted. Of course, only a fraction of this money went into Westminster Abbey: Henry also had his court favourites and a disastrous foreign policy to finance. But on some occasions Jews were specifically fined for the work at Westminster. Thus in 1245, the year Henry began the rebuilding, Moses of Hereford contributed £3000, Licoricia of Oxford £2500, and Elias le Eveske a silver gilt chalice. These men and their fellow sufferers deserve a thought from admirers of the Abbey.

THE CITY AND NATIONAL POLITICS

Inevitably the Crown's financial difficulties made for trouble with London, the richest town in the kingdom. Henry III soon discovered that the City's independent spirit was not to be easily curbed now that his father John had given it legal sanction. Londoners developed a tiresome tendency to haggle over the precise terms under which they paid taxes. Henry tried to cow them by suspending their privileges. On ten occasions between 1239 and 1257 he set aside mayor and aldermen and re-established direct royal rule, but the very number of times that he was compelled to restore their rights is an indication of his impotence. Ultimately the king always needed Londoners' loans too desperately to maintain a consistent attack on their freedom. In 1255, after years of harassment, the City was still capable of refusing point-blank to pay a compulsory 'tallage', or tax; as free men, the merchants argued, they were liable only for voluntary 'aids'.

In its essentials the struggle between the Crown and London followed the same pattern throughout the whole of the Middle Ages. As long as the king was in control nationally he could usually, as Edward I was to show, make the mayor respect his authority. But the Plantagenet line produced alternate weak and strong kings. When the Crown governed ineffectively Londoners were inclined to allow themselves to hope for better things from a change of regime.

There were, however, divisions within the City also, for the ruling élite was constantly under threat from the citizens who had been excluded. The rival parties of state, angling for support from the various interests within London, tended to being these internal tensions to a head, often with violent effect.

RISE OF THE CRAFTS

By the middle of the thirteenth century the dominance of the sixteen or so families who had led the commune was beginning to waver. To some extent they only had their own arrogance to blame. Like all the privileged they pushed their luck too far. 'Thomas Basing took a tallage from his ward', the complaint was heard in 1275, 'no one knows why'. Such high-handed behaviour invited retribution, as did the aldermen's habit of obtaining special exemption from taxes. But in any case the days of the old order were numbered: the energies of a booming City could not forever be contained in an oligarchic straitjacket. During the thirteenth century London's share of exports increased from roughly a seventh to a third of the country's mounting total. New men, like the fishmongers and the skinners who profited from the expanding Baltic trade, were making fortunes and seeking power, aspirations which gradually came to be expressed through craft associations.

Like town dwellers of any time medieval Londoners clubbed together for any number of purposes. There were purely convivial associations like the Feste de Pui, the aims of which were declared to be 'bon amour' and 'joly

desport': the members so reverenced women that they felt
bound to exclude the entire sex that they might learn to
'honour, cherish and love their dear wives, at all times and
in all places, as much in their absence as in their presence'.
The Feste, needless to say, was of French origin. Other
associations were sporting, like the Fraternity of Footballers,
or clerical, like the sinisterly entitled Secret Confederation
of London Rectors, formed in part to resist the encroach-
ments of curates. It would be difficult to find much in
common between so many different groups, beyond the
fact that each association was attached to a particular church.
Obviously, though, fraternities often originated from a
neighbourhood or street, and this geographical bias had
important implications because certain trades were concentrated into certain areas.

The saddlers, for instance, were to be found in Foster Lane,
the goldsmiths at the east end of Cheapside, and the plumbers
in Clement's Lane. Sometimes a district's ancient usage is
still preserved in a name. Cannon Street is a Cockney
shortening of Candlewick Street, once home of the candle-
makers and wax dealers: the old form, 'Candle wick', survives as a ward name. Similarly Cordwainer ward recalls
the cordwainers, or shoemakers, who clustered round St
Mary-le-Bow, while Vintry ward was the centre for wine
merchants. Street names like Ironmonger Lane, Bread
Street and Fish Street Hill (this last running down to old
London Bridge and conveniently sited for the landing
place at Billingsgate) speak for themselves; and Skinners
Lane actually still contains the premises of fur merchants
just as it did 700 and more years ago.

The local associations soon came to represent the particular
trades concentrated in their areas. As they began to seek
rights to control their own affairs, fix their own prices and
adjudicate their own disputes, the crafts naturally became

involved in City politics. Equally naturally the ruling élite, quite correctly sensing a threat, reacted to the new organizations with suspicion and hostility.

THE CRAFTS GAIN CONTROL (1263/64)

The emerging crafts were not without potential allies. One possibility was the king. In 1258 royal policy at last hit on an effective means of undermining London's rulers, making a direct appeal to popular opinion in the City by calling the folkmoot assembly of all the citizens. This line of attack succeeded in scaring the mayor and aldermen into temporary submission, but Henry's own power collapsed nationally before the policy could be developed. In the event it was in alliance with the baronial opposition to the king that the crafts first seized control from the aldermen. Left to themselves the solid and respectable tradesmen would probably never have dared to come out in open rebellion against the Crown. As things turned out, however, they were given no choice.

For beneath the industrious artisans lurked another class, the largest in London, that 'mass of destitution, misfortune and rascality' which swung unpredictably between listless despair and violent destructiveness, one moment a neglected multitude, the next a dangerous mob. What had such people to lose from chaos, where should they find hope save in anarchy, how could they profit but by plunder? 'Chattels and goods had he none', the coroners again and again recorded of medieval Londoners, and so they pass beyond history's ken, these men who were history's arbiters in the mass. Only occasional glimpses show what kind of conditions London's disinherited endured. Thus a report of an almsgiving at Blackfriars in 1322 casually mentions that fifty people were trampled to death in the scramble to receive the bounty. Such a rabble was at once irresistible and uncontrollable. For that reason the men of the crafts, who feared disorder, were wary of a deliberate alliance. On the other hand they would not hesitate to exploit whatever chaos the mob might cause. So it proved in 1263 when Simon de Montfort, leader of the baronial rebels against the king, appeared with an army outside the City gates, and fury erupted in the streets.

The king and queen were trapped in the Tower which Henry, who knew well the danger from the City, had prudently strengthened. Following Longchamp's lead, he had completed the surrounding stone wall, forming the great enclosure known as the Inner Ward, with the White Tower at the centre. This wall was interspersed with defensive bastions: the Wakefield, Bloody, Devereux, Flint, Bowyer, Brick, Martin, Constable, Broad Arrow and Salt towers all originally date from Henry's reign. The river frontage, meanwhile, was fortified with the St Thomas's (including Traitors' Gate) and Well towers. The construction of St Thomas's had caused some trouble. According to the chronicler, St Thomas à Becket, deeming this tower oppressive to his fellow Londoners, had twice flattened it with a blow of his crozier. When building the bastion a third time Henry was wise enough to dedicate an oratory in the south-east turret to the saint, a gesture which effectively diminished his concern for the citizens. The king needed all the protection he could get in 1263. When his formidable queen tried to escape to Windsor her barge was pelted with stones and mud and she was forced to take refuge in St Paul's.

The authority of the aldermen, no less than that of the king, disintegrated before the rabble in the streets. There was no chance to weigh the situation; they were compelled to accept de Montfort's terms to save their skins from the

City's own rioters. The mayor speedily and wisely discovered himself to be in sympathy with the popular mood,
and the craft leaders, responding to the intoxicating call of
public duty, assumed command. Gone were the exclusive
City councils and courts. The old folkmoot was again
resurrected, the rights of the crafts were acknowledged, and
the commune of all the citizens became an effective reality
for the first time since its institution.

The mayor's manner of proceeding reflected the new
mood. 'In all he did', reported the disgusted chronicler of
the displaced aldermen, 'he acted and determined through
them [the general assembly of citizens], saying "Is it your
will that so it should be?" And if they answered "Ya, Ya",
so it was done.' Even worse, 'from day to day individuals
of every craft *of themselves* made new statutes and pro-
visions. . . .' Such goings-on were outrageous to conservatives. After all, who were London's new rulers but
'ribalds with blue nails' and 'fools and ribalds of the lower
classes, servile sons of diverse mothers, caring nothing for
the welfare of the City'?

Faced with such hostility from the men they had displaced,
the 'servile sons' were irrevocably committed to de Montfort's rebel cause. In 1264 'those rustic Londoners' made a
powerful contribution to his victory at the battle of Lewes
by running away so precipitately when attacked that the
pursuing royal troops were never able to get back into the
fray. Such a triumph mightily improved the mayor's
courage and his oath of loyalty became impertinently
qualified. 'My lord,' he told the king, '*so long as unto us you
will be a good lord* we will be faithful and duteous unto you.'
He might have been wiser to hedge his bets.

DEFEAT OF THE CRAFTS: EDWARD I (1272–1307) IN COMMAND

In 1265, deprived of the Londoners' tactical assistance, de Montfort and his party perished at the battle of Evesham, and the City soon discovered that treason means backing the wrong side. The quality of Henry's mercy was not merely strained; it cost the City a fine of £17000 to obtain. A new crime appeared in the records: 'Offence – a Londoner'. Not until 1270 did the City regain the right of self-government and then it was the same few families as of old who resumed control. 'Whereas the commune ought to elect the mayor and sheriffs', the complaint arose in 1275, 'the aldermen meet and of their own will and no one else's elect their own friends.'

But this time their lease on power proved short-lived. The next king, Edward I, proved one of the strongest of medieval monarchs. Like Henry III he took away the City's privileges, but this policy, which had appeared petulant weakness in the father, meant virtual dictatorship when applied with the unrelenting determination of the son. For thirteen years (1284–97) Edward ruled the City through his own appointees. To make assurance doubly sure he continued his father's work at the Tower, building Byward and Beauchamp towers as well as the Middle Tower through which visitors enter the fort today.

Edward deprived the City's hereditary leadership of more than power; his economic policies sapped their wealth as well. The king could no longer turn to the Jews for funds. After Henry III had ruined them, Edward was able without undue sacrifice to win the plaudits of the church by expelling them from the country, a ban which was to last nearly 400 years. There remained, however, the problem of raising money, which he solved by turning to foreign merchants, in particular to the Italians who were then giving their name to Lombard Street. In return he granted them all kinds of trading privileges, in flat contradiction of the City's regulations. He also placed with foreigners those lucrative contracts, on which the aldermen's prosperity had been built, for the supply of the royal household. By the time that financial crisis compelled even Edward to accept an elected mayor again, the standing of London's great families had been completely undermined. Street names like Basinghall and Bucklersbury still commemorate their ancient power, but the Basings and the Bukerils vanished into obscurity after the thirteenth century.

CRAFT LEADERS AS ALDERMEN: A NEW ÉLITE

After the disappearance of these families the craft leaders no longer needed to overthrow the City's government; they were already becoming aldermen themselves. It was left to Edward II, another weak king whose reign was beset with baronial revolts, to reap the consequences of his father's policies. For after Edward I's rule the City had everything – and notably the restoration of the old trading laws against foreigners – to gain from espousing the barons' cause. The new regime in the City restricted its loyalty to Edward II to such occasions as the king could muster an army with which to threaten the capital. But, just as had happened under Henry III, the City's association with the national movement of revolt unleashed the radicals within its own bounds. During the years of baronial ascendancy from 1309 to 1312 the number of Londoners possessing citizen rights greatly increased, as membership of a craft became the sole effective qualification. Moreover it was decreed that all offices in City government should be elected by all the citizens. After all, the cry went up in 1312, 'the City ought to be governed by the aid of men engaged in trade and handicrafts'.

Or should it? There turned out to be no unanimity on that point. No sooner were the new City leaders in office than they became infected with the same oligarchic spirit as their predecessors. Of course it had been necessary for masters to make common cause with the workmen of their crafts during their sweep to power, but really, the new aldermen asked themselves, what had *they* to do with such a crowd? As great merchants and capitalists they did not soil their hands with manufacture. Had they captured the City's government only to be told that the mayor must rule with a council drawn from the crafts and wards? Perish the thought. It was enough that artisans should be classed as citizens without their presuming to claim the privileges thereof. So, just as the commune's first rulers had ignored King John's instructions over the election of the mayor, the craft leaders of the fourteenth century quietly set aside the democratic decrees of Edward II's reign. The aldermen were no longer all related but they remained a self-elected clique of great merchants rather than the choice of the artisans. As such they tended to come from organizations like the Mercers, who dealt in silk and cloth, or from the Fishmongers and Grocers who prospered by keeping the expanding population supplied with food. But a fierce resentment simmered among their former allies and before the end of the century they would be made to feel it.

THE LONDON MOB DEPOSES EDWARD II

The mob, meanwhile, was ever a smouldering threat which occasionally erupted into an angry and consuming blaze. In 1326–7 the rabble arose in London and struck

Edward II from his throne. Certainly the City leaders, who could hardly afford to contemplate the restoration of Edward's power when they had sided so consistently against him, were willing accomplices, but there was never any sign that they were in control of events.

As the rebels (though perhaps the presence of the queen and her son Prince Edward at their head gainsays that description) approached London the atmosphere in the City rapidly became so ugly that Edward II fled to the west. He was just in time. His treasurer, the bishop of Exeter, was confronted by angry swarms in Newgate. He ran for the sanctuary of St Paul's, but the crowd was in no mood for legal niceties. 'Kill, kill,' they chanted, dragging him through the cathedral churchyard to Cheapside where they hacked off his head with a breadknife. Several foreigners suffered similar fates. The mayor decided not to reason with the mob, but headed a deputation to Westminster. Was Parliament, he threatened, 'willing to be in accord with the City' in deposing Edward? In the circumstances Parliament decided that it was. During the next few days the great men of the land processed to the City where, with rioters daring them to refuse, they swore loyalty to Edward III. The archbishop of Canterbury even took the precaution of presenting the City with fifty tuns of wine. Not surprisingly the new reign began with Edward III issuing a charter confirming the liberties of London. As for Edward II, he would have done better to face the breadknives rather than the red-hot poker which scorched out his existence at Berkeley Castle in Gloucestershire.

RICHARD II AND THE PEASANTS' REVOLT (1381)

Not until the end of the century did the royal authority again come under such deadly attack from London. But

Richard II (1377–99) was blessed, or cursed, with the same artistic nature as Henry III. Likewise posterity gained the same architectural profit (notably the marvellous hammer-beam roof in Westminster Hall), his favourites the same perks, and his subjects the same immense taxes. Not that the City necessarily suffered by kingly extravagance, for the money which Richard took from merchants often found its way back into their pockets. In 1361 the Great Wardrobe, the department which ordered supplies for the court, had been permanently established within the City at a house near Baynard's Castle. (The church of St Andrew-by-the-Wardrobe in Queen Victoria Street takes its name from this institution.) Between 1392 and 1394 the Wardrobe spent £13 000 in the City, more than a quarter of that sum going to Richard Whittington (Dick Whittington of legend) who made his fortune by selling the king expensive silks and his reputation by spending his profits on City charities.

As Richard was only ten at the beginning of his reign the government was headed by his uncle John of Gaunt who quickly aroused London's hostility. It was not so much that the merchants disapproved of Gaunt's policies; indeed they subscribed generously to a campaign against French privateers who had been interfering with trade. The trouble with Gaunt was simply that he was ineffective. The mayor was driven to fitting out a fleet himself, and its capture of a celebrated pirate made a telling contrast with the dismal failure of Gaunt's own expedition to Brittany.

The popular opinion of Gaunt was made flagrantly clear during the Peasants' Revolt when his palace, the Savoy off the Strand, was burnt to the ground with all its contents, even plunder being eschewed in the universal zest for destruction. How the peasant rabble got into London is something of a mystery: after the revolt some prominent

City men were accused by their opponents of having deliberately allowed them to enter. It seems unlikely, though, that anyone with something to lose could have abetted such a raging horde, for the consequences were entirely predictable. Soon, the City's record relates, 'hardly was there a street . . . in which there were no bodies lying of those who had been slain'. As ever, foreigners were popular targets and thirty-five Flemings were killed in Cheapside alone. The London mob also seized the opportunity to pay off some old scores. A typical victim was Roger Legett, who had put 'hidden engines of iron' to trap people in Fittersfield (the site of Lincoln's Inn Fields) some years before and now found himself dragged from sanctuary and butchered.

When the king went to parley with the peasants at Mile End to the east of the City, the mob was allowed, through some extraordinary but unrecorded act of carelessness or treachery, to enter the Tower, with the result that the archbishop of Canterbury and other ministers parted company with their heads, which were subsequently displayed on London Bridge. John of Gaunt's son, destined to depose Richard in 1399 and reign as Henry IV, was in the Tower and only narrowly escaped a like fate, a deliverance which Richard may have rued in later years. In 1381 Henry was only one of many who owed their lives to the cool nerve of the boy king. Accompanied only by a tiny retinue which included the mayor, Richard bearded the peasant army by St Bartholomew the Great in Smithfield, where occurred one of the most dramatic scenes of the Middle Ages. Mayor Walworth tried to arrest the rebel leader Wat Tyler, who was badly wounded in the ensuing scuffle. The peasants looked on their hero's downfall in gaping disbelief; if one of them had moved it would all have been over for the king. But Richard calmly stepped forward to tell them that he was their true leader. The peasants, stunned by this gesture, meekly followed him to Clerkenwell where even the City militia proved equal to the task of dispersing them.

THE 'MUCHEL SMALE PEOPLE' DEFEATED (1382/83)

Mayor Walworth was a member of the Fishmongers' Company which still possesses the dagger with which he reputedly assailed Wat Tyler. But it is doubtful whether many Londoners regarded him with admiration. He was, after all, the very type of great capitalist that men of less privileged callings resented. The Fishmongers in particular incurred the enmity of the whole City by using their trading monopoly to keep their prices artificially high. Moreover as they possessed their own court, in which they themselves decided all charges against them, there was little hope of bringing a corrupt fishmonger to justice.

Walworth's successor as mayor, John of Northampton, embodied the inevitable reaction to such high-handed behaviour. Not only did he abolish the monopolies and privileges of the Fishmongers; he turned to the long-excluded artisan crafts for support against the great merchants. All the radical proposals of Edward II's reign – annual election of aldermen by the crafts and the establishment of a permanent elected council of citizens to advise the mayor – were implemented. For a year or two it really seemed as though the domination of the wealthy might be at an end, a prospect which moved them to expressions of outrage strikingly similar in tone to those used by the threatened élite in the previous century. Instead of 'servile sons of diverse mothers', John of Northampton's followers were designated 'muchel smale people that konne non skyl of governaunce'.

Northampton, though, was a bigot who antagonized too many interests with his reforming zeal, and his revolution did not last. By the end of the century the measures which he had introduced to involve all the citizens in government had nearly all been reversed. But the Fishmongers never recovered their former dominance and the general assembly which Northampton had rescued from obsolescence survived, the origin of the Common Council which now runs the City.

FLUID POPULATION: ENTRENCHED INSTITUTIONS

For the remainder of the Middle Ages London was ruled exclusively by rich men. That is not to say, though, that the aldermanic ranks were impenetrable. It was always possible for newcomers to force their way into the City élite if only because of the increasing tendency of successful merchants to leave London and set up as country gentlemen, an urge that still afflicts wealthy Londoners, and the country, today. The most famous merchant of all, Richard Whittington, mayor four times between 1397 and 1420, preferred to remain in London, but his early career was typical of the reverse process whereby new blood was drawn into the City from the country. He came from a Gloucestershire family which, like many of the landed gentry, solved the problem of finding careers for younger sons by apprenticing them in London. The constant movement in and out of London, however, was not confined to any one class. At all social levels the City's population was ever-shifting and few fourteenth- or fifteenth-century Londoners could have claimed more than two or three generations' residence there.

It was institutions rather than families which became entrenched. During the fourteenth century the craft associations began to acquire royal charters which gave them the right to hold property in perpetuity. That is why, several hundred years after the extinction of their original purpose, City companies can still celebrate their multifarious charities over distinctly adequate feasts in their grand halls. The Merchant Tailors were one of the first companies to possess a hall (today their premises in Threadneedle Street still include stonework from the original fourteenth-century building) and it was a sign of the times that they took over this site from a feudal lord called Sir Oliver Ingham. Similarly the Grocers bought land from the mighty Fitz-walter family, formerly lords of Baynard's Castle.

By 1500 nearly thirty companies owned halls and several, like the Merchant Tailors, still occupy their original sites. The Skinners, for instance, have been on Dowgate Hill to the south of Cannon Street for nearly seven centuries and the Saddlers are still to be found off Foster Lane, both places being the ancient centres of the respective crafts. By the fifteenth century, however, it was already becoming possible to be admitted to a company by inheritance, without going through an apprenticeship, so that gradually the membership became dissociated from actual work of the craft. Certainly one would not fancy the chances of the twentieth-century Ironmongers, Goldsmiths, Skinners and others of earning a living from their titular trades. As the character of the companies began to change the artisans were increasingly made to feel their place. Whereas once the entire membership had been entitled to wear the distinctive uniforms, or 'liveries', of their guild, in the fifteenth century this became a privilege restricted to an élite, the 'Liverymen', who in turn gave their name to the Livery Companies.

RICHARD II AND LONDON: ANOTHER KING DEPOSED

Richard II's reign did not live up to the brilliant promise which he had displayed in the Peasants' Revolt. Like Edward II's, his rule degenerated into an extended bicker with the barons, and once more the hostility of London played a major part in the king's downfall. Yet initially Richard had shown a shrewd grasp of the necessity of cultivating good relations with the City: Mayor Brembre, by virtue of the riches under his sway, had become a key figure in the king's government. But it is impossible to please all the people all the time. Brembre's high standing in affairs of state was an affront to the great lords who regarded themselves as the king's 'natural' counsellors. The situation presented an early example of one of the great themes of English history, namely the contest between landed and commercial wealth for the control of government. This has always been a bitter struggle and when the barons triumphed in 1388 they did not spare Brembre, who was executed after a mockery of a trial in Westminster Hall. In that crisis the City lived up to the chronicler's judgement that Londoners were 'as fickle as seed'. Having sworn an oath of loyalty to Richard in May, the mayor and aldermen welcomed the baronial army in June.

Thereafter many City merchants were too cautious to lend money to a king of doubtful permanence, while Richard, when he regained authority, made no effort to conciliate them. In his last years he illegally and sometimes forcibly extorted money from every class in London so it was not surprising that the City provided decisive backing for Henry of Lancaster when he claimed the throne. When Henry had triumphed, the mayor and aldermen, showing the magnanimous spirit of commerce, sent a special deputation begging for Richard's death, a request to which the new king, showing the mercy of an insecure usurper, was happy to accede.

PRESTIGE OF LONDON: THE GUILDHALL

Henry IV (1399–1413) summoned three Londoners to early meetings of his council, among them Richard Whittington, whose apparently effortless transfer to the new star was a reminder that financiers (for so the great merchant had now become) can be less expendable than kings. Henry's involvement of prominent City men in affairs of state was a more open version of Richard's dealings with Brembre. Both monarchs might have agreed with Froissart that Londoners were 'the most dangerous branch of a proud and dangerous people', and though it would have gone against the royal grain to have accepted Froissart's judgement that by this branch 'the whole kingdom of England orders and regulates itself', they could scarcely have denied that to govern in the teeth of London's enmity was to risk not governing at all.

For their part the mayor and aldermen did not fail to show themselves fully alive to the importance of their positions. In the fifteenth century *Lord* Mayor became the accepted form of address and if the aldermen possessed no personal title that did not prevent their wives from calling themselves 'Lady' or from clinging to that prefix even after remarriage to a mere commoner. To mayor and aldermen alike, moreover, it was becoming irresistibly evident that, if the king had a grand hall at Westminster, officers of their dignity could scarcely merit a lesser one within the City.

In 1411, then, work began on a new Guildhall in Aldermanbury, an area which, as the name suggests, has been associated with London's government from earliest times. The City's munificence did not always match its conception of its own grandeur so the building work dragged on and was not completed until 1439. Although the roof has been replaced several times since then and the entrance was entirely remodelled in the eighteenth century, the walls are still largely fifteenth-century work. The Guildhall remains the administrative centre of the City. The prime minister goes there once a year to give an account of government policy to the mayor and aldermen, an occasion which symbolizes the City's long and continuing involvement in matters of state.

NATIONAL CHAOS: EDWARD IV (1461–83) GAINS LONDON'S SUPPORT

In the Middle Ages London's loyalty to the Crown was always conditional on the king maintaining the order in which business and trade could flourish. There could be no argument with Henry V (1413–21), the successful warrior; but when, under Henry VI (1421–61), England not merely endured humiliation in France but also drifted towards the internal chaos of the Wars of the Roses (1455–85), during which the throne was contested between the rival houses of York and Lancaster, London's allegiance inevitably began to waver. This was particularly true of the merchants, who, though by no means suffering the same eclipse as the nation, longed for a government strong enough to enforce a policy of rigorous protection backed by a powerful navy. So, though the City was careful not to take sides when the Lancastrian Henry VI was deposed, there was a huge and attentive audience in March 1461 at an open-air sermon by St Paul's Cross (site of the ancient folkmoot) where the preacher canvassed the Yorkist claim to the throne.

Later, London's wary welcome for the Yorkist Edward IV was to turn to genuine enthusiasm. No doubt this was partly because the new king's talent for winning battles simplified the tricky problem of taking sides in those troubled times, but there was more to it than that. The flattering interest which Edward bestowed on merchants' wives was compounded by constant attentions to the husbands also. Before 1461 only eleven London citizens had been knighted: in the first decade of his reign Edward added another eighteen to this total. In 1482 he laid on a hunting party in Waltham Forest at which his guests from the City were plied 'right plenteously with all manner of dainties as if' (the reporter can find no more telling compliment) 'they had been in London'. The king himself was a member of the Merchant Tailors' Company and actively engaged in trade on his own account. Nor were the lesser crafts, many of which received charters of incorporation in this reign, forgotten. In short, Edward IV showed more concern for Londoners' interests and attributes than any of his predecessors and, although he was unable to indulge the full measure of their hostility towards foreigners after he had bargained with German merchants for help in regaining his throne in 1471, at least he invariably consulted them on commercial questions. With so many of the great feudal lords having been slaughtered in the Wars of the Roses this policy involved less risk than it had done for his predecessors. For centuries the Crown and City had indulged a fruitless antagonism: Edward IV pointed the way towards a mutually profitable alliance that was to sustain the Tudor monarchs of the sixteenth century.

WESTMINSTER AS CAPITAL

Not the least of Edward IV's services to London, after years of Lancastrian attachment to the Midlands, was finally to re-establish Westminster as the centre of government, as the capital in fact. For the Crown's association with Westminster had not by any means been continuous since the death of Henry III. As Edward I and Edward II had been preoccupied with Scotland for much of their reigns they had made York the centre of their operations, and the government departments had duly followed them there. Westminster, which possessed no trades to cushion the blow of the royal exodus, became a ghost town, and rents plunged to such an extent that the great lords actually pulled down their houses. Even the Confessor proved no irresistible draw: after Henry's death, takings at the shrine, at £30 a year, were only a tenth of what Becket pulled in at Canterbury.

Salvation for Westminster came not from heaven but from the Hundred Years War. In 1338 Edward III ordered the Exchequer back to Westminster 'so that it might be nearer to him in the parts beyond the sea', and other departments soon followed. Even more important for the future, Westminster became the regular meeting place of Parliament, which before Edward III (1327-77) had been as likely to assemble elsewhere. Full sessions of Lords and Commons together were held in the painted chamber in Westminster Palace, but the emerging Commons would also meet by themselves in the Abbey Chapter House. The proximity of the powerful was valuable to London, and when Richard II summoned Parliament to Gloucester the City found it worthwhile to subscribe £600 in order to tempt them back.

During the same period royal justice became established at Westminster and three separate courts would sit in the Hall at the same time. Since there was a shortage of housing in the area some of the Chancellor's staff found lodging in the House for Converted Jews which Henry III had founded and Edward I rendered superfluous: it was on the site of the public record office in Chancery (Chancellor's) Lane. The Holborn district was already a legal centre and in Fittersfield the royal clerks (by definition in orders – hence 'clerical' work) found their sporting and professional honour alike under constant challenge from the young bloods of Lincoln's and Gray's Inns, which in the fourteenth century were becoming the first English institutions to offer higher education to laymen. Both Inns had originally been the London estates of famous lawyers, Lord Grey de Wilton, who died in 1308, and Henry Lacy Earl of Lincoln, a royal Justice under Edward I.

There was still little enough building between Holborn and Westminster, although from the thirteenth century bishops – Exeter, Bath, Llandaff, Durham and York – possessed grand town houses along the Strand and further towards Westminster. (The archbishops of Canterbury have achieved longer tenure of their site across the river in Lambeth, where they presciently acquired land in the twelfth century and then, as Henry III's obsession with Westminster became evident, began the palace which is still their London home.) Westminster's *physical* distinctness was politically reinforced by the manner in which kings espoused its cause against the City. In 1248, for instance, Henry III ordered that all City shops should be closed during a Westminster fair, so that London's tradesmen were forced to bring their wares to Westminster in pouring rain. Again, in 1353, Edward III made Westminster a boom town by establishing it, and not London, as one of the places exclusively licensed to market wool for export. But as London provided the cash London ultimately called the tune, so that after twelve years the king had to allow the City to export directly.

The rivalry between the two places penetrated well below official level. Whoever organized a City *v.* Westminster wrestling match in 1222 was asking for trouble, and sure enough the event quickly degenerated into a running battle during which the City mob pulled down the house of the Abbey's steward. Thirty-odd years later a group of Westminster courtiers was unwise enough to jeer at the efforts of the unknightly City dwellers to tilt at the quintain, whereupon the Londoners, 'not able to bear so to be misused, fell upon the king's servants and beat them shrewdly'. The most spectacular crime of the Middle Ages was perpetrated by a City man at Westminster's expense. A character called Podlicote managed to burgle the royal treasury, and although he was eventually caught and executed, he lived long enough to savour the news that a furious Edward I had gaoled ten monks for his jape.

CRIME AND PUNISHMENT

The task of keeping public order constantly engaged the authorities of medieval London. Perhaps we receive an exaggerated impression of violence because City records naturally concentrate on the lawbreakers rather than the peaceful and virtuous. One would not, after all, judge the tone of New York exclusively by Harlem police reports. Accounts of medieval London, however, make it clear that, rather as in modern New York, the peaceful and virtuous found violence familiar enough to ignore. In 1325, for instance, a man was knifed off Milk Street; he staggered through Cheapside; rang the bell of St Peter's church; fell down dead . . . and only then, apparently, did his condition attract public notice. Again, though perhaps this was understandable enough, no one troubled to interfere when three goldsmiths attacked a saddler in the middle of Cheapside: one gashed open the unfortunate man's head, another chopped off his leg with an axe, while the third applied himself to some handy work with his staff. Such antagonism between crafts could flare up into pitched battles, like that between the Fishmongers and the Skinners in 1340, during which several were killed and a fishmonger so far forgot himself as to lay hands on the mayor. He was executed of course. Such brawls were frequent in the fourteenth century, though perhaps not frequent enough for a man like William Woodcock who turned up at the old Guildhall armed with buckler and pole-axe '*hoping* that a riot would arise'. Still Woodcock might have won good citizenship prizes in competition with John le Furber of Cornhill, who had a weakness for using church towers as targets for shooting practice. Clearly dangerous characters were in good supply, and they must often have been drunk in a City with over a thousand brew shops, where the smallest measure was apparently a quart.

Foreigners were especially favoured as victims of attack. London was 'overflowing' with Poitevins, Provençals, Italians and Spaniards, complained a thirteenth-century writer, apparently heedless that their presence was the basis of the town's prosperity. No one could have accused Londoners of encouraging foreign traders. In particular the Italians, who succeeded the Jews as royal financiers, and who remained as merchants bringing in spices, drugs, silks, jewels and other luxuries long after the king had ruined them as bankers, came in for rough treatment. Lombard Street was the scene of numerous riots in the late Middle Ages. It was at a hostel there in 1301, for instance, that some Italians were rash enough (if English sources are to be believed) to discuss the Anglo-French war, praising the French king and making slighting references to his English rival. This was too much for the bluff English spirit. A riot ensued and the Italians, having delivered themselves of the telling insult, 'English houndes', decided to beat a hasty retreat. There were also complaints at this time of the Lombards dragging fair specimens of London womanhood into their hostel and 'shamefully maltreating them'. The women's objections went unrecorded, but the men considered that this behaviour showed 'contempt of the English', an unforgivable offence.

In the fifteenth century the riots assumed the proportions of a campaign to drive the Italians out. 'Londoners have such fierce tempers and wicked dispositions,' one Italian reported at the end of this century, 'that they not only despise the way in which Italians live, but actually pursue them with uncontrolled hatred. They look askance at us by day and at night sometimes drive us off with kicks and blows of the truncheon.' Notwithstanding complaints of silks being 'falsely and deceivably wrought' and spices being improperly cleaned, one suspects that the real cause of trouble was that Londoners could not bear to see others making money. In 1456, after a particularly bad riot in which several Italians were killed, the Lombards determined to leave London for Winchester, while the Venetian senate retaliated by forbidding all trade with England. But the commercial lure of London was too strong for these threats to prove effective: the Italians were more easily seduced by London's wealth than repelled by the hostile citizenry. 'In one single street, named the Strand, leading to St Paul's', a visitor breathlessly recorded in the late fifteenth century, 'there are fifty-two goldsmiths shops, so rich and full of silver vessels, great and small, that in all the shops in Milan, Rome, Venice and Florence put together I do not think there would be found so many of the magnificence that are to be seen in London.'

Violence was far from being the only crime. The long

catalogue of petty trading frauds makes such dreary reading
that it is good to know that occasionally the biters were bit.
In the fifteenth century a Londoner called William passed
himself off as a sergeant and arrested two bakerwomen for
selling short-weight loaves: after receiving his severe
warning they were grateful to be let off with a fine. Official
justice tended to proceed on the principle that the punishment should be designed to fit the crime. Thus a cook who
killed sixteen people by poisoning was boiled to death at
Smithfield. Often, though, the mayor's judgements were
relatively merciful, their aim being to inflict humiliation
rather than torture. A vintner who sold bad wine was made
to drink it. A fraudulent doctor was paraded through the
streets back to front on a horse, with his prescription hung
about his neck with a whetstone (to symbolize deceit), 'a
urinal also being hung before him and another urinal on his
back'. A priest caught *in flagrante* with a grocer's wife was
marched along with his breeches hanging about his knees
and his clerical trappings solemnly carried behind. It was left
to the church to burn a man on Tower Hill in 1430 for
eating meat on Fridays.

The existence of several competing jurisdictions – mayor's,
king's and church's, not to mention a multitude of legal
rights and exemptions belonging to particular individuals –
made the task of keeping the peace much more difficult. The
rival courts were instinctively hostile to each other's claims,
and the more they wrangled, the less likely was the conviction of the criminal. Any clerk could demand trial in a
church court, with its lighter penalties for unheretical
crimes like murder; and any felon who could read stood a
fair chance of being accepted as a clerk. A man on the run,
moreover, could claim sanctuary in a church, where he
would be beyond the mayor's reach for forty days. When
the mayor dragged a criminal out of the sanctuary of St

Paul's in 1344 he was immediately summoned to explain his sacrilege before the archbishop of Canterbury. The most notorious sanctuary area of all was at St Martin's-le-Grand, where the forty-day limitation did not apply, so that fraudulent goldsmiths and jewellers actually set up business within the precincts.

Another haven for criminals was just across the bridge in Southwark, which, not being legally part of the City, was outside the scope of its justice. The king had a court there and did not always resist the temptation to spite the mayor by extending his protection to London offenders. Naturally the City authorities longed to bring Southwark within their sway, but although Edward III's charter gave them some rights there they had to wait until 1550 before the borough became Bridge Ward Without. So medieval Southwark presented strange contrasts. On the one hand the greater part was owned by three dignitaries of the church, the archbishop of Canterbury, the abbot of Bermondsey and the bishop of Winchester (today the decaying warehouses of Winchester Square outline the courtyard of the old bishop's palace); on the other hand it was the mecca of low life. Not for nothing were prostitutes known as 'Winchester geese'.

SLUM LIFE IN A COUNTRY TOWN

If Southwark was a raffish slum, the City itself was scarcely salubrious. Of course, especially after 1400, there were grand City houses, like that in Bishopsgate belonging to the vastly rich Sir John Crosby, the hall from which has been rebuilt off Cheyne Walk in Chelsea. Moving down the social scale, the house of a successful grocer like Richard Toky, Member of Parliament, a list of whose effects has by chance survived, was certainly abundantly furnished. His taste in colours (bright red canopy, orange wall) would not commend itself to the tyrants of modern décor, but then his choice of wall-hangings (pole-axe, crossbow, lance and shield) suggests that their distaste might have been effectively reciprocated. Such luxury, however, was completely untypical. Whereas Toky's family all slept in one room with six beds, the ordinary London family only *had* one room and certainly no beds. Many lived over their shops in flimsy lath-and-plaster constructions which were no more than ten feet wide. From John's reign on, the City issued a stream of regulations designed to check fires by enforcing building in stone with tiled roofs, but no one could afford to take any notice. Not until the fifteenth century did a few more substantial houses, built of brick from the kilns of Limehouse and Whitechapel, and up to five storeys high with glazed windows, begin to replace the earlier hovels.

There were compensations for the general squalor. The countryside was right at the gates and when the great bell of St Mary-le-Bow sounded the curfew every night it did so in part to reclaim those 'benighted in the fields'. On May Day, we are told, Londoners 'would walk into the sweet meadows and green woods, there to rejoice their spirits with the beauty and savour of sweet flowers, and with the harmony of birds, praising God in their kind'. Another kind rejoiced their spirits slaughtering the foxes which made themselves obligingly available to the City's pack of hounds. 'After dinner to the hunting of the fox', one sportsmen recorded as late as 1562, 'and there was a goodly cry for a mile and after the hounds killed the fox at the end of St Giles [in-the-Fields].' There is a memory to be treasured amongst the rush-hour crowds at Tottenham Court Road tube station! Nearby Soho was also probably connected with the chase, since its name was once a hunting cry used when the fox was found.

So whatever the deprivations of medieval urban life there

was at least no shortage of play-space. On holidays – and Saints' Days were most scrupulously observed as such – Londoners were avid for sport. Their games were energetic rather than subtle, generally including some form of fighting and only sometimes a friendly spirit. Football, 'a bloody and murthering practice' as a sixteenth-century writer described it, was especially popular, although in 1479 the mayor had banned labourers, servants and apprentices from playing this game on pain of six months' imprisonment. His purpose was not so much humanitarian as to encourage archery in Finsbury Fields: after all, England's security depended on the prowess of her bowmen. But the very number of times between the fourteenth and the seventeenth centuries that mayors issued regulations enjoining archery suggests that the sport aroused little enthusiasm, lacking the essential stimulus of physical combat. But even though archery was not over-popular, it was still worth a fight. When the inhabitants of Shoreditch, Islington and Hoxton enclosed some fields used for shooting, Londoners sallied forth with shovels and spades to tear down the hedges and fill in the ditches.

Up to the sixteenth century there was still plenty of open space within the walls. To the monastic grounds mentioned in the last chapter must be added those of the friars who came to London in the thirteenth century. Their dedication to poverty and humility was so impressive that the rich and the mighty vied with each other to heap wealth upon them. Although the City wall had to be moved to the west in order to accommodate the precinct of the Dominican, or Black, friars; and although the Carmelite, or White, friars lived nearby just outside the wall (where a vault from the prior's house survives in Britton's Court off Whitefriars Street), there was more than ample room for two other orders *inside* the ancient City. The Franciscan, known as

Grey, friars possessed a 300-foot-long church off Newgate, the largest in the City after St Paul's. It was destroyed in the Great Fire: the replacement, Wren's Christ Church, covered only the choir of its predecessor, although the tower (all that remains after the bombing of 1940) shows that this too was a considerable building. Yet in medieval London the Grey friars still had room for an orchard beside their church. Similarly, the lands of the Austin friars were a huge tract stretching across the north of the City from Colman Street to Broad Street, and included the biggest of all City gardens. The English passion for vegetable-growing had already asserted itself, and, besides the monasteries, guilds and other institutions many individuals also boasted their patch of green. The streets were often bounded by garden walls, and John Stow recorded in the sixteenth century that the City had formerly been self-sufficient for 'garden ware', although then 'but a few herbs were used at table in comparison to what are spent now'.

But medieval London was certainly not picturesque. True, the houses were set at crazy angles to the street; granted, they were painted in garish colours; accepted, they jutted out further at each storey so as to be almost touching their opposite at the top. On this diminutive grounding of fact any number of sentimental reveries have been constructed. The truth is that medieval London stank. Its inhabitants were not indifferent to the disgusting smells amongst which they lived, nor did they fail to make the connection between the filth in the streets (or in the houses too for that matter) and the brevity of life.

A whole network of officials, from the mayor down to the four rakers attached to each ward, were continuously battling with the problems of street cleaning. City carts laden with refuse hourly trundled out to muck-heaps such as 'the laystall called Islington'. People like William atte Ward, who caused 'great nuisance and discomfort to his neighbours by throwing out horrible filth onto the highway, the stench of which is so odious that none of his neighbours can remain in their shops', were prosecuted as public menaces. Some areas were relatively clean; a few, like the spice market in Bucklersbury, positively sweet-smelling. For pageants and processions even greater efforts than usual would be made to clear the streets.

Yet when all these qualifications have been made the fact remains that the extent of the problem was way beyond the resources or techniques available for coping with it. The flushing lavatory is possibly the greatest contribution of the English to world civilization, but it had not yet been made. One did not have to be as unlucky as Richard the Raker, who drowned in a cesspit when the floorboards gave way, to appreciate the limitations of this form of sewage disposal. To what purpose did the authorities provide a public lavatory in every ward when that at Ludgate became so 'ful defectif and perlus' that 'the ordur rotith the stone walls'? No wonder so many people defied regulations and simply emptied their slops into the street, or, like one ingenious fellow, piped them into the cellar of a neighbour.

Sewage was only part of the trouble. An experienced City man could have found his way around London blindfolded simply from the distinctive smells which the various trades gave their districts, although he would have found it difficult to avoid tripping over the pigs and poultry which roamed in the streets. The most powerful direction finders would have been the three meat markets, the Shambles in Newgate, the Stocks Market and East Cheap. In 1290 the Carmelites, who lived over 100 yards from the Shambles, and were after all in the flesh mortification business, were driven to complain of the butchers' habit of chucking offal into the Fleet. However thoroughly the stream was cleared it soon became blocked again. A sentence to the Fleet prison was retribution indeed.

Yet some travellers found these conditions alluring enough, notably 'rattus rattus', the black rat on which plague-bearing fleas made their journey of destruction from the heart of Asia. In 1348 the bacillus reached London and soon the one great stench of the City had bred the myriad nauseating symptoms ('sweat, excrement, spittle, breath, so foetid as to be overpowering') of the Black Death. In the next two years probably half the City population of 50000 or 60000 died: between February and April 1349 the victims were being shovelled into pits at Smithfield at the rate of 200 a day. But the historian of London's development must callously record that the most significant feature of the Black Death was the astonishing resilience which the City showed in the face of such a catastrophe. Within fifty years the lost numbers had been largely replaced, which is the more remarkable when it is considered that there were at least six further outbreaks of plague in the fourteenth century, and one in 1407 of a destructive power on almost the same scale as the Black Death. The City's life-force was match even for its sanitation.

LONDON INCREASES ITS SHARE OF TRADE

The fount of this extraordinary vitality was, as ever, the port. The development of English commerce in the Middle Ages could not have favoured London more if it had been ordered by the Lord Mayor himself. We have seen that London was a port for wool from earliest times, but before 1350 its share of the trade was far from exclusive. In the thirteenth century the East Anglian port of Boston exported nearly twice as much wool. Not more than a third of the City's overseas trade, moreover, had been handled by native merchants. However much Londoners might discriminate against foreigners *within* the City they were responsible for only a fraction of the shipping in the port during the early Middle Ages. Then in 1275 the king embarked on a policy which, notwithstanding its lack of glamour, was to prove one of the decisive turning points of English, and of London, history. In 1275 Edward I began to tax the export of wool.

The first important development was that in order to make the collection of this tax easier the wool trade was restricted to specific places. The first time this policy was followed, in 1294, Edward I designated Brabant, right across the narrow seas from London, as the market to which sellers should take their wool. Immediately London became the most convenient English port from which to ship wool and its part in the trade increased dramatically. At this stage, however, the king was still obliged to suit his foreign creditors and various other schemes were tried after the Brabant staple was abandoned. Sometimes the markets were abroad; sometimes they were at home, as when Westminster became a staple town. But after the 1340s, when the exigencies of financing the Hundred Years War had bankrupted his Italian financiers, Edward III was forced to work out a staple system at the behest of English merchants. By the arrangement which emerged after 1363 the staple was fixed at Calais and the trade vested in a monopoly company, the Merchants of the Staple, the majority of whom were Londoners.

But the taxation system which gave London and Londoners control of wool exports was also sending the trade into decline. As England had a virtual monopoly of wool the Crown yielded to the temptation to increase the tax again and again. The great poet Geoffrey Chaucer, who was employed as a Customs Officer in the port of London (artists not having yet discovered that work was alien to their inspiration), was one of those who implemented this policy. By the beginning of the fifteenth century customs were accounting for over half the royal revenue, but the wool trade was in decline. It had become much more profitable to export woven cloths, the wool for which could be bought at home by English clothmakers for far less than their overseas rivals were paying, and the shipping of which bore little duty. For the first time England had a significant export that was manufactured.

Fortunately for London the old geographical factor which had made it a wool centre operated with redoubled force in the case of cloth. The chief market for cloth was Germany, where political weakness prevented any effective protective measures being taken against English imports. The natural route into Germany was down the Rhine, and the best port from which to reach the Rhine from England was London. So the Middle Ages ended with the cloth trade, on which England's wealth would be built, almost entirely in the hands of London. No other port could compete: Bristol and Southampton went into decline, and the City drew cloth from all over England. 'God give you good winning', a London merchant wrote to one of his fellows in 1471. As far as London was concerned God could usually be relied upon to do just that.

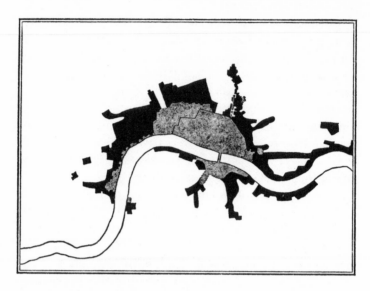

5. 'Out of the gates to the suburbs'
[1485-1666]

RICHES FROM THE PORT

Between 1500 and 1650 London achieved a commercial and
political ascendancy over the rest of the country which has
never been matched before or since. Indeed one eminent
historian has claimed that the despotism of the Tudor
dynasty which ruled from 1485 to 1603 was in essence the
dominance of London over the remainder of England.
Conversely, the ruin of the succeeding Stuart family,
accomplished between 1603 and 1649, might be ascribed
to their failure to gain the support of the capital.

To rivals like the merchants of Bristol it seemed as though 'God had no sons to whom he gave the benefits of the earth but in London'. Well they might complain: for most of this period the City handled nine-tenths of the entire country's overseas trade. The grouses of Bristol were echoed in many a coastal town, but there was to be no cure for them until after 1650 when new trade routes began to emerge from the chrysalis of Empire. For the greater part of the sixteenth century English exports were directed towards Antwerp, and London's position directly across the North Sea gave it such a monopolistic hold over this traffic that even after 1572, when Antwerp was sacked by Spanish troops and English cloth obliged to seek other markets in the Mediterranean and the Baltic, the capital's dominance was hardly challenged.

On the Thames the statistics of commerce appeared in bobbing, jostling reality. 'A man would say, that seeth the shipping there,' wrote a contemporary, 'that it is, as it were, a very wood of trees disbranched to make glades and let in light; so shaded is it with masts and sails.' Being London's own main highway as well as the route of international trade the Thames was also choked with rivercraft ferrying passengers along and across its course. Upright visitors were shocked by the easily misinterpreted cry of 'Oars, oars' with which the watermen advertised their services. In the early seventeenth century, though, river transport within London was menaced by the advent of coaches, against which, as against the sedan chair, that 'mere engine of pride', the watermen directed torrents of abuse. The crush on the Thames, however, did not diminish, and life became ever more hazardous for the swans which still wove their way through the multitude of boats. Conditions must have worsened after 1558, when a law passed to combat smuggling ordained that all dutiable goods from abroad should be

unloaded only at 'legal quays' established on the north bank
of the Thames between London Bridge and the Tower. The
result was that virtually all England's imports were confined
to a landing frontage of just 1464 feet.

Here indeed were infinite riches in a little room; and
infinite also were the consequences for the City which was
the distribution centre of such immense wealth. Of course
the great fortunes remained with a select few, merchant
princes like Sir Thomas Gresham, who knocked down
four streets and eighty houses to build the first Royal
Exchange (on the same site as the present building) as a
meeting place for traders: there were no problems with
planning permission in those days. But the lesser figures who
frequented the Exchange also had money to spend, albeit
not on such a princely scale. 'The private riches of London',
noted John Stow at the end of the sixteenth century, though
he might have been referring to any period, 'resteth chiefly
in the hands of merchants and retailers, for the artificers have
not much to spare, and labourers have need that it were
given unto them.' Nevertheless, industries sprang up to
cater to the merchants' needs, and silk-weavers, shoemakers,
glass-makers and fan-makers, together with manufacturers
of the minutiae of civilization like pins, buckles and buttons,
all found a ready market for their goods. The general
pattern of London's industry – relatively small in scale,
multifarious in kind – has remained the same ever since. But
there were no 'factories' in the sixteenth century; most of
the work was done in private houses.

Some of the new workers were foreigners, who escaped
City regulations but not citizen hostility by lodging in the
outskirts. 'And further,' a preacher fulminated in 1517, 'the
strangers compass the City about in Southwark, in Westminster, Temple Bar, Holborn, St Martin's, St John's
Gate, Aldgate, Tower Hill [and] St Katharine's.' These

pulpit remonstrations produced an anti-alien riot, mild enough by previous standards – nobody was killed – but which nevertheless became remembered as Evil May Day owing to the savagery of Henry VIII's reaction. Thirteen 'poor younglings' were hanged, before the king, with what he doubtless conceived to be a magnanimous gesture, spared 400 other offenders paraded in front of him with halters around their necks.

After the Reformation had provided Christian zealots with a whole new set of reasons for burning, massacring, torturing and otherwise persecuting each other, the flow of refugees from the Continent increased, and the skills which they brought with them sparked off something of an industrial renaissance in London. But even the shared bigotry of Protestantism rarely sufficed to overcome the traditional London prejudice against foreigners. And when, after the loss of Calais in 1558, families from the nearby Hammes and Guisnes came to the City, the lanes where they lived soon became known as Hangman's Gains. Clearly Londoners had no time for these fancy foreign names.

POPULATION EXPLOSION: FOOD AND HOUSING

The majority of new arrivals, however, were still English, drawn by hope of wealth or simply of work, and frequently failing to find either. Nevertheless, London's population had begun a mushroom growth that was not to cease until this century. In 1500 there were about 75000 Londoners; in 1600 about 220000; and by 1650 perhaps 450000. For the first time London was on the way to becoming the largest European town, while the next biggest in England, Norwich, had a population of only about 29000 in 1650.

Obviously feeding and housing London's multitudes presented immense problems. Whereas before 1600 the

City's food had nearly all been supplied from immediately surrounding counties, by 1650 it was coming from as far afield as Berwick-on-Tweed, Cornwall and Wales. Cheese and butter arrived from Norfolk, Lincolnshire, Yorkshire and Northumberland; eggs and poultry from Bedfordshire and Northamptonshire; and cattle trekked towards the capital from all parts of the kingdom to end up as meat on City plates. In fact, with food supplies hardly less than with cloth exports, the produce of the entire country was brought into mutual dependence on the vast market of the capital.

The housing shortage, by contrast, was never solved. In the 1530s Henry VIII's Reformation brought the end of the monasteries, the properties of which were given to courtiers or sold to the highest bidders. As a result, large areas became available for building and afforded some temporary relief from the overcrowding. St Katharine's by the Tower, for instance, was 'inclosed about or pestered with small tenements and homely cottages, having inhabitants, English and strangers, more in number than in some cities in England'. Thus recorded John Stow, the City's greatest historian, whose *Survey of London*, first published in 1598, is a mine of fascinating material. (He is buried in the church of St Andrew's Undershaft, where the monument depicting him writing is provided with a new quill pen every year.) Like most antiquaries Stow was no enthusiast for his own times, 'the most scoffing, respectless and unthankful age that ever was'.

If he disliked scruffy development like that at St Katharine's, he hated still more the 'bad and greedy men of spoil' who reserved the former monastic properties for their exclusive profit and use. Such a man was the unscrupulous Sir Richard Rich, who acquired St Bartholomew's and pulled down the nave in order to increase space for a market.

Other private owners, like the Marquess of Winchester, who was granted Austin Friars, might be less objectionable, but their tenure of such areas hardly represented a housing gain. By 1660 the City was more densely packed than ever. Rents soared and communal living became more and more communal: one moderate-sized house in Dowgate sheltered no fewer than eleven married couples and fifteen single persons. Shops which began as mere sheds spilling over on to the pavements ended up by supporting four storeys of lodgings. Even the churchyards at last began to yield to the pressure for housing. St Michael's Cornhill actually sold its plate in order to recoup its fortunes by building in the churchyard, 'whereby the church is darkened and other ways annoyed'.

WATER SUPPLIES

Inevitably building began to spread out to east and west, despite all the efforts of City authorities to restrict development to areas within its control. In fact, the lack of sufficient springs in the heavy London clay proved a far more effective restraint than the copious regulations against building. Water supplies were wholly inadequate in the middle of the sixteenth century. Each of the three available sources had disadvantages. Wells were frequently polluted with sewage; wooden conduits bringing water from various springs outside the City to a dozen or so street cisterns (the best known was in Cheapside) were leaky and unreliable; and the Thames, forever 'sparkling' in the fancy of romantic commentators, stank to such a degree that the Venetian ambassador complained that its 'odour remains even in clean linen'.

It was, however, absence of pumps rather than considerations of hygiene which limited the use of the river's water.

Then in 1572 a German called Peter Morris, using a wheel turned by the tidal rush through London Bridge, greatly impressed the assembled mayor and aldermen by shooting a jet of water over St Magnus church. Morris and his descendants were granted a 500-year lease of an arch of the bridge (later extended to other arches) at ten shillings a year, after which water was pumped regularly up to Leadenhall, the highest ground in the City, where a standard discharged through four spouts 'plentifully serving to the commodity of the inhabitants near adjoining in their houses'. Over the next two centuries several other pumps installed along the river made its water far more widely available. The York Buildings Company, which operated on the site of Charing Cross station, introduced a 'fire engine' as early as 1712–13. Before that most of the pumps had been tidal- or horse-driven, although at the end of the seventeenth century one ingenious device actually used the downfall of a sewer to turn its mill wheels.

By that time, however, the water shortage was no longer critical, for London was drawing more than half its supplies from another source entirely. Early in the seventeenth century a wealthy City man called Hugh Myddleton, with financial help from the king, succeeded in bringing water to London from springs in Hertfordshire by means of a channel over forty miles long. To this day the 'New River' – as it is still known after 360-odd years – supplies water to much of north London. Although the 'river' now ends at Stoke Newington, it originally flowed into a reservoir near Sadler's Wells in Rosebery Avenue, on the site of which the Metropolitan Water Board has appropriately built its headquarters. The Board still owns much property in the area, which was developed early in the nineteenth century – hence Myddleton Square.

EXPANSION TO EAST AND WEST

With the arrival of reliable water supplies – notwithstanding continuing difficulties with wooden pipes – a major obstacle to London's expansion had been removed. Already in the sixteenth century there had been two ribbon developments in the east, along the river bank (Wapping High Street) and beside the Ratcliffe highway in Stepney. Fifty years before, complained John Stow in 1598, there had been open country between the Tower and Wapping; now there was 'a continual street, or filthy straight passage, with alleys of small tenements or cottages . . . inhabited by sailors and victuallers'. The establishment of the East India Company's anchorage at Blackwall in 1614 (though cargoes still had to be taken to the legal quays in lighters for Customs clearance) encouraged further extensions. Stepney became the chief resort of all connected with shipping – of shipwrights, anchorsmiths, carpenters and ropemakers, as well as of sailors. Officers lived there too, but on the whole building in the east was ramshackle, with bricks the exception rather than the rule. The quality of construction was not improved by an Act of Parliament of 1617, which stipulated leases of not more than thirty-one years in Hackney and Stepney.

There was to be some much smarter development to the west. According to the diarist John Evelyn (1620–1706) this was 'because the winds blowing near three quarters of the year from the west, the dwellings of the west end are so much the more free of fumes, steams and stinks of the whole easterly pile; which where seacoal is burnt is a great matter'. But, as the concluding phrase suggests, Evelyn was writing a polemic against the evil effects of smoke from coal fires and wanted to make the most of his argument. The allure

of the royal court is surely a sufficient reason for the fashionable world being drawn to the west of the city.

After the Reformation the bishops' palaces along the
Thames were taken over by great aristocrats (see map on
p. 148). The houses of the bishops of Exeter, Bath and Wells,
Carlisle and Durham became respectively the homes of the
Pagets, the Earl of Southampton, the Earl of Bedford and
Sir Walter Ralegh. The Earl of Somerset, more ambitious,
demolished the residences of the bishops of Lichfield and
Llandaff to build the first Somerset House, which was still
uncompleted at the time of his execution in 1552. Great
houses were still being constructed along the river in the
seventeenth century, like Northumberland House which
actually survived to be photographed. Street names are
generally the only remaining memory of the Thames
palaces, although there is still a Somerset House, and a
watergate for the Earl of Buckingham's mansion stands in
the gardens by Embankment underground station. Its
present distance from the river shows how much land was
gained by nineteenth-century embankment of the Thames.

The most princely of all pre-Reformation bishops had
been Henry VIII's minister Cardinal Wolsey, who somewhat untactfully began to develop York Place into a far
grander palace, covering twenty-three acres, than the king
possessed at Westminster, where the royal apartments
were 'in utter ruin and decay'. The sweetest-natured monarch might have found this hard to take and Henry VIII, to
do him justice, did not even make the attempt. After ruining
Wolsey he himself moved into York Place, which was
renamed Whitehall. (The present street of that name was
once a public thoroughfare running through the middle of
the palace; the Horseguards building covers the ancient
tiltyard.)

Henry VIII hardly lacked space to lay his head for he

owned no fewer than thirteen palaces within easy reach of London. But throughout the Tudor and Stuart periods, or at least until the Civil War, Whitehall and Greenwich were the main royal residences. Whitehall remained the centre for government offices even after Charles II had moved west to St James's Palace. Although fire destroyed much of Whitehall Palace in 1698 and Greenwich was rebuilt after 1660, an exquisite building by Inigo Jones (1573-1652), who introduced the classical Palladian style into England, has survived at each of these places – the Banqueting House at Whitehall (1622) and the Queen's House at Greenwich (1635). Inigo Jones also designed the Queen's Chapel at Marlborough Gate (1623-7), the first church in England to break completely away from the traditional Gothic styles – in contrast to the contemporary Lincoln's Inn Chapel (1619-23) with its Perpendicular window tracing.

BEGINNINGS OF THE WEST END

Westminster was still distinct from London in the sixteenth century and the furthest development of Whitehall was the royal stables on the site of Trafalgar Square. Thus a proclamation of 1545 could announce that the king was 'desirous to have the games of hare, partridge, pheasant and heron preserved in and about . . . the honour of his palace of Westminster' and forbid hunting and hawking 'from the palace of Westminster to St Giles-in-the-Fields,. and from thence to Islington, to our Lodge of the Oak, to Highgate, to Hornsey Park and to Hampstead Heath'. Much of the land between Westminster and the City was used as sheep pasturage and had belonged to the Abbey before the Crown acquired it at the Dissolution.

There was no early development of the West End

because those who might have organized and financed it were hardly troubled by the crowding within the City. When Thomas Cromwell, who was the brains behind Henry VIII's attack on the monasteries, wished to extend his garden, later the Draper's garden, further down Throgmorton Street, he simply dug up John Stow's father's house and moved it twenty feet away on rollers – without either warning or compensation. Even in Elizabeth's reign noblemen and notables remained content to live in the City. Only after 1600 did the aristocracy begin to apprehend that their dignity might suffer from the proximity of tradesmen. When in 1602 the Marquess of Winchester sold

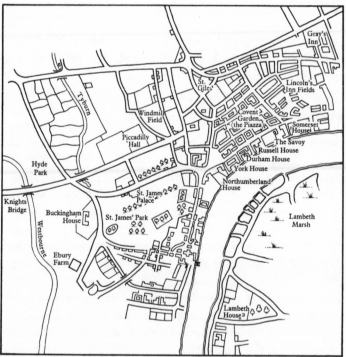

The West End about 1660.

his plot in Austin Friars to 'one Swinnerton, merchant' the Countess of Shrewsbury, who had been a tenant, received a letter of sympathy from a friend: of course she would be moving now as one would not 'willingly become a tenant to such a fellow'.

Indeed not. How fortunate, then, that relief should so often have been provided by the very best class of developer. In 1608, for example, James I gave some land near St Martin-in-the-Fields to Robert Cecil, Earl of Salisbury, that impecunious monarch having no other means to reward his ministers after he had satisfied their craving for titles. On his plot Salisbury built 'many gentle fair houses in a row' and so created St Martin's Lane, which soon became a fashionable street for courtiers. The Cecil family has since given up property development but its ancient involvement with the area is commemorated by names like Cecil Court and Cranbourn Street.

In 1610 Salisbury had tried unsuccessfully to purchase the neighbouring 'Convent Garden', which lay between St Martin's and Drury lanes. This land had formerly been part of Westminster Abbey's property – hence the name – and had been acquired after the Dissolution by the Earl of Bedford, probably for no other purpose than to provide pasture for his horses and dairy produce for his house which lay off the Strand. Innocence is often a prerequisite of the most lucrative property dealing and this happy inspiration of the first earl helped to keep his family in clover for centuries. In 1631 the fourth earl began to develop Covent Garden, although his Puritan sympathies meant that he encountered some difficulty getting the appropriate licences from the Crown. Still, it was very likely Charles I's involvement with the project that was responsible for the appointment of Inigo Jones, who was the king's Surveyor General, as overall designer. The magnificent piazza, based on

Italian models, which resulted was not only the first but the best large-scale plan ever effected in London.

Apart from St Paul's church, 'the handsomest barn in England', no original buildings survive from the Covent Garden piazza, although the porticoed form was incorporated into Bedford Chambers in the late nineteenth century. The façade was allowed to disappear bit by bit with a typically English indifference to its splendours. The rot really began in 1670, when the fifth Earl of Bedford, determined to squeeze every last penny from the site, obtained a licence to sell fruit and vegetables over the whole area of the piazza. The resulting clangour and bustle was no encouragement to smart householders and by the middle of the eighteenth century the buildings 'instead of being inhabited by Persons of the greatest Distinction, as formerly . . . were now obliged to take up with Vintners, Coffee-men and such other inhabitants'. When the market was finally moved to Nine Elms, Wandsworth, in 1974 it had long survived all Inigo Jones's work in Covent Garden.

One of the refuges to which the fashionable inhabitants of the piazza fled was Leicester Square, built up in the 1670s but taking its name from the great house which the Earl of Leicester had raised forty years earlier, where the Empire cinema now stands. It would be quite misleading, however, to give the impression that all early development to the west of London was grand and aristocratic. In 1606, two years before the Earl of Salisbury obtained his land there, the parishioners of St Martin's had already complained that the church was no longer big enough to hold the local population. And half a mile to the west of St Martin's Lane, no one grander than Robert Baker, tailor, bought the plot, 'very fit and necessary for building', beside the windmill which is still remembered in the name of a theatre and street. Nothing, though, exalts the humble and meek like property; by 1616, four years after his purchase, Mr Baker was styling himself 'Gent.', which appears to have caused his neighbours some merriment. At any rate, they dubbed his house 'Pickadilly Hall', very likely in allusion to his former calling since a 'pickadil' was the hem at the skirt of a garment. So, but for the pretensions of a tailor, Piccadilly might be Baker Street.

Property breeds worse evils than vanity, and the housing crisis in London gave birth to a new bogeyman – the building speculator. 'The desire of profit', pronounced an anonymous tract of James I's reign (1603–25), 'greatly increaseth buildings and so much the more, for that this great concourse of all sorts of people drawing near unto the City, every man seeketh out places, highways, lanes and covert corners to build upon, if it be but sheds, cottages and small tenements for people to lodge in. . . . These sort of covetous builders exact great rents, and daily do increase them in so much that a poor handscraftman is not able by his painful labours to pay the rent of a small tenement and feed his family.' John Stow had also made some sharp comments on the way of the world. Describing how a shark named Russell screwed tenants and builders alike for his dreadful houses in Spitalfields, he concludes ' . . . and yet in honour of his name it is now called Russell's Row'.

Mind, it was difficult for the speculator to win approval. When William Newton built substantial houses in Lincoln's Inn Fields, he fell under the hideous suspicion of being in league with the papists, 'for of himself he was never able to build the hundredth part of them'. The same charge was levelled against the builders who helped the Earl of Bedford to finance the Covent Garden piazza. But, in general, sympathy for the speculators would be misplaced. Betwixt and between the showpiece developments, they set the tone for the appalling slums which bedevilled central London right up to this century. It was no accident that the Great Plague which desolated London in 1665 first broke out in the slums surrounding the City. Yet although this proved to be the last catastrophic visitation of bubonic plague to London, the regular death rate in the suburbs remained appallingly high.

THE UNGOVERNED SUBURBS

The fundamental trouble was that there was no authority to govern the new development between the City and Westminster. Indeed, the City's jurisdiction was limited even within its own bounds because the new owners of monastic property claimed all the same exemptions that the monks had once enjoyed. John Stow was shocked by the presumption of the *canaille* (mostly foreign too) who swarmed over St Martin's-le-Grand. 'Privileges granted to canons serving God day and night . . . may hardly be wrested to artificers, buyers and sellers, otherwise than is mentioned in the 21st of St Matthew's gospel', he sniffed, conveniently forgetting that the canons themselves had been notable neither for godliness nor for the casting out of those that bought and sold in the temple.

The case of the suburbs, however, was worse than that of the monastic properties, for whereas the mayor and aldermen would always contest any denial of their authority on home ground they wanted nothing to do with the chaos in the outskirts. In fact the City was divided on the issue of the suburbs. The guilds and Livery Companies deeply resented workers escaping from their control. 'The freedom of London, which was heretofore of very great esteem,' they complained to the king in 1632, 'is grown to be of little worth, by reason of the extraordinary enlargement of the suburbs, where great numbers of traders and handicraftsmen do enjoy, without charge, equal benefit with the freemen and citizens of London'. To remedy this state of affairs many companies sought and obtained charters which widened their jurisdiction to cover the new areas of building. On the other hand the mayor and aldermen, the City government, resolutely shirked any responsibility for the suburbs. Charles I (1625-49) pressed them to assume control there, but their repeated refusals meant that in 1636 the king was forced to incorporate the suburbs as a separate and independent authority. Although the City had only itself to blame for this outcome, that did not make it any more appreciative of the potentially formidable rival on its own doorstep. During the Civil War the new authority was allowed to lapse by a Parliament which needed the City's help against the king. It was never resurrected, and the suburbs, which even by 1640 were becoming as populous as the old walled City, remained without any proper government for the next 200 years.

PURITANISM IN LONDON

In the early seventeenth century only one power proved effective in this suburban no-man's-land – the sermons which issued at such inordinate length from Puritan pulpits. The doctrines of Puritanism were derived from John Calvin, but the term 'Puritan' gradually became a blanket expression applied to almost any opponent of the narrow base of privilege on which Stuart government rested. Indeed, the great advantage of the word as a revolutionary rallying cry was that it embraced both radical and conservative ideas and could therefore be used, before the Civil War, to cover a multitude of differences. Only when the common enemy had been defeated, and opposition had been transformed

into government, did Puritan trouble to look at Puritan –
and recoil in horror.

The breadth of Puritanism's appeal was especially evident
in London. In the outskirts it was the radical aspect that
attracted. Many suburban dwellers were craftsmen who
could no longer afford to live in the City, where their
trades had fallen increasingly under capitalist control. A
contemporary pamphlet explained the plight of the 'poor
handicraft people' who made pins, girdles, gloves and
suchlike, and who had once had their own shops and
servants. But 'a sort began to buy and sell all such handicraft wares called haberdashers . . . whereby many rich men
is risen upon destruction of the poor people'. The craftsmen
were forced out of their shops and direct contact with their
customers into alleys where they slaved all week and on
Saturday tried to sell their work to the haberdashers 'which
would not give them so much winning for their wares to
find them meat and drink, saying they had no need thereof;
their ships lay stored of wares from beyond the sea'. Here,
then, was inflammable material for Puritan preachers to
work on.

The dispossessed of London heard with approval that 'the
profession of religion is no such gentlemanlike life or trade,
whose rents come in by their stewards, whether they sleep
or wake, work or play'. On the contrary, virtue demanded
unwavering self-control and – a key Puritan word – discipline. Surely a poor man might possess these qualities as well
as a rich one. If he did, moreover, he would not remain
poor for long. 'They put it into the people's heads', it was
noted of Puritans even in Elizabeth's reign, 'that, if discipline
were planted, there should be no beggars nor vagabonds: a
thing very plausible.'

But the same doctrines viewed from a different angle
appealed to the hated City capitalist. The rich never find it

hard to credit that their wealth is the product of exceptional talent; how intoxicating for the merchants to learn that it was also evidence of extraordinary virtue. Obviously the poor were not blessed at all; they were just bone idle. We have seen that before the Reformation merchants had been ready enough to request 'good winning' of the Almighty. Now the Puritans no longer accorded Him any choice in the matter. As godliness involved sobriety, thrift, hard work and dedication, godliness would inevitably provide good winning. The two were inextricable.

PURITANISM AND THE THEATRE

So Puritanism proved formidable in opposition and intolerant in authority. Qualities of self-reliance, daring and independence which the preachers brought to the suburbs were distorted within the Guildhall into complacency, inflexibility and repressiveness. Joylessness became the animating spirit of City government so that a ceremony as innocent as May Day dancing round the maypole was regarded as a symbol of idolatrous heathenism. As early as 1549, after a sermon had denounced this practice with more than usual virulence, the maypole was taken down and burnt, although its memory lives on in the church name of St Andrew Undershaft, Leadenhall Street.

The heaviest Puritan guns were reserved for the theatres, not least because they predictably proved to be a bigger draw than the preachers. 'Will not a filthy play, with the blast of the trumpet, sooner call thither a thousand, than an hour's tolling of the bell bring to the sermon an hundred?' The 'winking and glancing of wanton eyes' among the audience also much exercised the Puritans, while even their opponents could agree that theatres helped to spread the plague. Altogether, the Lord Mayor concluded in 1580, players were 'a very superfluous sort of men' and every effort was made to ban their performances. The earliest theatres therefore had to be established in places beyond the City's jurisdiction, first in Shoreditch and then in the liberty of Paris Garden in Southwark, where the Rose playhouse was built in 1587 and the Globe in 1599. One of the Globe shareholders (he owned a tenth part) was William Shakespeare.

There's the rub. If the City had objected only to bear-baiting and similar spectacles exhibited in the bear garden beside the Globe (and doubtless sharing much the same audience), its attitude would command some sympathy. But the 'superfluous sort of men' included the brightest galaxy of literary talent that ever graced a single place at one epoch. Even without its most brilliant luminary the list would be impressive enough: Marlowe, Jonson, Beaumont, Fletcher, Webster and Ford all wrote plays which are still regularly performed. Nevertheless it is the spirit of Shakespeare's work, rather than a catalogue of names, which best confounds the Puritan censoriousness. In one play, *Twelfth Night* (first performed, incidentally, in the still existing Middle Temple Hall), he specifically pilloried Puritan attitudes in the person of Malvolio: 'Dost thou think that because thou art virtuous there shall be no more cakes and ale?' Of course that is precisely what the mayor and aldermen thought.

Not just *Twelfth Night*, but all Shakespeare's plays, with their rejection of an excluding morality for a comprehensive humanity, and with their indifference to the formalities of religion, were at odds with Puritanism. It was possibly only his profession which kept Shakespeare in London, for as soon as he was rich enough to escape he did so. A window in the church of St Helen's Bishopsgate recalls that he was assessed for tax in that parish from 1597 to 1599, a claim on posterity's attention which doubtless he would have been glad to forfeit; at any rate he made the tax collectors work for their money, because the returns refer the matter to the bishop of Winchester, suggesting Shakespeare's removal to Southwark. Later, in 1613, after he had retired to Stratford, he invested £140 in the house above the old priory gatehouse at Blackfriars, where his company had acquired a theatre four years before. One of the witnesses to that transaction was the landlord of the famous Mermaid Inn, which was in Bread Street off Cheapside. With Shakespeare, Jonson, Ralegh, Donne and Beaumont among its clientele we may guess that the conversation compared favourably with that heard in London pubs today. Clearly the Puritans did not have everything their own way. Even so, the theatre could never have withstood their antagonism for so long without support and patronage in the highest circles. Elizabeth I, James I and Charles I all loved plays, and the value of their protection was made clear when the opposition gained power in 1640 and immediately closed all theatres.

TUDORS CONCILIATE, STUARTS ANTAGONIZE LONDON

By the 1630s Charles I could not even open Hyde Park to the public without provoking an outcry about defilement of the Sabbath. Although the struggle between the Crown and the Puritans involved the whole country, nowhere was it more intense or significant than in London. The Tudors' alliance with the City had always been a fundamental element in their control of England. The exception which proved the rule was the reign of Queen Mary 1553-8), who attempted to restore Catholicism. Her cause perished above all at Smithfield, where the spectacle of the Protestant martyrs – for the most part humble shopkeepers

and tradesmen with whom Londoners could easily identify –
being burnt for the good of their souls instilled a revulsion
from Catholicism not yet utterly extinguished in England.
The date of Elizabeth's accession was celebrated as a national
holiday for 150 years. Her reign (1558–1603) was the most
glorious in English history and not least because, apart from
the occasional tiff, Londoners were amongst her most
devout worshippers. Yet within forty years of her death the
City found itself not only at war with the Crown but the
driving force of the rebellion. What on earth went wrong?

Of course the Stuarts were quite as aware as Elizabeth of
the need to cultivate the goodwill of City leaders, and in
several respects they followed similar policies to gain it. The
trouble was not just that they were far less able than the
great queen, but also that problems like the spread of the
suburbs and the growth of Puritanism, which Elizabeth only
had to face in embryo, became ever more intractable after
her death. In tackling such threats the Stuarts left themselves
too little room for manoeuvre.

For where Elizabeth had been parsimonious, James I and
Charles I were nearly always broke. As a result they were all
too often tempted to pervert policies from their original
purpose. Take the matter of Building Proclamations for
instance. The mayor and aldermen wanted to limit the
growth of the City in order to keep it within their control,
and Elizabeth had been so anxious to conciliate them that she
got herself the reputation as the first town planner. In 1580
she ordered that no new houses should be built within three
miles of the City unless there had been another house on the
spot within living memory. But Crown and City alike
lacked surveyors to enforce this prohibition, so that development proceeded more or less without hindrance. (One man,
though, did take the elephantine precaution of raising a wall
in Cursitor's Alley, off Chancery Lane; he claimed to be

keeping rabbits behind it while he was actually building houses.) In any case, as Elizabeth's main concern had been to please the mayor and aldermen, she soon exempted 'the better sort of men' from this legislation. But the Stuarts could not resist going one further: the restrictions should not apply to the 'better sort', *providing* they paid hard cash for their privilege. Thus an Elizabethan device for attaching the propertied classes to her cause had become, under her successors, a mere money-making swindle that antagonized them. The Earl of Bedford, for example, was not only obliged to pay £2000 for a licence to build in Covent Garden; he was also stung for a further £2000 on the grounds that the original licence was not sufficiently comprehensive, a fine which in no way increased his monarchical zeal.

James I's and Charles I's good intentions for London buildings were always at the mercy of their financial needs. It was all very well for James I to proclaim his ambition to have 'found our City of London and suburbs of sticks, and left them of brick', but he did not mention how such regulations could be enforced without an army of officials whom he could not afford. Building policies would always be reversed for ready cash, and generally hostility was aroused in the process. In 1613, for example, the Crown supported the lawyers of Lincoln's Inn who wanted the nearby fields converted into walks 'after the same manner as Moorfields', but Charles I was finally tempted to increase his income therefrom by granting a licence to build. To be fair, the king was responsible for the grand scale on which the buildings were laid out, and for No. 59/60 being designed by Inigo Jones, but it takes more than good planning to mollify outraged lawyers.

The same fatal tendency whereby almost every Stuart policy became a species of extortion was also responsible for undermining the goodwill which the Tudors had gained in the City by their organization of overseas trade. From Henry VII on the Tudors had ensured that the cloth trade remained under the control of the London Merchant Adventurers. Monopoly rights were also granted to great City merchants in the formation of trading companies like the Russia Company (1555), the Levant Company (1581) and, most famous of all, the East India Company (1601). Obviously the lesser merchants who were excluded resented this system, but powerful links were forged between the Crown and the company directors.

Even this bond, however, was loosened under the Stuarts. In 1622 the Venetian ambassador reported that 'although favoured by various privileges, the companies are declining owing to the charges laid upon them by sovereigns . . . and because to maintain themselves they are compelled to disburse great sums to the favourites, the lords of the Council and other ministers. . . .' By retaining the monopolies and antagonizing the monopolists, James I and Charles I were inviting hostility from every kind of merchant. In the Civil War the Merchant Adventurers supported Parliament.

Tudor foreign and commercial policies had also been popular with the City. Traders naturally appreciate the security of a strong navy. Whereas Henry VIII had established the royal shipyards at Deptford and Woolwich, and Elizabeth's ships had defeated the Spanish Armada (1588), the Stuarts allowed the navy to decline to such an extent that it could no longer even protect English shipping against pirates; indeed, in James I's reign the Lord Admiral was actually in the pay of pirates. The Tudors had sought to promote the City's trading interests, from Henry VII's treaty which secured free trade with the Netherlands (1496) to Elizabeth's expulsion of the Hanseatic merchants (1598):

they expected and received a return for their pains. London contributed generously in men, money and materials to the force which defeated the Armada because the war against Spain, with its opportunities for the plunder of rich fleets from Spain's American Empire was thoroughly popular with the merchant class. Elizabeth acknowledged their support with characteristic style: 'Tell them I thank them for it, and desire them to pray for me and I will pray for them, and that I would be sorry mine enemies should have the like subjects for I think no prince in Christendom hath the like, or can have better.' The queen was not descended from a Lord Mayor for nothing. Frugal as she was, she could not always resist a dabble in the commercial and colonial projects which she encouraged. Yet she was not just stylish and shrewd; she was successful. By contrast the only consistent thread in the foreign policy of the first two Stuarts, apart from a pro-Spanish bias which hindered colonial development, was abject failure.

LONDON IN THE GREAT REBELLION

In the circumstances it is remarkable that the mayor and aldermen remained loyal to the Crown almost up to the Civil War between King and Parliament (1642–6). As late as November 1641 they greeted Charles I enthusiastically at a City banquet and presented him with £20000. Perhaps they were beginning to fear worse from the breakdown of order; if so the event proved them correct. For the 'ribalds with blue nails' were surfacing again. As the national crisis mounted throughout 1641 it was the 'men of a mean or middle quality', hitherto excluded alike from City councils, monopoly companies and guild government, who seized control. Working with the Puritan preachers, they whipped up the disinherited suburban masses into a frenzy which not merely toppled the mayoral regime but also provoked the English Revolution.

The irresistible nature of the force at their command first became evident in May 1641 when Parliament presented Charles with a bill for the execution of his chief minister, the Earl of Strafford. The king hesitated to sign, but the London rabble soon made up his mind. He was, a contemporary reports, 'so frighted with these burghers, that if justice were not done, and the bill passed for the Earl of Strafford's execution, the multitude would come the next day and pull down Whitehall (and God knows what might become of the king himself)'. Parliament soon became just as scared as the king. Their sittings at Westminster were besieged by riotous mobs who terrorized the more conservative members into accepting measures which made compromise with Charles impossible; the Commons, we hear, 'were more afraid of them than of the ruin of the kingdom'. The point of no return came when Charles tried to arrest five of his leading opponents in the House of Commons and they fled into the City. Bravely the king went there to reclaim them. His reception at the Guildhall was mixed: there was even an odd cry of 'God Save the King'. In the streets, however, a furious crowd surrounded Charles, shouting 'Privilege of Parliament, privilege of Parliament'. 'The good king', reported the Venetian ambassador, 'was somewhat moved and I believe was glad when he was at home.'

That night the City lay in terror of a royal attack. 'We heard (as we lay in our beds) . . . that there was horse and foot coming against the City. So the gates were shut and the cullises let down, and the chains put across the corners of our streets, and every man ready on his arms.' One of the alderman's wives apparently died from shock; other women, of tougher spirit, busied themselves preparing boiling cauldrons to upset on the king's horsemen. But London escaped the royal wrath. The king, it transpired, had been more than 'somewhat moved' by the mob; on 10 January 1642 he fled from Whitehall. The Civil War had begun.

It remained for the radicals to take official control of the City which they had dominated for the previous year. They had controlled the mob through Puritan pulpits; now they overthrew the City's government through their command of its militia. The power of the aldermen to veto proposals of the Common Council was abolished – again, here were echoes from earlier struggles. Then, in July 1642, the royalist Lord Mayor was impeached in Parliament, stripped of his office, and imprisoned in the Tower, where he died five years later. A radical was elected in his stead: London was ready for the fray.

In the first months of the Civil War there could hardly have been a fray at all without the City's provision of men and money. The necks of the new leadership had been stuck out so far in the Parliamentary cause that nothing short of victory could keep them in one piece. Clearly Charles's first aim would be to capture London, and his best chance of achieving this was early in the war, before the Parliamentary forces were properly organized. On 12 November 1642 (it was still only a year since Charles had attended that City banquet) the advancing royalists overwhelmed the Parliamentary regiments at Brentford and it seemed that an attack on the City must follow. Sheer terror, however, had concentrated Londoners' minds most wonderfully. Their trained bands assembled in such force – 24000 – at Turnham Green, just by Chiswick Common, that Charles foolishly decided to retire to Reading. He was never again to have such a fine opportunity to win the Civil War.

Not that Londoners could have known this. Before Turnham Green they had already begun to ring the City with a vast and complex system of forts and ditches (see the map below). From the pulpits the edict went forth that all, women and children included, must help to build the defences: the measure of Puritan fear may be gauged from the fact that the preachers even encouraged work on Sundays. One hundred thousand people helped in con-

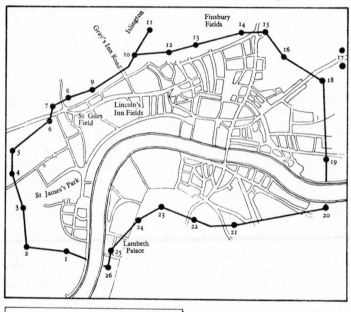

1 Tothill Fort	14 Hoxton Fort
2 Milkfield Fort	15 Shoreditch Fort
3 Goring House Fort	16 Brick Lane Fort
4 Hyde Park Corner Fort	17 Mile End Fort's
5 Serjeants Fort	18 Whitechapel Fort
6 Wardour Street Fort	19 Gravel Lane Fort
7 Crabtree Fort	20 Redriff Fort
8 St Giles' Fort	21 Kent Street Fort
9 Southampton Fort	22 Newington Fort
10 Pinder of Wakefield's Fort	23 St. George's Fort
11 Strawes Fort	24 Halfway Fort
12 Waterfield Fort	25 Vauxhall Fort
13 Mount Mill Fort	26 Nine Elms Fort

The line of forts built around London in the Civil War.

structing the fortifications, the greatest communal effort in London's history. As in the blitz of 1940, the shared danger lowered class barriers. At Hyde Park Corner no lesser personages than Lady Middlesex, Lady Foster and Lady Anne Walker 'lent material aid' to the work, such efforts inspiring the royalists to sing, 'Roundhead cuckolds, come dig'. By May 1643 the Venetian ambassador reported 'the forts completed and admirably designed. They are now beginning the connecting lines. . . .' Later that year it took an observer twelve hours to make the circuit of the fortifications, some of which remained visible into the nineteenth century. The site of one of the forts is now covered, appropriately enough, by the Imperial War Museum off Lambeth Road.

Ironically it was London's riches which ensured that these fortifications were never needed. 'What means had he [the king] to pay,' wrote Thomas Hobbes, 'what provision had he to arm, nay, means to levy, any army able to resist the army of Parliament, maintained by the great purse of the City of London. . . . Those that helped the king in that kind were only lords and gentlemen.' Charles's supporters could only sell capital; Parliament had the City's income at its disposal. When the king did not win quickly he could not win at all. 'If posterity shall asked who pulled the Crown from the King's head,' commented a royalist, 'say, 'twas the proud, unthankful, schismatical, rebellious, bloody City of London.'

Victory for the City was defeat for Westminster and Whitehall. At Westminster George Withers, 'noted for a bad poet', paraded in the royal vestments and 'with a thousand apish and ridiculous actions exposed those sacred ornaments to contempt and laughter'. The Abbey had already suffered once from Calvinist zeal against superstition and idolatry under Edward VI. Now its priceless medieval glass was subjected to a process called 'cleansing out of the pictures', and Henry Wilson, freemason, received £7.16.0 for 'taking down the Altar in Henry VII's chapel [and] for rassing out the painted images'. (The altar in question was a work of incomparable richness by the Italian Torrigiano.) In 1643 soldiers were quartered in the Abbey, where they displayed a truly military sense of decorum. They took their meals on the altar, smashed down the altar rails for firewood and broke up the organ in order to flog the pipes for beer. According to one account they even 'introduced their whores into the church, laying their filth and excrement about it'. Westminster School was lucky to escape: 'it will never be well with this nation', proclaimed a Puritan, 'till Westminster School is repressed', a programme of national rehabilitation which has yet to be tried. At Whitehall the grass grew high in the empty court-yards. 'You may walk in the presence chamber with your hat, spurs and sword on. And if you will presume to be so unmannerly, you may sit down in the chair of state.' Charles I only returned there to be executed in 1649. There was a gruesome appropriateness about the scaffold on which he died being placed outside Inigo Jones's Banqueting House, a symbol of the Stuarts' taste, pride and extravagance.

THE REWARDS OF VICTORY

The next tenant, Oliver Cromwell, was less aesthetically appreciative. There was, however, the compensation that he proved an infinitely more efficient ruler. London in particular discovered that the king had not been opposed in vain, for commerce now became a major determinant of foreign policy. Cromwell recognized that colonial trade, not European territory, was the spoil for which wars were worth fighting. In the 1650s 200 ships were added to the navy, Spain's American empire was attacked and Jamaica captured, and the first English challenge was issued to Dutch shipping supremacy. As a result of Cromwell's policies London began to rival Amsterdam as the entrepôt of Europe.

Prospering merchants do not make dangerous revolutionaries. Up to the 1650s the City's radical mood had not abated and the attack on the great merchants had been sustained by efforts to lessen the exclusiveness of the guilds and trading companies. Immediately after the king's execution Parliament had even debated the possibility of abolishing the office of Lord Mayor altogether, and of handing over control of the City to the Common Council alone. Thereafter, however, a conservative reaction was evident in the City no less than in Cromwell's government. In particular property owners heard with horror the wild notions, such as votes for all men (even the lunatic fringe did not suggest a vote for any woman), which circulated among City apprentices and small tradesmen, and, still more alarming, in Cromwell's army.

The Protector himself could maintain control, but after his death in September 1658 the void opened. 'Either the fanatics must now be undone', wrote Samuel Pepys in his diary on 18 April 1660, 'or the gentry and citizens throughout England . . . must fall.' Faced with such a choice the City did not hesitate: its willingness to provide the loans required to pay off Cromwell's army was the vital prerequisite of the Restoration of Charles II. On 29 May 1660 the king entered London, being received there with rejoicings which belied the part which the City had played in the struggle against his father. The roads, we hear, were strewn with flowers, the streets hung with tapestry and the fountains flowed with wine. These acclamations were all the more heartfelt for the relief which they expressed. Amidst the universal joy, however, the City's Common Council did not forget to strike a line through their records of the previous twenty years' proceedings.

ORDEAL BY PLAGUE AND FIRE

Five years later nearly one in four Londoners, and six years later the medieval City itself, were struck from the record. Contemporaries believed that the Great Plague of 1665 and the Great Fire of 1666 were associated by more than their dates. For the godly the two calamities were expressions of a single divine judgement on the wickedness of London's life. For the knowing gossip, however, the fire had been started for an essentially secular purpose. Even a sage and sober antiquary could seriously advance the view that 'London was burnt by Government to annihilate the Plague, which was grafted in every crevice of the hateful old houses consumed in the Fire'.

In fact his premise, no less than his conclusion, was false. The fire scarcely touched the suburbs on the City's periphery, places like Holborn, Finsbury, Shoreditch, Southwark and Whitechapel which, as they contained the filthiest slums, had been the parts where the plague was at its most virulent. All these areas, and Westminster, had higher death rates than the City in 1665, terrible though the number of victims was within the walls. Not for nothing was the disease known as 'the poor's Plague'. The slums suffered worst because they provided the most favourable environment for the black rat, which had continued to flourish in London ever since the Black Death of 1348. Its presence had ensured that the plague remained endemic in the town for over 300 years, from time to time flaring up into an epidemic. The outbreak of 1665 was the dreadful climax of a long history of affliction. Already in the seventeeth century there had been two disastrous attacks in London, coinciding with the beginnings of the reigns of James I and Charles I. The plague of 1603 had claimed 30 000, and that of 1625, 40 000, deaths within the town. By 1665, as its inhabitants well knew, London was due for another visitation.

It was grimly predictable that the plague would erupt in the worst slum of all. St Giles was still partly 'in the fields', with meadows stretching away to the north and west, but the fresh country air was no match for the urban squalor that existed there. The parish was well known for epidemics: only in 1664 there had been an outbreak of smallpox. So when, during February and March 1665, plague cases began to be reported in St Giles, the news was at first accepted elsewhere in London more as a matter of routine than as a terrible warning. Up to the end of May the death rate for the town as a whole remained only marginally higher than for the previous year. And if there were forty-three deaths from plague in the first week of June, thirty-one of them were in St Giles parish.

Thenceforward, however, it became alarmingly clear that this epidemic was not going to be containable in any one place. The better-off Londoners, determined that the disease should remain an affliction of the poor, began to flee: on 21 June Pepys noted 'all the town almost going out of town, the coaches and waggons being all full of people going into the country'. It was a particularly ominous sign when, also in that June, the canny lawyers at the Inns of Court began to seek pastoral shades. Early in July the king and courtiers followed them. To their eternal credit George Monck, Duke of Albemarle, the most respected man in the country, and his friend the Earl of Craven, stayed behind to lead the fight against the plague. Otherwise, only the black rats did not leave the sinking ship. Contemporaries marvelled that not a single magistrate died in the plague. Yet few exposed themselves to the risk, with one happy effect at least. For the first time in centuries the gallows bore no fruit for seven months, from July to February.

So the town was abandoned by those who might have helped to organize and enforce preventative measures against the plague. The churchyard at St Giles was soon affording utterly insufficient lodging for the dead, although five pits were dug there and the corpses 'piled up like faggots for the society of their future resurrection'. Still, though, the City appeared relatively immune and, a contemporary relates, 'so few of the religious sort were taken away that (according to the mode of many such) they began to be puffed up and to boast the great difference that God did make'. But God, after all, proved to be no respecter of persons; within a short space even his elect were being struck down. From July the plague began to assume unprecedented proportions and the number of victims soared until in September over 6000 were lost in a single week.

There was no one way of dying. Some simply became sleepy and never woke up. The less fortunate endured an agonizing series of symptoms – shivering, violent vomiting, searing headache, fever and delirium – from which death came as a merciful deliverance. The buboes, or swellings, appeared in the groin and under the arms. Only if these tumours burst and let forth their evil might the stricken recover, but victims were driven crazy by the pain involved in lancing their sores. There was one sign, a rash which could spread over the whole body, which was regarded as a certain indication of approaching death, even though the patient was sometimes feeling perfectly well when he first noticed it. 'The tokens', as these spots were called, are commemorated in what has now become an innocent children's rhyme:

Ring a-ring a-Roses,
A pocketful of posies,
'Tishoo, 'tishoo
We all fall down.

'A pocketful of posies' refers to the herbs which people used to carry in order to ward off the plague. It was also believed that strong fumes might drive away the epidemic, and the City burnt disinfectants in the streets. Possibly this remedy, when applied to houses, produced some benefit by persuading the black rat to move on. But another precaution taken, killing all cats and dogs, can only have been to the rodents' advantage. The importance of isolating plague victims was well understood but since the pest houses were quickly filled to overflowing there was no alternative to shutting up whole families in their houses, so that the uninfected members were exposed to the disease. Sometimes the healthy were smuggled away from under the eyes of the watchmen, but doors marked with red crosses could only legally be opened to remove corpses on to the carts which trundled out at the dead of night to the pits at Finsbury, Shoreditch, Tothill Fields (south-west of Westminster) and elsewhere. There were gruesome stories about these carts; the drivers might fall dead on the way, leaving the horses to plunge where they would with their dreadful cargo, or to stand stock still in the streets awaiting discovery at dawn. It was all the town could manage to bury its dead. Pepys, who stayed in London to carry on the business of the Navy Office (England was at war with Holland), recorded the desolate scene on 20 September: 'But, Lord! what a sad time to see no boats upon the river; and grass all up and down White Hall court, and nobody but poor wretches in the streets.'

In October the plague began to wane, although it was

still dangerous enough to carry off those who ventured back into London too early. No one can say with certainty how many the Great Plague killed altogether: the inadequate mortality lists of the time recorded about 68000 victims, but modern historians have inclined towards a figure of 100000. On any reckoning it was a monstrous catastrophe, and contemporaries were denied the consolation of knowing it would be the last of its kind. As the plague flickered on through the winter and into the following spring, it seemed that the threat had not retired but only become dormant, ready to burst forth again at any time. Londoners were still buying specifics against plague in the eighteenth century, and indeed it is not obvious why their fears proved unfounded. 'That one parish of St Giles hath done us all this mischief', a contemporary concluded with some justice; yet St Giles was to remain a sink of squalor for another two centuries. Of course in some parts of London living conditions improved, but a more plausible explanation for the plague's disappearance is that the brown rat, less amenable to the plague fleas, began to chase out its black fellow.

But there were still golden days ahead for the doom merchants. 'London, go on still in thy presumptuous wickedness,' one of them had cried a few years before, 'put the evil day from thee, and repent not, do so London! But if the Fire makes not ashes of the City, and thy bones also, conclude me a liar for ever.' Unhappily no such conclusion would be justified.

Actually it needed very little foresight to predict that London might burn. City houses were nearly all flimsy lath and plaster constructions the timbers of which were coated with pitch. The streets and lanes were generally so narrow that it was possible to converse with one's neighbour in the opposite house without even raising one's voice. The possibility of fire was constantly in mind. In April 1666 eight army officers had been executed for plotting to burn the City, and by an extraordinary chance the date which they had chosen for the deed, following the best astrological advice, was 3 September. In 1665 the king had expressed concern about the fire risk in the City, and had written to the Mayor urging him to enforce regulations which would ensure a less inflammable fabric. Brick was rare in the City where the gabled houses huddled together all higgledy-piggledy.

Despite the slums, the western suburbs were better provided with modern buildings. Great Queen Street in Holborn, laid out at the beginning of the seventeenth century, has been called 'the first regular street in London' on account of the uniform façades of its original brick houses, all of which have now disappeared. It was in such West End streets at the very edge of the country that, well before the Great Fire, courtiers and government officials were tending to live. Pepys was a rare exception to this rule. 'I believe there will be no City left shortly,' the Spanish ambassador wrote home at the time Great Queen Street was rising, 'for all will run out of the gates to the suburbs.' His Excellency's 'all' clearly embraced only the smart world, because at the time of the fire, notwithstanding the ravages of the plague, there were probably more than 200000 people living within the City's bars, albeit mere merchants, artisans and labourers.

In 1666 the City was still entirely medieval in appearance. The City wall was preserved almost in its entirety. Even several monastic buildings remained, despite Henry VIII's depredations. The churches of the Black and White friars had been levelled, but the Greyfriars precinct had passed to Christ's Hospital school, which used the chancel of the great church for worship while the huge nave was let off as a warehouse. Likewise the refectory of the Austin Friars had survived as the hall of the Pinners' Company. As for the City's 107 churches, they appear in all their amazing profusion on Wenceslaus Hollar's magnificent panorama of 1647.

Even without its spire Old St Paul's towered over all else. The cathedral was in ruinous condition, though, and its reputation for godliness lower than ever before. During the Civil War the brutal and licentious soldiery had subjected the building to new humiliations, of which playing ninepins in the nave was among the more respectful. Under Cromwell only the east end was reserved for any religious purpose, and rumour had it that the Protector meant to sell the whole building lock, stock and barrel to the Jews whom he had allowed back into the country. After the Restoration, however, there had been signs of a more determined effort to repair the cathedral, and only eight days before the fire broke out Dr Christopher Wren and some colleagues had made a thorough survey. Old St Paul's was an apt symbol for the City it dominated – awe-inspiring from a distance, but really in a dangerously advanced state of decay.

Londoners had their last complete glimpse of the medieval City on Saturday 1 September 1666. At three o'clock in the morning of Sunday, 2 September, Samuel Pepys was roused by a maid at his house in Seething Lane, near Tower Hill, and told that a fire was raging to the west. 'So I rose and slipped on my nightgown, and went to her window, and thought it to be at the backside of Mark Lane at the farthest; and so to bed again and asleep.'

The blaze which Pepys saw had started a quarter of a mile away in the singularly unsalubrious Pudding Lane, known as Red Rose Lane in better days but since the fifteenth century a mere dumping ground for offal cast off by the butchers of East Cheap market. Whereas its western neighbour, Fish Street Hill, was then the main highway leading

to old London Bridge, Pudding Lane only achieved significance on this September night. Although he strenuously
denied the charge, it seems that the king's baker, one
Farynor, who lived there, had failed to damp down his
oven properly: at any rate there is no disputing that his
house was ablaze between 1 and 2 a.m. Sparks therefrom
set alight some hay stored in the yard of the Star inn on
Fish Street Hill and by morning 300 houses and London
Bridge (including Morris's water wheel) were on fire. The
mayor, though, was apparently unimpressed when first
called to the scene. 'Pish,' he expostulated, 'a woman might
piss it out.' Fires were common enough in London and that
Sunday morning the citizens, by no means unduly alarmed,
filled the churches as usual. And not until 11 o'clock, when
Pepys arrived in Whitehall, did news of the blaze reach the
king – a good indication of how cut off the court was from
the City.

Two factors combined to make the fire not just another
disaster but the greatest physical catastrophe that the world
had yet seen. The first was the spread of the flames to Thames
Street, where the cellars and warehouses were piled high
with combustible materials landed from the river – tallow,
oil, spirits, hemp, hay, timber and coal. Although on
Sunday the fire remained chiefly on the riverside, it kindled
there an appetite that grew hungry by what it fed on. The
other factor was the wind which, following a long dry
spell, blew increasingly hard from the east over the next
three days. Thus the flames, unlike the plague which had
spread towards the east, were always driven towards the
west: it was Monday night before the blaze reached Billingsgate, only 150 yards from Pudding Lane, although by that
time the fire was already devouring Baynard's Castle on
the other side of the City. The wind not only fanned the
flames to an ever-greater intensity, but also carried aloft

brands which set alight houses well away from the main conflagration. 'With one's face in the wind', Pepys reported, 'you were almost burned with a shower of fire drops.' So although the fire never crossed London Bridge, exhausting itself in a space between the houses thereon some distance from the north bank, the sparks still set alight a stable in Southwark, where St Thomas's Hospital also burnt for a while.

Once Thames Street had caught, there was little hope of extinguishing such a fire until the wind dropped. On Sunday afternoon the flames were coursing through the

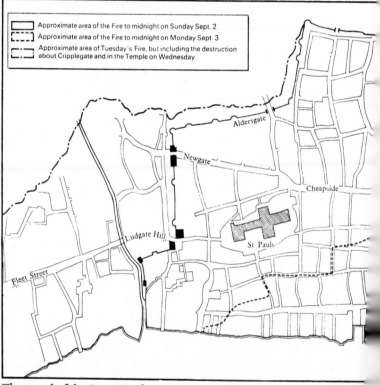

The spread of the Great Fire from 2 to 5 September 1666.

Steelyard, the ancient precinct of the Hanseatic merchants, today the site of Cannon Street station. The heat was so intense that no one could get close to what Pepys called the 'most horrid, malicious, bloody flame'. Yet even if Londoners had been able to stand the heat, how could they have fought such an inferno with the leather buckets and primitive 'squirts' which were flatteringly designated the City's fire-fighting equipment? In any case, during the fret of that Sunday the wooden pipes carrying the New River's water had been hacked to pieces in order to fill the buckets more quickly, with the result that the supply simply went to waste.

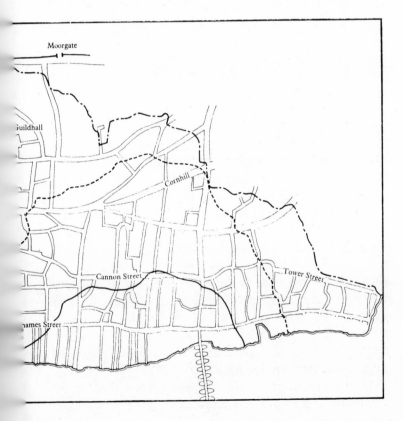

With the London Bridge wheel burnt there was no other water available.

The best hope was to pull down houses in the way of the fire, although this policy was liable to be defeated by the airborne sparks. In the event it was not applied early enough or with sufficient rigour. For after his early confidence the mayor lost his nerve. When advised to demolish buildings on Sunday morning he could only wonder 'who shall pay the cost of rebuilding the houses'. Pepys, returning from Whitehall with a message from the king urging the levelling of buildings and promising troops to assist, encountered the mayor in Canning Street looking 'like a man spent, with a handkercher around his neck. To the King's message, he cried like a fainting woman, "Lord, what can I do? I am spent. People will not obey me. I have been pulling down houses. But the fire overtakes us faster than we can do it." ' Another report suggests that the mayor's difficulties were compounded by merchants, 'tenacious and avaricious men, Aldermen etc.' who would not allow demolition 'because their houses might have been first'. The seamen called in from the dockyards at Deptford and Woolwich wanted to use gunpowder, but this, by far the best means available for creating fire gaps, was not permitted until the last day of the fire. Very likely, though, it would have made little difference. On Monday hopes were entertained that the demon could be contained at Queenhythe, an inlet in the Thames that had served as the principal landing place above the bridge since Saxon times. But, a contemporary records, 'After two hours expectation we saw all their endeavours slighted by a leap which the Fire made over twenty houses upon the turret of a house in Thames Street.' Exactly the same disappointment was experienced at the Fleet Ditch on the following day.

The unconcern of Sunday morning had vanished by the afternoon. There was a desperate scramble for carts on which to carry belongings to safety, and the laws of supply and demand operated with their accustomed rigour. The longer the fire burned, the more pressing became people's needs, and the higher soared the price of carts. By Tuesday the going rate was half the value of the goods to be carried. There were appalling jams at the exits from the City. Pepys finally got his money, plate and 'best things' away at 4 o'clock on Monday morning, 'which I did, riding myself in my nightgown in the cart; and Lord! to see how the streets and the highways are crowded with people running and riding, and getting of carts at any rate to carry away things.' The rest of Pepys's goods (what did he do with his diary? one wonders) were committed to lighters on Tuesday. The Thames was crowded with boats piled high with household effects: 'hardly one lighter or boat in three', Pepys noted, 'but there was a pair of virginals on it'. Those who failed to obtain a lighter simply chucked their furniture into the Thames on the chance that they might be able to reclaim it on another day.

But Londoners still did not know the worst. That Sunday night those whose houses had been burnt sought shelter in old St Paul's and other buildings that were themselves destined for destruction. Pepys saw 'my little goldsmith Stokes receiving some friends' goods, whose house itself was burned the day after'. Monday dawned another bright morning but nobody in London noticed the fact. The dying City was enshrouded in 'a smoke so great as darkened the sun at noonday; if at any time the sun peeped forth, it looked red like blood'. For miles beyond London, travellers went in the shade of its pall. The flames appeared less dramatic by day than at night but they were not a wit less destructive. That Monday the fire struck north 'with the noise of the whirlwind in it', paralysing the citizens with its intensity and power. First Lombard Street, the City's financial centre, then, in the afternoon, Cornhill, were lost to the flames, Gresham's

Royal Exchange perishing in clouds of incense as the East India Company's spices stored in the vaults caught fire.

Helpless in their plight, Londoners began to seek scapegoats for their ruin. Rumours abounded: the Papists had fired the City; an army of 50000 French and Dutchmen (England was at war with these countries) were at the gates ready to put to the sword those spared by the fire. In such an atmosphere foreigners did well to keep silent. London's women were on the rampage. 'They had a corps de garde in each street', reported a quavering Frenchman, 'and did knock down several strangers for not speaking good Engish.' A blacksmith felled an innocent Frenchman with an iron bar, while in Moorfields the mob almost dismembered another for carrying 'balls of fire' in his chest. In the nick of time the unfortunate man was able to convince his assailants that they were in fact only tennis balls.

To Charles II's credit he refused to countenance any of the wild allegations. The official court verdict, expressed in the *London Gazette*, was that the fire was 'an effect of an unhappy chance, or to speak better, the heavy hand of God upon us for our sins. . . .' In fact the disaster was the king's finest hour. From Sunday onwards he took control of counter-measures from the wavering mayor, not disdaining to take up buckets and spades himself or to endanger his life in his attempts to stem the blaze. His brother the Duke of York played an equally distinguished part: 'had not the Duke been present', one of his attendants reported, 'and forced all people to submit to his demands, by this time I am confident there had not been a house standing in Whitehall.' 'If the Lord Mayor had done as much', commented another, 'his example might have gone far towards saving the City.' But the Duke's services weighed less heavily than his Catholicism in the eyes of some, who spread ugly libels that he had himself been responsible for the fire.

That Monday night Pepys had to make do with the remains of Sunday's dinner – 'having no fire', he explained. But others suffered more serious deprivations as there was no longer any space for the refugees within the walls. In their thousands the homeless camped out in Moorfields outside the north wall. For centuries marsh had prevented building here but the ground had at last been drained during the Civil War, for the purpose of practising artillery manoeuvres.

Still, though, the work of the fire was but half done. On Tuesday, 4 September, the wind blew into a gale so that the gardens of Kensington were covered with ash, while charred debris from the fire reached Windsor Great Park, Beaconsfield and even Henley over thirty miles away. The day began with the blaze approaching Cheapside, the grandest thoroughfare in the old City and the avenue used for all processions and ceremonials. As a street, a foreigner wrote at the end of Queen Elizabeth's reign, 'it surpasseth all the rest. There are to be seen . . . all sorts of gold and silver vessels exposed to sale, as well as ancient and modern medals, as must surprise a man the first time he sees and considers them.' But Cheapside was not wide enough to stop the fire engulfing it and passing on to the north. Once more the destruction was total. 'You may stand in Cheapside and see the Thames', an amazed visitor noted after the fire.

The next great building to be consumed was the Guildhall, which proved to be a most recalcitrant victim, so well had the medieval builders done their work. The roof beams were of such solid oak that instead of bursting into flame they glowed 'in a bright shining coal', as one witness described it, 'as if it had been a palace of gold or a great building of burnished brass'. The stone walls withstood the heat and it is still possible to see the change in colour of the interior where they have been increased in height since the fire. Moreover the crypt, containing all the records of medieval London, survived undamaged. No wonder that such careful attention was paid to the Guildhall's design in considering regulations for the rebuilding of London after the fire.

Even while the Guildhall was burning, the fire, driven by the tempest, was reducing the western half of the City to ashes. Only the massive stonework of Newgate offered any bar to its progress, and a little beyond the gate the blaze was halted at Pie Corner in Cock Lane. The fire 'began at Pudding Lane and ended at Pie Corner', noted one preacher, arguing that this was clear evidence that the catastrophe had been occasioned by the sin of gluttony. In reality, Pie Corner was the furthest limit of the fire neither as regards position (for the Temple is considerably further from Pudding Lane) nor as regards time (for the conflagration continued another twenty hours after being stopped at this point). Still, the little gilt figure of the Fat Boy, which can be seen high on the wall in Cock Lane, keeps alive the theory of the fire's gluttonous origins; and Pie Corner was, after all, the first place in which counter-measures achieved any success downwind of the main blaze. The workmen there received £50 to divide among themselves – generous compensation by some of the standards prevailing in the fire. Alderman Starling, one of the City's richest men, rewarded thirty workmen who had saved his house with 2/6d. (12½ pence) between them, while Alderman Sir Richard Browne was moved to bestow £4 on men who risked their lives saving his chest, the contents of which were valued at over £10000.

Meanwhile the fire had crossed the western wall and was racing down Fleet Street, so that Charles II deemed it wise to order the removal of the Exchequer from Whitehall to Nonsuch Palace in Surrey. And now, with the wind blowing harder than ever, and Tuesday night closing in, occurred the grand climax.

For some time it seemed as though old St Paul's, though hemmed in by flames, would itself escape burning, as its successor was to do in 1940-1. The cathedral rose so high above the surrounding buildings that it had looked impregnable to Londoners. The Stationers had demonstrated their confidence by storing all their books in its crypt for safety. And perhaps St Paul's might have escaped but for the scaffolding which had been erected for Wren's survey shortly before. Once this was kindled by sparks borne on the wind the roof was soon ablaze. As it fell into the nave six acres of molten lead cascaded down nearby streets, while huge stones splintered by the heat flew about 'like grenadoes'. Well over a mile away at Westminster, a scholar who should have been better employed found that he could read his Terence by the light of the burning St Paul's.

The end of the cathedral was like a vision of the apocalypse, even down to the tombs bursting open. Robert de Braybroke, Chancellor of England under Richard II and as bishop of London the very same man who had in 1385 crusaded against playing ball and shooting at birds in the cathedral, now made a reappearance in the world, and in fine fettle. His teeth, beard, hair and nails were still complete, 'the flesh, sinews and skin cleaving fast to the bones', so that when set on his feet the bishop stood 'as stiff as a plank, the skin being tough like leather and not at all inclined to putrefaction, which some attributed to the sanctity of his person'. Only the shrouded effigy of John Donne, the poet, survived unscathed from the old cathedral and is now housed in Wren's successor.

That Tuesday evening a Mr Locke, an amateur meteorologist living in Oxford, more than fifty miles from the City, noted 'a dim reddish sunshine. This unusual colour of the Air, which without a cloud appearing made the sunbeams of a strange dim light, was very remarkable. We then heard nothing of the Fire of London.' At last, though, the wind which had kindled the blaze began to drop. It was by no means the end of the fire, for St Paul's was still in flames on the night of Thursday, 6 September, while Cripplegate and the Temple burnt throughout Wednesday, the churches of both places only narrowly escaping destruction. In the small hours of Wednesday morning Pepys's wife heard new cries of 'fire', which was in fact licking the church of All Hallows Barking at the bottom of Seething Lane. Pepys promptly packed her off to Woolwich, but in the event neither the church nor his house were burnt. On the morning of 5 September, Pepys ascended All Hallows tower to survey the scene, 'the saddest sight of desolation that ever I saw'. Five-sixths of the area within the wall had been burnt, whilst to the west the devastation stretched as far as Fetter Lane. Later that day Pepys ventured into the ruined City with some companions. They found 'Fenchurch Street, Gracechurch Street, and Lombard Street all in dust. The Exchange a sad sight, nothing standing there of all the statues or pillars but Sir Thomas Gresham's picture in the corner. Walked into Moorfields (our feet ready to burn, walking through the town among the hot coals) and find that full of people, and poor wretches carrying their goods there. . . . Thence homeward, having passed through Cheapside and Newgate market, all burned. . . .' A contemporary print appears to show a surprising amount of the City still standing, but the distant view, taken from across the river, is deceptive. In reality only stone or brick husks remained; of the houses nothing but door porches and chimney breasts; of the churches nothing but empty towers and gutted naves open to the sky.

More than six months later, in March 1667, there were still cellars smoking in the City despite an exceptionally harsh winter. But in just four days the work of centuries had been destroyed, so that today the visitor has to be as far west as Staple Inn, by Chancery Lane tube station, to get any idea of what old London must have looked like. Surprisingly few people had died in the Great Fire – only eight deaths have been recorded as directly attributable to the flames. But for the tens of thousands who huddled in tents on the perimeter of the smoking devastation, the City's story must have appeared at an end. John Evelyn reduced the catastrophe to a single sentence, affecting in its simplicity, staggering in its implications: 'London was, but is no more.' In the aftermath of disaster, though, he forgot that 'London' and 'the City' were no longer interchangeable terms.

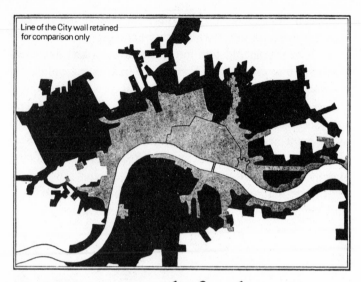

Line of the City wall retained
for comparison only

6. 'How much further it may spread God knows'

[1666-1800]

REBUILDING THE CITY

Even while the Great Fire was still burning there were some, who saw in the desolation a rebuilding opportunity hitherto beyond the scope of fantasy. On 10 September, only five days after the flames had become controllable, a young professor of astronomy called Christopher Wren, not yet widely known as an architect, presented his scheme for rebuilding the City to the king. Wren's plan took no

account whatever of the medieval street plan. He superimposed his grandiose vision of wide avenues radiating in
straight lines from the Royal Exchange, and intersecting with
streets leading north from the river, on what he conceived
to be the blank space of the ruined City.

The difficulty was that the space was only blank to the
eye. In law it was criss-crossed with property rights which
would certainly be protected by a Parliament of landowners.
For a few days Charles II appeared to share Wren's enthusiasm for an entirely fresh start but as an intelligent man
determined never to go on his travels again he had a keen
grasp of the practical. On 13 September he issued a proclamation assuring the City that 'though every man must
not be suffered to erect what buildings and where he
pleases, he shall not in any degree be debarred from receiving the reasonable benefit of what ought to accrue to
him from such Houses or Lands, there being nothing less in
Our thoughts than that any particular person's right and
interest should be sacrificed to the public benefit and convenience, without such recompense as in justice he ought
to receive for the same. . . .' When a Mr Valentine Knight
produced a scheme whereby each inhabitant should pay a
rent to the king in proportion to the value of his building
site, Charles, who would have liked nothing better than a
personal income of over £200000 a year, seized the opportunity to make a public parade of virtue. Knight was
imprisoned merely for venturing such a suggestion, 'as if',
in the words of a royalist report, 'his Majesty would draw
benefit to himself from so public a calamity of his people, of
which his Majesty is known to have so deep a sense, that he
is pleased to seek rather by all means to give them ease under
it'. The rejection of Wren's plan was a powerful demonstra-
tion of the way in which private ownership has always
dominated London's development, rendering it, for all its

size, a town of intimate rather than magnificent appeal, a succession of many and various small-scale delights rather than one overwhelming and integrated spectacle. The scope of its vistas has always been limited by the size of its estates.

As soon as it was recognized that new building would have to conform in great measure to the ancient pattern of the City, the problem was no longer *where* but *how* the houses should be rebuilt. The question needed resolving quickly because the authorities harboured the terrifying suspicion that unless the City was rebuilt immediately it might never be rebuilt at all. City merchants had been forced into the rival suburbs by the fire and there was alarm that the port would permanently lose its trade in the commercial vacuum that must necessarily follow the disaster. Officials made brave efforts to ensure continuity by holding parish meetings amidst the ruins but the very gallantry of such gestures reflected a gnawing uncertainty about the future. 'The City less and less likely to be rebuilt', thought Pepys on the last day of 1666, 'everybody settling elsewhere and nobody encouraged to trade.'

England's enemies took no pains to conceal their delight at London's misfortune. Throughout Europe, Catholics and Protestants alike were lost in admiration for the justice of the Almighty's ways. The Calvinist Dutch sniffed increased profit and blessed him, while the Spanish could only wonder at the wisdom of a God who had been as eager as they to associate fire with heresy. A Spaniard in London wrote home with sweet Catholic charity that there was now but one hope left to Londoners. 'Having recognized the true Roman church let them pray to God that he may save them from a greater fire, namely, the fire of Hell.' Louis XIV, by contrast, behaved with exemplary restraint. Although France was at war with England he forbad any celebration and offered to send food and relief. But then there was alarm abroad in

Paris: 'A proud and barbarous nation reduced to despair leaves some reason for apprehension that some of them may resolve to come forth out of the country in great numbers and provide additional travail and peril for their enemies.'

This matter of population loss also worried the mayor and aldermen, in more urgent though in somewhat less dramatic form. Even so, rebuilding could not start immediately. The rejection of a comprehensive plan certainly did not mean that all controls were forsworn. On the contrary, private rebuilding was to be subjected to the strictest public surveillance. The king forbad work to start before rules governing reconstruction had been agreed, and the royal word was reinforced by the unusually cold winter. A commission of Crown and City experts, of which Wren was a member, used the breathing space to produce regulations which were passed by Parliament in February 1667.

Naturally the first object of the laws was to ensure that such a catastrophe could never occur again. The City was to be rebuilt in brick and stone, and this time the prohibition of wooden houses finally stuck – to the benefit of the brick kilns which sprang up on the outskirts of the City. Moreover the authorities were determined to prevent slapdash building: rules governing every aspect of house construction were to be enforced by 'knowing and intelligent persons in buildings'. Four different types of house, each related to particular street widths, were prescribed. Thus four-storey houses were limited to the 'high and principal streets', three-storey houses to 'streets and lanes of note', and two storeys to 'by-lanes'.

Once these regulations had been settled, rebuilding proceeded apace. Preachers declared the work to be not merely virtuous but very likely more profitable than trade. A special court was set up to decide whether landlords or tenants should be responsible for reconstruction in cases where former houses had been let, and its judgements reflected the urgency of the times. Generally, where the landlord lacked means to rebuild, the tenant was encouraged to do so by the extension of his lease and a reduction in his rent. On the other hand, if the tenant was broke, the court would declare his lease forfeit on payment of compensation from the landlord. Where no one had rebuilt within three years (a period subsequently extended) the Acts provided compulsory powers of acquisition to ensure resale to those able to build. This threat must have been a marvellous encouragement: at any rate much of the house rebuilding had been completed by the end of 1670, and nearly all by 1672. In its enthusiasm for the task the City even relaxed for seven years the exclusive privileges possessed by its freemen craftsmen so that workmen flooded in from all parts of the country.

The houses which they built presented no monotonous façades for there was scope for variation within the limits prescribed. Numbers 5 and 6 Crane Court, just to the east of Fetter Lane, are the earliest remaining post-fire City houses: few others from this period survived the last war. Some company halls – those of the Apothecaries at Blackfriars, Vintners by Southwark Bridge and Skinners on Dowgate Hill – have fared better, at least in part, and such buildings typify the resilience with which the City reacted to the fire. Many of the companies had been in bad financial shape before 1666 – Charles I's enemies had proved no better than he at repaying loans – but nearly all managed to rebuild their halls, even at the cost of steeping themselves in debt for the next century.

The character of the streets altered as dramatically as that of the houses. It was not merely that the laws ordained minimum widths – of sixteen feet for alleys and up to sixty feet for main routes. For the first time since Roman London the City streets acquired a straight and definite frontage, so that instead of being tortuous paths to individual houses they became clear highways. This improvement was all the more welcome because after 1600 the advent of coaches had added to the chaos in the medieval streets. Royal proclamations banning coach hire had proved no more effective than those attempting to curb the growth of the suburbs. On the very day of Charles II's proclamation against the use of hackney coaches Pepys triumphantly boasted, 'I got one to carry me home.' Now that the streets were wider and paved, the number of carriages multiplied.

In the years after the fire the City spent nearly £75000 on street widening, the greater part in buying properties which had previously obstructed the way. The money for all such public expenditure on reconstruction was raised by taxes on coal coming into the port. By 1688 these dues had produced £736804, of which £382848 went to the City, £265467 to the parish churches (as an example it cost about £15000 to rebuild St Mary-le-Bow) and the remaining £88489 was devoted towards the new St Paul's Cathedral. (After 1687 the entire proceeds of the tax went to St Paul's.) The only project which tempted the king to dig deep in the royal pocket was the Custom House: one does not need to be unduly cynical to guess the reason. Yet as plans for the Custom House presupposed continued activity in the port, the City shared the royal enthusiasm for seeing it in action again. Naturally, though, the City's first priority, and one of the most expensive, was the repair and rebuilding of the Guildhall, which was given direct access to the river by the creation of King and Queen Streets, the only considerable alteration to the old street plan. The Guildhall was ready in time for the Lord Mayor's Banquet of 1671, but the nearest occasion to a ceremonial rebirth of the City had been three years before, when

Charles II came to lay the first stone of the new Royal
Exchange and was fêted in a 'shed' erected on the ruins, to
the accompaniment of trumpets and kettledrums.

Two projects to improve the port deserve mention.
Rubble from the burnt City was used to build up wharves
so that a forty-foot-wide quay ran uninterruptedly between
London Bridge and the Tower. There were plans to extend
it to the Temple, but these were never effected. In truth
there was not much incentive since traffic above the bridge
had long been confined to river barges bringing corn and
fruit from upriver, and lighters carrying bulky cargoes,
especially coal, through the bridge (Sea Coal Lane survives
as a witness to this ancient traffic). None the less it was still
deemed worth while to make a highly extravagant attempt
to render the Fleet navigable in its lower half-mile through
the construction of a cutting with wharves alongside. After
countless difficulties the canal was completed, but eventually
the Fleet's filth overcame the City's willingness to pay for
continuous dredging. The works were arched over in 1733
and the river Fleet finally hidden from view.

WREN'S CHURCHES

So much of the restoration work carried out after the Great
Fire has perished that the part survival of its most glorious
aspect must be counted as singular good fortune. Eighty-
seven churches had been burnt, of which fifty-two were
rebuilt, nearly all of them to the designs, or at least under
the general supervision, of Sir Christopher Wren. Although
most of his City churches which were still standing in 1939
were damaged or destroyed in the blitz, all but seven have
been reconstructed since the war, more or less according to
the original plan. The shame is that the Church of England
proved more permanently destructive of Wren's churches

in the nineteenth century than did the Germans in the
twentieth. The happy accident that associated an architect of
genius with these merchant temples did not commend
itself to Victorian sensibility. It was decreed, with a degree
of philistine bigotry perhaps only attainable by aesthetes,
that churches must, almost by definition, be built in the
Gothic style, from which it followed that Wren's baroque
was pagan and could be destroyed with a good conscience.

Between 1782 and 1939, therefore, seventeen of Wren's
City churches were pulled down and the land sold to finance
churches in the suburbs. Many of the remainder were
subjected to 'Christian' improvements, which meant ripping
out the fittings. This was especially disastrous. As the
churches' exteriors were so often hidden by surrounding
buildings the skills of Wren and his craftsmen had been concentrated, the steeples apart, on the interiors. The Victorians
felt no compunction about removing the furniture or about
fitting stained-glass windows in direct contradiction to his
guiding principle that 'nothing could add beauty to light'.
Although the Germans shattered this stained glass, it was
replaced in many cases after the war. At least, though, that is
a reversible error, whereas the high-backed pews and other
woodwork, treated with equal disrespect by Victorians
and Germans alike, are irrecoverable. Moreover Wren's
steeples, now dwarfed by tower blocks, can never again
provide the distinctive and varied City skyline which
he intended and which is evident in eighteenth-century
pictures.

Still, when all is said and done, twenty-three Wren
churches, apart from St Paul's, remain in the City, and their
different sizes and designs (one, St Mary Aldermary in
Queen Victoria Street is even in the Gothic style) together
with their shared elegance and practicality bear witness to
the extraordinary fertility of their creator's invention.

Surviving Wren churches in London

St Michael, Cornhill (1670–2)
St Mary-at-Hill, Thames Street (1670–6)
*St Edmund the Martyr, Lombard Street (1670–9, spire 1706–7)
St Olave, Jewry (1670–9; tower only remains)
*St Mary-le-Bow, Cheapside (1670–80)
*St Bride, Fleet Street (1670–84, spire 1701–3)
St Magnus the Martyr, Lower Thames Street (1671–6, steeple 1705)
*St Lawrence, Jewry (1671–7)
*St Nicholas Cole Abbey, Queen Victoria Street (1671–7)
*St Stephen, Walbrook (1672–9, steeple 1717)
St Paul's Cathedral (1675–1710)
*St James Garlickhythe (1676–83, spire 1713–17)
*St James, Piccadilly (1676–84)
*St Anne and St Agnes, Gresham Street (1677–80)
St Peter, Cornhill (1677–81)
St Benet Paul's Wharf, Upper Thames Street (1677–83)
St Martin, Ludgate Hill (1677–84)
Christ Church, Newgate Street (1677–87; tower, 1703–4, and part of outer wall only remain)
*St Clement Danes, Strand (1680–2)
St Anne, Soho (1680–6; a ruin save for nineteenth-century tower)
*St Mary Abchurch, Cannon Street (1681–7)
*St Mary Aldermary, Queen Victoria Street (1681–2, tower 1701–4)
St Clement, Eastcheap (1683–7)
St Margaret Pattens, Eastcheap (1684–7, spire 1698–1702)
*St Andrew, Holborn (1684–90)
*St Andrew by the Wardrobe, Queen Victoria Street (1685–95)
St Margaret, Lothbury (1686–90)
St Mary Somerset, Upper Thames Street (1686–94; tower only remains)

*St Michael Paternoster Royal, College Street (1686–94, steeple 1713)
*St Vedast, Foster Lane (1695–1700, steeple 1709–12)
 St Alban, Wood Street (tower only, 1697–8, remains)
 St Dunstan in the East, Great Tower Street (tower only, 1702, remains)

In addition Wren was concerned with twenty-two City churches which have disappeared, mainly by Victorian or German action.

---

* Indicates that the church has been restored after being badly bombed in the last war.

Perhaps the most famous of the steeples, which were generally built after the main body of the church, are those at St Mary-le-Bow Cheapside, St Bride Fleet Street, and Christchurch Newgate, at which last the tower is all that remains. There are also lead spires like that of St Martin Ludgate, which is meant to be seen in the context of the dome of St Paul's. It is invidious to single out examples, but of other Wren churches St James Garlickhythe off Upper Thames Street, St Mary Abchurch in Cannon Street, and St Mary-at-Hill in Eastcheap possess interiors which, if not all original, at least reflect their designer's spirit and contain magnificent fittings; while St Stephen Walbrook demonstrates his ingenuity in creating a variety of different vistas on a plain rectangular ground-plan.

Like Anglicanism itself, Wren's churches reflect a compromise between extreme Catholic and Protestant ideals. The altars are generally railed off as in a Catholic church, but they are placed flat against the east wall rather than in a special apse. At the same time the Protestant emphasis on the sermon made Wren determined that all parts of the congregation should be able to hear. 'The Romanists', he wrote, 'may build larger churches, it is enough if they hear the murmur of the Mass and see the Elevation of the Host, but ours are fitted to be Auditories.' Hence his City churches contained fine pulpits, some with sounding boards above them.

THE NEW ST PAUL'S

In the case of St Paul's Cathedral, however, Wren was committed to rebuild on the Romanist scale. Immediately after the fire the ruined hulk of old St Paul's retained sufficient grandeur to encourage notions that it could be repatched. In January 1668 orders were given for the construction of a temporary choir within the west end, which had been given Inigo Jones's classical refronting only thirty years previously. By May, however, some ominous cracks had set the Dean to write to Dr Wren. 'It is the opinion of all men', he related, 'that we can proceed no further at the west end. What we are to do next is the present deliberation, in which you are so absolutely and indispensably necessary to us that we can do nothing, re-solve on nothing, without you. . . .' Even before the fire Wren had been asked to prepare plans for restoring old St Paul's and had made a drawing which capped the cath-edral with a dome. Now, apparently, he was to be given a freer hand. 'The way their Lordships resolve upon . . . is to frame a design, handsome and noble, and suitable to all the Ends of it, and to the Reputation of the City, and the Nation, and to take it for granted that money will be had to accomplish it.'

Wren soon discovered, though, that it is no simple task to satisfy every interest involved in such a vast project, and another seven years passed before he produced a design which won general consent. The cathedral which was finally built is a tribute to his character and cunning as much as to his genius, because his favourite plan, incorporated in the Great Model of 1673 which is on display in St Paul's museum, was rejected by the clergy on the grounds that it was not in the original cruciform shape. Wren masked his disappointment and soon produced another design – 'the oddest mongrel product ever recommended by a great architect', Sir Nikolaus Pevsner calls it – which he probably had no intention of following but which he correctly judged would obtain the necessary approval by its conservative form.

The remnants of old St Paul's took two years to remove. At first gunpowder was used to break down the massive piers but after some masonry had ended up in the front room of a nearby house this method was abandoned in favour of a battering ram manned by thirty labourers. When Wren, clambering over the rubble, asked a surveyor to mark a spot for him he was delighted to observe that the stone picked up for this purpose came from a tomb and bore the word, *Resurgam* – 'I will rise again'. It was soon obvious that the building which was rising differed considerably from the plan which had been accepted, and that Wren intended to stretch to its full, and beyond, a proviso in the king's consent which allowed him 'to make variations, rather ornamental than essential, as from time to time he should see proper'. Perhaps Wren interpreted the substitution of a massive dome for the plan's low one topped by a large steeple as a merely 'ornamental' variation; at any rate he made his real intentions clear from an early stage by adding two feet to the thickness of the walls, thus enabling them to bear the heavier weight. In fact the dome's final design was only settled after 1702, over thirty years after Wren began work on the cathedral, by which time the choir had already been consecrated (1697) and the west front well advanced.

Here again Wren was forced to compromise. He would have preferred a single gigantic portico rather than the two-storeyed design which was built, but the Portland quarries which provided stone for the exterior were unable to produce blocks sufficiently large to span his projected columns. The two western towers were completed in 1708 and two years later the ball and cross placed on top of the dome.

At this point the accounts recorded with somewhat pedantic accuracy that the work had cost £738845.5.2½d, but Wren still found it necessary to petition for the arrears of his salary which had been withheld after 1697 due to concern about the slow progress. Thereafter he had to submit to a balustrade being placed along the top of his cathedral in direct defiance of his wishes ('Ladies think nothing well without an edging', he commented bitterly), and of 1718 suffered the indignity of being dismissed from his post of Surveyor General. But perhaps the old man who occasionally shuffled into the cathedral to ponder silently in the crossing beneath the dome considered it sufficient reward to have been spared long enough to see his thirty-five-year task through to its conclusion.

No man has ever served London better. St Paul's was only the crowning glory of his prodigious labours on behalf of the City's reconstruction. Writing to congratulate Wren, a contemporary reflected that the fire, 'however disastrous it might have been to the then inhabitants, had prov'd infinetly beneficial to their posterity; conducing vastly to the Improvement and Increase, as well as the Riches and Opulency of this City. Then, which I and every Body must observe with great Satisfaction, by means of the Inlargement of the Streets; of the great Plenty of good Water, convey'd to all Parts; of the common Sewers, and other like Contrivances, such Provision is made for a free

Access and Passage of the Air, for Sweetness, for Cleanness and for Salubrity, that it is not only the finest, but the most healthy City in the world.' It is entirely fitting that Wren should have designed the Monument erected to the memory of the Great Fire, the height of which (202 feet) is supposed to measure the distance between its position and the site of the baker's house in Pudding Lane where the conflagration began. Wren wanted to crown the Monument with a statue of the king but the story has it that Charles II objected to this idea on the grounds that he was not responsible for the fire.

CHANGING CHARACTER OF THE CITY

The snag about the rebuilding was that the former in- habitants did not all flock back to the new City. To that extent the fears which had been expressed for its future immediately after the fire proved well-founded. Although the street widening meant that only 9000 of the 13 000 burnt houses had been rebuilt, many stood empty for years after completion, so that the mayor and aldermen were compelled to relax the conditions governing citizenship in order to tempt people to fill them. By 1700 there were 208 000 living under their rule, but the City's population never reached its former proportions. It was bad enough that some merchants moved to other ports, but perhaps even more ominous for the future was the tendency of the prosperous to live away from their businesses. Beautiful City houses like those at 1–2 Laurence Pountney Hill, dating from 1702, were no longer a sufficient lure. Even aldermen were choosing to live in nearby country houses or in the more fashionable suburbs to the west.

Many of the deserters belonged to the new breed of City capitalist, no longer the merchant venturers of old but bankers and directors whose power centres were not so much the Livery Companies, with their ancient local attachments and their long traditions of hospitality, but more soulless new institutions like the Bank of England (founded in 1694). In the eighteenth century many wealthy men found City office a chore to be avoided rather than a privilege to be sought; and the Mansion House, the Lord Mayor's residence which was completed in 1753, was largely paid for by fines elicited from those anxious to avoid office. These were as yet only straws in the wind, but with hindsight it is possible to discern the first inklings of the process which over the next two centuries was to transform the City from a place to live into a conglomeration of offices deserted every night.

The changing character of the City did not affect its pretensions. The medieval town and environment had both vanished, but the medieval sense of privilege was still very much alive. Although ruling only about a third of the capital's total population in 1700 the mayor and aldermen continued to act as though 'London' and 'the City' were interchangeable terms. They shut their official eyes to the suburbs by which they were engulfed (and where some of them lived) and continued to petition against new building there as though still surrounded by green fields. Market rights outside City bounds were sternly contested and a timely loan of £100000 to the ever eager Charles II delayed the building of a rival bridge at Westminster by another sixty years.

EIGHTEENTH-CENTURY POPULATION GROWTH: COMMERCE AND INDUSTRY

Notwithstanding such negative achievements the City was blowing into the wind: as long as London's population went on rising nothing could prevent its area expanding in order to accommodate the increase. Already in the late seventeenth century it was becoming hard to set a limit on future numbers. Sir William Petty, one of the cleverest men of that time, when there were only half a million people in the capital, projected that this figure would reach ten million by 1842. His timing but not his vision was incorrect. London's population grew from 575000 in 1700 to 675000 in 1750 to 900000 (nearly twice the size of Paris) at the end of the eighteenth century. 'I have twice this spring been going to stop my coach in Piccadilly, to inquire what was the matter', wrote Horace Walpole in 1791, 'thinking there was a mob – not at all; it was only passengers.' During the eighteenth century, one in six Englishmen was either living or had lived in London.

Yet there were far more deaths than births in the capital: the increase in numbers was entirely due to new arrivals from outside. For the first time, town life was offering diversions sufficiently alluring to drag the English gentleman from his shire, so that a town house became a desirable adjunct, even in some cases a replacement, of the country seat. Hordes of servants were imported to sustain the life of fashion, and a particularly opulent aristocrat like the Duke of Bedford kept a staff of forty servants at his Bloomsbury home even when he was out of town. But of course the vast majority of immigrants came to the capital in order to find work. For all kinds of people – younger sons compelled to earn their keep; artists in search of a patron; political refugees like the Huguenots in flight from Le Roi Très Chrétien; all manner of workmen, both skilled craftsmen and casual labourers; criminals escaping from justice – for all these the road to London appeared to offer the best means of supporting existence.

Many of them drifted towards the eastern suburbs because in 1700 a quarter of London's jobs were still related directly or indirectly to the shipping which crowded into the port. The capital, wrote Defoe in 1724, 'sucks the vitals of trade in this island to itself'. The amount of traffic handled there doubled in the course of the eighteenth century; and although London lost some of its relative predominance due to the rise of western ports like Bristol or Liverpool, it still accounted for a healthy 65 per cent of the nation's foreign trade in the 1790s. The character of that trade had entirely altered: London's prosperity no longer depended, as it had done for centuries, on the export of wool and woollen cloth across the narrow seas. Yet the port's easy communication with Europe was still the basis of its attraction, even now that England was the head of a far-flung commercial empire. The colonies were forced to send their produce to England in order that the mother country might profit by re-exporting it. Cargoes came to London from distant east and west at least partly because it was the most convenient place from which they could be sold to the European market. The port became the centre of exchange between the new world and the old, so that in the eighteenth century it was a fair bet that any tobacco, coffee or rice consumed on the Continent had passed through London. A vast labour force was needed on the Thames to handle all this traffic. Besides the thousands of musclemen who loaded and unloaded the cargoes, there were countless others employed in industries closely associated with the port, like ship-building and sugar refining. Naturally the great trading companies had their head offices nearby, while the insurance and banking services for which the City is still famous developed in the first instance to provide the cover and credit required by the port's vast international commerce.

Trades unconnected with the port were increasingly to be found outside the City, which, indeed, became ringed with industries anxious to be at once beyond its bounds and its medieval regulations. Perhaps the word 'industries' conveys the wrong impression because most of the work was still done in individual houses rather than in factories: nevertheless, certain areas still became identified with certain trades. Thus, silk-weavers congregated in Spitalfields (where some houses still have tall attic windows which were designed to light the looms), clock-makers and jewellers in Clerkenwell, and tanners in Bermondsey.

By the end of the eighteenth century some trades – knitting and shoemaking are examples – were beginning to migrate northwards, but even after the Industrial Revolution London remained, and still remains, the greatest manufacturing centre in the country. Today that fact is obscured because London's industries are many, scattered and relatively small-scale, rather than concentrated into a few vast factories as in some other towns. Before 1750, when *all* industries were small-scale, London's manufacturing pre-eminence must have been more obvious. There was no trade that was not represented there. In particular the capital was famous for high-class luxury trades such as coach-building, furniture-making and watch-making, which found a ready market among the many wealthy inhabitants and visitors. The whims of the fashionable also called into being a host of services, from haircutting to coach-painting, from wig-making to chocolate-making.

PHYSICAL GROWTH: THE SURROUNDING VILLAGES

No trade offered such opportunities, both for making and for losing money, as building the houses which the new population required. Defoe, in the early eighteenth century, reckoned that 'London' was already thirty-six miles in

circumference, with a diameter stretching across its middle
from Blackwall in the east to Tothill Fields (where St
James's Park station now is) in the west. Its limits extended
as far as 'Hide Park Corner in the Brentford Road, and
almost to Marylebone in the Acton Road; and how much
further it may spread God knows'. Eighteenth-century
observers were left bemused by the rate of growth. 'Rows
of houses shoot out every day like a polypus', wrote
Horace Walpole in 1786, 'and so great is the rage of building
everywhere, that, if I stay here [Twickenham] a fortnight
without going to town, I look about to see if no new house is
built since I went last.' Five years later he was predicting
that 'there will soon be one street from London to Brentford; ay, and from London to every village for ten miles
around'. By that time the western villages of Knightsbridge and Marylebone were hardly distinct from the great
urban mass, while Paddington and St Pancras were about
to expand and be engulfed.

As the brick lines crept relentlessly outwards, a more
distant range of villages, hitherto beyond the City's ambit,
developed as retreats for Londoners who wanted a sniff of
the country about their homes. Hampstead was especially
popular due to the supposedly curative effects of its waters:
lovely terraces like Church Row (*c.* 1720) and fine residences like Fenton House (*c.* 1697) still bear witness to its
vogue. Nearby Highgate also contains much of the eighteenth century at its heart, around the Green. To the west of
London, Kensington Square suddenly appeared in the midst
of fields at the end of the seventeenth century, in order to
house the courtiers who attended William III in his palace
there. And all around London, in Hackney, Islington,
Chelsea, Battersea, Wandsworth, Clapham and Roe-
hampton, urban terraces sprouted as a result of eighteenth-
century Londoners' search for country retreats.

THE GREAT ESTATES: THE GROSVENORS

Within the town itself, the distinction between the smart West End and the shabby East End became ever more marked. This contrast was not simply attributable to the port being in the east and the court in the west. There was another factor at work. Since all development was carried through by the owners of the land, grand schemes were only feasible where a considerable area belonged to one proprietor. As it happened, holdings to the east of the City were mainly small and scattered, while most of the land to the west of Holborn, formerly the property of Westminster Abbey, was divided by the seventeenth century into big estates owned by the Crown and private individuals (see the map on p. 207). It was therefore possible to meet the demand for fashionable houses in that quarter by building squares and streets in large-scale comprehensive schemes. Nor did the estate owners need much encouragement to do so, since

> The richest crop for any field
> Is a crop of bricks for it to yield.
> The richest crop that it can grow,
> Is a crop of houses in a row.

By the middle of the seventeenth century the potentially golden fertility of the fields on the west side of the expanding town had become obvious enough to render their ownership a prized object of familial ambition. The origin of the greatest of all London estates, that of the Grosvenor family, shows the determination and unscrupulousness which the scramble for fortune engendered.

The Grosvenor estate was once the Manor of Ebury, a collection of farmsteads between the rivers Tyburn and

Westbourne, bounded by the Thames at Pimlico and, two miles away to the north, by Oxford Street. This property was divided into two separate sections, the northern, which was narrowed by the protrusion of Hyde Park from the west, being cut off from the swampy southern meadows by the Crown land attached to St James's Palace. In 1626 the whole of Ebury Manor had been bought for £9400 by a lawyer called Hugh Awdeley (hence Audley Street) who had made a fortune out of helping the Stuarts to fleece their subjects. Having no children, and lacking better employment in his declining years, Awdeley amused himself by making frequent changes in his will. Ebury Manor, which was only a small part of his total estate, was devised in turn to several people, with an obscure great-nephew called Alexander Davies finally emerging as the beneficiary in favour at the time of Awdeley's death in 1662. Wealth came suddenly to the Davies family. Alexander himself, the son of a draper, had been a clerk; and his brother Thomas's subsequent elevation was to amaze the envious Pepys. 'Davis [*sic*], the little fellow, my school-fellow, the book-seller, who was one of Audley's Executors, . . . [is] now become Sheriff; which is a strange turn methinks.'

But Alexander Davies did not enjoy his good fortune for long since he died of plague in 1665; his headstone may still be seen in the churchyard of St Margaret's, Westminster. He left, however, a capable and determined widow in charge of a daughter called Mary, who thus became, at the age of seven months, one of the hottest properties on the marriage market. But there was opportunity for suitors to bargain as Mrs Davies desperately needed ready cash in order to fend off her brother-in-law's claims to the Awdeley inheritance.

After another candidate had fallen by the wayside through lack of means, Sir Thomas Grosvenor, a well-off young

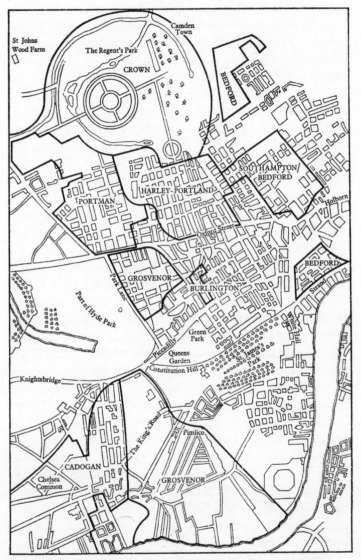

The West End about 1800, showing the areas of some of the family estates.

baronet from Cheshire, managed to buy Mrs Davies's favour
and Mary Davies's hand. At St Clement Danes on 10 October
1677 he claimed his twelve-year-old bride, thus unknowingly
setting his family on the road to a dukedom. There were
three sons and a daughter from the marriage, but although
he was always affectionate Sir Thomas must have been
increasingly worried by his wife's behaviour. Some time
around 1685 she became a Catholic, a harsh blow for the
conventionally Protestant Grosvenor family. Then in the
1690s she began to manifest signs of serious mental instability,
developing, among other alarming habits, a tendency to
shut her servants up in cupboards, or even, in one case, in a
convent. After Sir Thomas's death in 1700 these symptoms
combined to present the Grosvenors with a deadly threat to
their entire Davies inheritance.

For Mary Grosvenor fell under the influence of a Catholic
priest, Father Fenwick, who accompanied her on a visit to
Rome in the year of her husband's death. On the way back,
in Paris, she suffered a total breakdown, and while she was
immured in an hotel under treatments which included
regular doses of opium the Catholic mafia struck. It was
claimed, and attested by witnesses, that Father Fenwick had
married Mary Grosvenor to his brother Edward, although
the bride, on her return to England, disavowed any knowledge of these proceedings – 'for I never saw book, or heard
marriage words, nor said any'.

Nevertheless Edward Fenwick took his marital duties
seriously enough to begin collecting rents from the Ebury
estate, a move which helped to convince the Grosvenors, who
had meanwhile packed Sir Thomas's widow smartly off to
Eaton Hall in Cheshire, of their duty to rid her of this
pretended spouse. Lawyers were martialled by both sides
and extended battle was joined in the courts, where the
struggle was conducted as ruthlessly as one might have

expected with so much at stake. The Grosvenors scored a notable triumph in 1702, when they had Fenwick imprisoned in Paris on the charge of coercing a woman into matrimony, an offence which bore the death penalty. But with the aid of some judicious bribery their redoubtable antagonist escaped to win a verdict in England's Court of Queen's Bench in favour of the validity of his marriage. The Grosvenors had to go to an ecclesiastical court to get this judgement reversed in 1705, a decision which in effect secured them final victory. It was as well, for by that time the northern part of Ebury Manor was ready for its crop of houses.

THE BUILDING LEASE

The pattern of estate development had been established over forty years before in 1661, when the Earl of Southampton had set about creating Bloomsbury Square to the south of his own house. The scheme which he devised had the considerable attraction of limiting his own expenditure to a minimum while guaranteeing him control over the design, an ultimate share in the profits, and an increased income in the interim. The land was divided into plots which were let for forty-two years at low rents on condition that the tenant of each plot should construct a house thereon in a prescribed style. In fact the first tenants were mainly building speculators, whether workmen or financiers, who had no intention of living there but who realized their profits by selling either house or lease or both as soon as the work was finished.

It is easy to see why this system of building leases was adopted, with variations in the length of term, by all other great London landowners. The device, however, could not have been used so generally if it had not also suited the building workers. How else could they have obtained the use of prime development land at such cheap rates without losing their independence? Moreover the different kinds of craftsmen could operate a system of barter with their various skills, so that, for instance, a plumber would work in a plasterer's house and vice versa. With labour charges thus reduced to a minimum and the ground costing him a pittance, a speculative builder only needed sufficient capital to pay for the cost of materials. This reduction of capital outlay was important because the wealthy were not noticeably eager to risk their money building London houses. Indeed it is hard to see how the West End could have been developed without the building lease. The Earl of St Albans met this problem when, at about the same time as the Earl of Southampton's Bloomsbury scheme, he tried to build St James's Square as an exclusively aristocratic quarter of about ten grand houses.

ST JAMES'S

There could be no complaints about the Earl of St Albans' site. The area had been made fashionable by Charles II's preference for the palace which Henry VIII had built after taking over the old leper hospital of St James. The Tudor gateway still stands at the bottom of St James's Street, but the buildings of the palace have always been unremarkable: a Frenchman wrote that 'the kings of England are lodged like invalids at the palace of St James, and the invalids of the Army and Navy like kings at Chelsea and Greenwich'. (There is still not a palace in England to match Wren's buildings for the 'invalids'.) Perhaps Charles II found his pleasures a little harder to take at Whitehall, the scene of his father's death; at any rate it was at St James's that he installed his various mistresses and there that he applied himself assiduously to the business of peopling the English aristocracy with his bastards. Frequently he would sally forth with his partners in this enterprise, a sight which Sir William Petty numbered amongst the major attractions of London. 'There is greater liberty at the Court, in St James' and Hide Parks, in churches, at theatres and elsewhere, to see beautiful women, with and without impunity.' Or there was the more innocent diversion of *palla a maglio*, a kind of cross between croquet and bowls, which gave its name to Pall Mall. The easy informal association of king and subjects in the park appears strange to the present generation, but Charles II was never sensitive about the vulgar gaze. There was, in any case, no avoiding it as long as monarchs chose to use the parks: when George II's Queen Caroline asked Sir Robert Walpole how much it would cost to close them to the public the prime minister replied, 'Only three *Crowns*.'

Charles II had asked Le Notre to landscape St James's Park, but the Frenchman professed himself content to let well alone. All the same, the Gallic manner with nature was evident enough in a dead straight canal, flanked on both sides by equally straight lines of trees. Fortunately John Nash created rather more subtle scenery there in 1828, and today St James's is perhaps the most beautiful of all the parks. Yet its smartest days were in Charles II's reign, especially after the king, with royal hypocrisy as breathtaking as Henry VIII's closure of the brothels in Southwark, banned St James's Fair on the grounds that it tended 'rather to the advantage of looseness and irregularity than to the substantial promoting of any good'.

So the position of the Earl of St Albans' projected square for aristocrats was perfect. Moreover as a long-standing crony of the king he was able to obtain a free grant of the land. Only one thing was wrong: the very grand people whom he had envisaged as neighbours were reluctant themselves to fork out the sums needed to build the huge houses which had been planned. So the earl was compelled to tone down his ideas and act in much the same way as the Earl of Southampton. He cut down the size of the plots in order to reduce the expense of building, and let them not just to the titled, as he had originally intended, but to anyone prepared to undertake the task of putting up houses. The development was still grand – St Albans commissioned Wren to design a church, St James's Piccadilly, which the architect regarded among his best – but the work was no longer financed only by the eventual residents. Even at St James's the speculator had proved a necessity.

SPECULATIVE DEVELOPERS: NICHOLAS BARBON

Many familiar London street names – like Bond, Clarges, Storey, Panton and Frith – once belonged to late seventeenth-century developers who exploited land through the device of the building lease. The biggest operator of them all, and one of the least sensitive men ever to grace the property business, was Dr Nicholas Barbon (the title 'Doctor' was pretty suspect), or 'rogue, knave, damned Barbon' in the estimation of those who did business with him. Oddly enough there are no streets named after him, although his works extended all over London. Bedford Row, Essex Street, Theobalds Row and Red Lion Square were just some of his projects. It is not a bit surprising to find his name cropping up as one of the house builders in St James's Square, although he did not usually care to involve himself in such isolated ventures. 'It was not worth his while to deal little,' Barbon loftily announced, '*that* a bricklayer could do, The gain he expected was out of great undertakings.'

That sounds suspiciously like the bluster of a fantasist, and it is certainly true that the Doctor did leave huge debts, together with instructions that they should not be paid. But debt was merely his means of gaining credit, much cheaper, he reckoned, than borrowing at 10 per cent. No man was ever less of a fool: besides his property schemes he wrote economic treatises quoted with approval by Marx, and was a pioneer in banking and insurance. But 'all his aim was profit', to which end he consecrated his talent and nastiness in equal measure. He loved a scrap, and when his Red Lion Square project aroused the hostility of the lawyers of Gray's Inn he led 200 of his workmen into the intervening fields 'shouting and hollowing and waving their hats to the gentlemen of the Society to come out and encounter them'. This summons the lawyers eventually obeyed, and indeed had the better of the fisticuffs – which made a change from being outsmarted by Barbon on their own ground of the law.

For no one ever bettered the Doctor with words. A contemporary brilliantly described how he handled meetings with those who owned properties which obstructed his ambitions.

They would certainly be early at the place, and confirm and hearten one another to stand it out, for the Doctor must come to their terms. . . . Then he would make his entry, as fine and as richly dressed as a lord of the bedchamber . . . [and] these hard-headed fellows that had prepared to give him all the affronts and opposition that their brutal way suggested, truly seeing such a brave man, pulled off their hats and knew not what to think of it. And the Doctor also being (forsooth) much of a gentleman then . . . proposed his terms, which . . . were ever plausible, and terminated in their interest. . . . It mattered not a litigious knave or two, if any such did stand out, for the first thing he did was to pull down their houses about their ears, and build upon their ground, and stand it out at law till their hearts ached, and at last they would truckle and take any terms for peace and a quiet life.

The houses which Barbon built were designed to ensnare the *nouveaux riches* with a slick smartness, and rarely gave lasting satisfaction. 'All the vaults fell in and the houses came down most scandalously', rose the plaintive cry from Mincing Lane. Nevertheless a few of his houses have endured, like those in Crane Court, numbers 36–43 Bedford Row, and 7–10 Denmark Street; and one could wish that all modern property sharks built so elegantly.

In fact the system of building leases enforced the basic design of the London terrace house. Inevitably the landlord marked off his ground in narrow plots in order to obtain as many rents as possible, so the only way to gain space in each house was to build upwards. Londoners have thus been condemned to running up and down stairs to the various parts of their houses instead of living 'horizontally' in flats like the inhabitants of most other capitals. With the plan of the London house largely predetermined there was little scope for architects: indeed before 1750 the breed hardly existed in the sense of a separate, defined profession. The greater part of the West End was designed by its builders and the only qualification required to make (say) a carpenter into an 'architect' was a flair for the job. The terrace houses which they produced were seemly, practical and eminently suited to the requirements of purchasers who did not generally set much store on outward displays of grandeur. As one writer has put it – 'The victorious English merchant had acquired such a feeling of superiority, that he might quite well live in a simple house.'

THE SMARTER LONDON HOUSES

Aristocrats who wanted magnificent town residences were generally obliged to build separate, detached mansions. Of these, Burlington House (1713–14) in Piccadilly, now the home of the Royal Academy, is a part survivor, although mauled by Victorian alterations. Better preserved is nearby Spencer House (1752–4) which looks over Green Park from St James's Place. Clubs have come to the rescue of one or two others: Derby House (1773) in Stratford Place off Oxford Street is now the Oriental Club, and Lansdowne House is fragmentarily preserved in the club of that name in Fitzmaurice Place off Berkeley Square. Most of the rest, like Chesterfield House, which once stood in South Audley Street, Devonshire House (Piccadilly) and Grosvenor, Dorchester and Londonderry houses (Park Lane) have fallen victims to the age of the common man.

No one ever cared less about the common man, or indeed about any other variety of the species, than the school of designers of which Lord Burlington was the doyen, and which was responsible for so many of these great mansions. They acknowledged only the rules of classical proportion and expected their patrons to order their lives accordingly. Even parties could arouse their wrath. 'Our forefathers were pleased with seeing their friends as they chanced to come and with entertaining them when they were there. The present custom is to see them all at once, and to entertain troups of them; this brings in the necessity of a great room which is opened only on occasions, and which loads and discredits the rest of the edifice.' It was tiresome for men of such rigorous views not to be able to design the people to live in their houses, but at least, by working for aristocrats, classical architects were generally able to liberate themselves from the tyranny of practical considerations. The state also proved an amenable employer, as Somerset House (1776 by William Chambers) and the Horse Guards (designed by William Kent in the 1740s) bear witness.

Apart from experiments on the Burlington Estate in Piccadilly, which became a trial ground for his lordship's stable of designers, it was unusual for the great architects to be concerned with terrace houses. Of course, there were exceptions. William Kent contrived to create a rich interior behind an unostentatious façade at 44 Berkeley Square; later in the century Robert Adam designed 20 Portman Square (now the Courtauld Institute) and 20 St James's Square, as well as the east side of Fitzroy Square, while his brother John built the original houses in Portland Place. Robert Adam was also responsible for the now sadly lost Adelphi development, off the Strand (see p. 221). Generally, however, the influence of famous architects was transmitted indirectly to building craftsmen through books of drawings which tended to standardize designs.

GEORGIAN BUILDING REGULATIONS

A series of Building Acts, reflecting a continuing fear of fire, also had a stereotyping effect on West End housing. The Act of 1709 ordered that window frames should be set back four inches from the front of the house, a measure that destroyed the Queen Anne (actually Dutch) style, in which the window surrounds were flush to the outside walls. The 1774 Building Act went further and banished window joinery into recesses, as well as introducing a series of restrictions which left the door-case as the only external wooden embellishment permissible.

Well before this last Act was passed some judges were finding the uniform rows of terrace houses both monotonous and dull. The new buildings at Marylebone, one writer declared in 1766, 'give no better idea to the spectator than of a plain brick wall of prodigious length'. With such strictures the Victorians entirely agreed and repeatedly set themselves to concealing both the plainness and the brick. For example, the houses in Great Russell Street, by the

British Museum, were stuccoed in the 1860s and those in nearby Gower Street ('the *nec plus ultra* of ugliness in street architecture', thought Ruskin) given heavy cement doorcases.

The twentieth century has been more appreciative but no less destructive of Georgian architecture. There are fewer complaints of its dullness now that the University of London has destroyed acres of Bloomsbury terraces in the cause of higher education, and a huge eighteenth-century development like Grosvenor Square contains not a single original house. Often, too, surviving terraces have been interrupted by later buildings which have marvellously enhanced appreciation of Georgian elegance and simplicity. Today, therefore, places like Lord North Street (*c.* 1720) and Bedford Square (*c.* 1770), which are both original and complete, are prized as rarities, not condemned for uniformity. It is not usually possible to point a visitor towards a particular place in London with the assurance that every building there is of one date. On the other hand, eighteenth-century building is not hard to recognize, and there are sufficient stylistic variations even in terrace houses (some of which are shown on pp. 218-19) to make dating a fascinating exercise.

EIGHTEENTH-CENTURY BUILDING PHASES

The fact that London's development was privately financed meant that the growth of the West End was not a continuous process but concentrated into bursts which coincided with times of prosperity. The great boom periods of the eighteenth century followed the successful conclusion of two wars, by the Treaty of Utrecht in 1713 and by the Peace of Paris in 1763.

The phase after Utrecht saw the development of Mayfair,

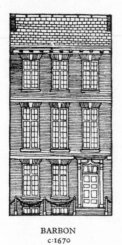

BARBON
c:1670

1715-30

1750-65

Some styles of terrace housing, 1670–1825.

1825

1789

as the quadrilateral bounded by Regent Street, Piccadilly, Park Lane and Oxford Street is known. Into this area has been crammed, or so a nineteenth-century diner-out satisfied himself, 'more intelligence, human ability, to say nothing of wealth and beauty, than the world ever collected in so small a space before'. Yet the event from which the district took its name was far from distinguished. Indeed the May Fair, which took place in Brook Field (where Curzon Street now runs by Shepherd Market) at the end of the seventeenth century, was an annual excuse for the bawdiest merrymaking. 'Can any rational man imagine', the voice of righteousness inquired, 'that her Majesty would permit so much lewdness as is committed at May Fair, for so many days together, so near to her royal palace, if she knew anything of the matter?' And indeed Queen Anne seemed disposed to permit no lewdness whatsoever, for the May Fair was banned in 1708, although it persisted furtively until Brook Field was built over in the 1750s. By that time respectability was no longer a stranger in the area.

Between 1717 and 1719 the Earl of Scarborough had built Hanover Square, the name expressing his delight at the accession of a German princeling to the throne of England. Indeed he did not thereby exhaust his enthusiasm, for the houses were built in a German style, still visible at Number 30 St George's Street. At much the same time Lord Burlington and Sir Richard Grosvenor, now uncontested heir to Ebury Manor, began building on their lands, while the Cavendish/Harley axis spread the names of their families and country estates (Welbeck, Wimpole, Wigmore, Mortimer, Weymouth, Clipstone, Carburton and others) about their territory to the north of Oxford Street. In Holborn, Bedford Row (with the exception of numbers 36–43, by Barbon) remains as an almost complete street from this period, while in Kensington numbers 18–26

Holland Street stand as a reminder that the building ripples spread out into the suburbs. But by 1738, when the east side of Berkeley Square was begun, the building impetus had slackened and the square stood half-finished for another decade.

Before the next boom got under way in the 1760s two new works had appeared to direct its course. First, the presence of Westminster Bridge, at last opened in 1750 and soon to be followed by another at Blackfriars, encouraged the development of Lambeth, Kennington and Vauxhall. Second, the construction in 1756–7 of a new road from Paddington to Islington (now the Marylebone, Euston and Pentonville roads) set a northern limit to the town's expansion for the rest of the century. Between Oxford Street and this New Road, and to the west of the Cavendish-Harley estate, were lands belonging to the Portman family, who in 1761 laid out the square bearing their name and over the next sixty years gradually pressed their building, much of which still exists, towards the Edgware Road.

Meanwhile in 1768 the Adam brothers had taken a lease of the site of Durham House on the Strand to the east of Charing Cross and hazarded their fortunes in creating a magnificent terrace, flanked by two further terraces running back at right angles to the main façade, on a vaulted embankment overlooking the river. They called the scheme Adelphi, which is Greek for 'brothers'. It was the finest riverside building which London has ever seen, but once again Londoners showed themselves wary of grandeur, so that the Adams had to resort to a public lottery for the houses in order to save their skins. The airy elegance of the Adelphi's decoration, still visible at Number 7 Adam Street, proved too much for the Victorians who encased the riverfront terrace in stucco and added a pediment and stone balconies. This block was demolished in 1936 and although a tiny piece of the vaulting can be seen in Lower Robert Street, and some original houses in Adam, John Adam, and Robert streets, nothing remains worthy of the name Adelphi.

The Adams' influence was partly responsible for a less austere attitude towards ornamentation, and in the late eighteenth century a firm called E. and W. Coade, based on the south side of Westminster Bridge, where County Hall now stands, flourished by virtue of their secret (and lost) formula for making a weather-proof artificial stone, ideal for decorative purposes. By 1776 Coade stone was a natural choice for the door surrounds of Bedford Square, the first and grandest development on the Duke of Bedford's estate. The family had acquired this vast tract, stretching north to the Euston Road between Tottenham Court Road and Southampton Row, in the seventeenth century through a judicious marriage (the couple even loved each other) to the Earl of Southampton's heiress, although all would have been lost if the spendthrift third duke had not had the grace to die before his order to sell could be executed. His successors made the most of this reprieve, and the estate, on which building slowly crept northwards, reaching the Euston Road early in the nineteenth century, became a model of good, if conservative, administration. Indeed, the Bedfords were so concerned to preserve the high tone of their squares that they put gates across the entrances, through which none but the most superior tradesmen were allowed to pass. Some of these gates were only removed in this century.

It would be wrong, however, to think of eighteenth-century London entirely in terms of smart West End development. Even the estates built less exclusive streets designed to complement the grandeur of the squares; and only just beyond the aristocratic borders there were appalling slums. St Giles Holborn, for instance, was on the southern fringe of the Bedford's Bloomsbury estate, where New Oxford Street now runs. Moreover in the heart of London, which was still nearer the City – 'the full tide of human existence', proclaimed Dr Johnson, 'is at Charing Cross' – smart and squalid areas were scarcely to be distinguished. 'If we look into the streets', wrote a journalist in 1748, 'what a medley do we see. Here lives a personage of high distinction; next door a butcher with his stinking shambles. A tallow chandler shall front my Lady's nice Venetian window; and two or three brawny naked Curriers [leather dressers] in their pits shall face a fine Lady in her back closet, and disturb her spiritual thoughts. . . .' Dr Johnson himself lived in Gough Square, off Fleet Street, which was hardly more than a stone's throw away from slum alleys of the kind that claimed twenty deaths from starvation in every week.

RICH AND POOR

What price existence? Opinions seemed to vary. The Duke of Kingston contrived to spend £2000 during a fortnight's stay in town; Dr Johnson considered that £30 a year was enough to make a man live without being contemptible; and in depressed times a silk-winder in Spitalfields might earn as little as three shillings a week. With tens of thousands of homeless in search of twopence with which to secure a night's lodging it did not do to haggle about wages. Not only were the poor obliged to be grateful for the privilege of staying alive by slaving from dawn to dusk; they were even required by some to refrain from enjoying their Sundays. 'Our common people', one journal complained, 'are very observant of that part of the commandment which enjoins them to do no work on that day; and which they also seem to understand as licence to devote it to pleasure.'

Doubtless such articles went down well in coffee houses where business men read newspapers, gossiped (the Stock Exchange originated in such a place) and otherwise passed the time of day. There was less reading, however, in the coffee houses of Covent Garden, where assembled devotees of a more ancient commerce, with ladies who did not care a fig about the disturbance of their spiritual thoughts.

For all the disapproval of popular pastimes, it cannot be said that the privileged set an inspiring example in the enriching use of leisure. Indeed sometimes they only seemed concerned to use their resources to ape and extend the amusements of their despised inferiors. If the masses ventured their pennies on the result of a cockfight, the smart gaming clubs like White's or Boodle's in St James's Street saw men lose £30000 in a single night on the turn of the cards; if the barbarous flocked to bull- and bear-baiting, the fashionable enjoyed an afternoon taunting the lunatics in Bedlam; if the mob was dangerous, a pack of rich thugs called the Mohocks, who flourished early in the century and amused themselves torturing old watchmen and prostitutes and otherwise 'doing all possible harm to their fellow creatures', were still more terrifying; if the vulgar settled scores with a quick thrust of the knive in dark alleys, the well-bred massacred one another in duels conducted according to the best possible taste. Brutality and prostitution, in fact, were the most effective dissolvents of class barriers. Where else could the high and lowly encounter each other on equal terms but in brothels, at public executions, or watching prize fighters·smash each other into pulp? There was not even any sex discrimination in the boxing ring: ladies' singles were a star turn, and woe betide any challenger of the famous Bruising Peg, who, it is reported, 'beat her antagonist in a terrible manner' when a new dress was at stake.

Of course the values of civilization were not altogether extinct. There were many who would not have been seen dead at such exhibitions. The fastidious Horace Walpole, for example, considered he was mingling with the masses if he visited the pleasure gardens at Vauxhall and Ranelagh, which attracted vast crowds with their music, balls, masquerades and fireworks. Vauxhall, on the south of the river, was so popular that on special nights there would be three-hour traffic jams on London Bridge. Ranelagh, with its great wooden rotunda near the Royal Hospital in Chelsea, opened later, in 1742. Although the lack of 'dark walks' disappointed the amorous, Edward Gibbon judged it 'the most convenient place for courtships of every kind. It is certainly the best market we have in England.' The entrance fee was half a crown, higher than Vauxhall, but if Ranelagh was more exclusive, Horace Walpole failed to register the fact. 'Much nobility, much mob', he wrote of the opening night; and, later, 'Every night I constantly go to Ranelagh, which has totally beat Vauxhall. Nobody goes anywhere else – everybody goes there. . . . You can't set your foot without treading on a Prince of Wales, or Duke of Cumberland. The company is universal; there is from his Grace of Grafton down to the children out of the Foundling Hospital. . . .'

This last reference was presumably a piece of upper-class whimsy. The Foundling Hospital was the fruit of Captain Coram's lifelong work on behalf of the hundreds of children abandoned in the streets each year (the building, now demolished, stood in Coram's Fields, Bloomsbury), and was accounted a success because only just over half the children admitted died in the first fifteen years of its existence. And success it was, for only one in 100 foundlings survived the alternative charity of being sent out to nurse in the parish or committed to the workhouse. The Industrial

Revolution was to provide another solution, the surviving foundlings being packed off in cartloads to the factories of the north.

Not that prospects were bright for any child in Georgian London. Rich and poor alike fell victim to the infections bred amongst the squalid slums, and in the second quarter of the eighteenth century three in four of all children born in London were dead before their fifth birthday. But there was one hazard – gin – to which the poor were especially prone. A populace condemned to lives of hopeless despair seized on a solace which sunk them even further into misery. Gin was cheap ('drunk for a penny, dead drunk for two-pence, straw for nothing', advertised one tavern); gin was readily available in over 8000 dram shops; and gin was drunk in staggering quantities. By the 1740s consumption was averaging two pints a week for every man, woman and child in London – and children were certainly making a sub-stantial contribution to that figure. Gin that was administered to quieten babies for the short term effectively did so for ever: in 1751 a deputation to the House of Commons reckoned that over 9000 children a year were being killed by spirits. Hogarth's *Gin Lane* portrayed no horrors that were not exceeded in reality. One mother confessed to having strangled her child and sold its clothes for one and fourpence to spend on gin.

No wonder the novelist Henry Fielding warned that 'a new kind of drunkenness . . . if not put a stop to, will infallibly destroy a great part of the inferior people'. Yet for a long time the government did not act for fear of the distilling interest which was powerful in the House of Commons. When at last a law of 1736 provided that those setting up to sell gin should take out a £50 licence, the measure proved wholly unenforceable: indeed several informers were actually stoned to death by angry mobs.

Not until 1751 were effective limits placed on retailers, and even after that Mother Geneva, as the drink was known, was a long time relinquishing her hold on her children.

THE AGE OF BRUTALITY

Drink exacerbated the problem of crime. No one was safe in the streets of Georgian London. Within the space of a few years in the 1770s and 1780s the Prince of Wales, the Prime Minister and the Lord Chancellor had all been robbed in broad daylight in the West End, while the Lord Mayor was held up at pistol point on Turnham Green. Highwaymen frequently attacked stage coaches in the middle of town, and even fixed notices to the doors of the rich threatening death to any who ventured forth without money. Since there was no police force capable of dealing with the situation Londoners were obliged to defend themselves. Pity the unfortunate thief who tried to take Dr Johnson's handkerchief in Grosvenor Square: the Doctor 'seized him by the collar, shook him violently and smacked him so hard in the face that the thief staggered off the pavement'.

Actually this was the most humane as well as the most effective treatment of crime, because the government had no counter beyond extending the death penalty to cover the most trivial offences. Even impersonating a Chelsea Hospital pensioner was a capital crime. Youths were hung for stealing sixpence, to the accompaniment of jeers from the crowds who regarded the eight hanging days a year at Tyburn (where Marble Arch now stands) as the ultimate in entertainment. Yet even these spectacles were not enough for some. A pamphlet entitled *Hanging Not Punishment Enough* (1701) advocated torture, followed by life servitude on Negro plantations, 'first marking them in the face to distinguish them from honest men'.

Notwithstanding such savageries, the conventional, Hollywood image of the eighteenth century so often consists of bluff country squires, devil-may-care rakes and roguishly amusing whores, all somehow associated with fine English concepts like roast beef, liberty and no-popery, and presented with the same untroubled conscience as a Gainsborough portrait. Another cliché represents the Victorians as smug hypocrites, totally blind or indifferent to the sufferings of the oppressed if golden-hearted masses. Ironically these distortions have arisen partly because there were more Victorians concerned to chronicle and rectify the degradations of London life, thus giving posterity ammunition to use against them.

Somehow information reaching us from the eighteenth century tends to be of another kind. Do you know, Charles James Fox actually spent thirty-six hours at the gambling tables, interrupted only by a trip to the House of Commons to deliver a brilliant oration on the thirty-nine articles of religion; heavens, you should have heard Johnson put down Goldsmith in the Turk's Head the other day; Sheridan's conversation is even funnier than his plays but the dear fellow always gets so fearfully tight. . . . The continuous flow of gossip is much more entertaining than a catalogue of human misery but it should not obscure the disagreeable fact that the life of the poor in eighteenth-century London transcended in sheer awfulness even the better-known horrors of the Victorian era. That people kept flocking into such a hell is the most telling possible comment on the myth of the pastoral idyll. It was the age of reason that was the real age of callousness.

Certainly there was precious little hope of comfort from the Church of England which, in the first half of the eighteenth century, before the challenge of Methodism restored to it a degree of moral earnestness, was sunk in a state of torpor unique even in its own history. One clergyman actually delivered a series of four sermons 'on the nature, folly, sin and anger of being righteous overmuch'; he must have been gratified by the eager response to his message. The only ecclesiastical achievement of this period was owed to Parliament. The Church Building Act of 1711 was responsible for six marvellous churches by Hawksmoor – St Alfege in Greenwich, St Anne's Limehouse, Christ Church Spitalfields, St George-in-the-East (Stepney), St George's Bloomsbury and the City church of St Mary Woolnoth. Among the other churches built under the Act were St Mary-le-Strand by James Gibbs (who also designed St Martin-in-the-Fields); St John's Smith Square by Thomas Archer who typified the gentleman-architect; and St Giles-in-the-Fields by Henry Flitcroft, who belonged to the craftsman category, having begun life as a joiner. Even after these churches had been built there was hardly space in London's pews for more than a quarter of the population. But although the fashionable churches were crammed, Hawksmoor's vast edifices in the slums, outposts of the establishment set in the midst of extreme distress, were rarely filled. The masses were not readily identifiable as Christians.

IMPROVEMENTS: LAW AND ORDER

For all their spiritual deprivation the condition of the poor had undoubtedly improved by the end of the century, when births in the capital actually began to exceed deaths. A certain Dr Price displayed classic middle-class ambivalence about the betterment of the lower orders when he wrote in 1773: 'The circumstances of the lower ranks of the people are altered in every respect for the worse, while tea, wheaten bread and other delicacies are necessaries which were formerly unknown to them.'

The improvement went beyond matters of diet: even the eighteenth century had its reformers. Several famous hospitals were founded at this time, including the Westminster (1720), Guy's (1725), St George's (1734), the London (1740) and the Middlesex (1745); and though inmates might have found the high tone a trifle oppressive (at St Thomas's patients could be expelled for swearing or abusing their neighbours, let alone taking God's name in vain), the proportion of cures was impressive. Further, the streets became less squalid, especially after the Westminster Paving Act of 1762, and visitors at the end of the century were greatly impressed by the oil lamps therein, feeble though their glow must have been. Whereas visitors to Paris had once been struck by its superior cleanliness, the boot was on the other foot after 1750. 'Mrs Gregory and I', reported a Londoner from Paris in 1776, 'are not yet cured of our astonishment at the dirtiness, the stinks and the narrowness of the streets.'

There were even signs of a more constructive approach to the problem of keeping order, thanks principally to Henry Fielding and his brother John, who succeeded one another as magistrates at the Bow Street Court from 1749. Both took their duties a lot more seriously than the common run of magistrate, whose main concern was to pocket the profits of justice. On the one hand they recognized that many of those who appeared before them were 'guilty of no crime but poverty'; indeed they were capable of giving the accused money to set up in a trade. On the other hand they were determined to bring hardened criminals to justice and therefore created a team of constables, known as the Bow Street Runners, to catch suspects. But the Runners never amounted to a police force, and the town's security continued to depend on watchmen appointed by the parishes. A French observer in 1765 recorded that 'London is guarded at night by old men chosen from the dregs of the people who have no other arms but a lantern and a pole, crying the hour every time the clock strikes ... and whom it is the custom of young rakes to beat and use ill when they come reeling out of the taverns where they have passed the night.'

Of course the watchmen were totally unable to cope when, as frequently occurred, the festering misery burst into angry riots. In fact during the 1780 Gordon Riots, the worst in London's history, when a distillery was sacked and drunken mobs ran amok for a week, firing the houses of the great, setting prisoners free, and smashing whatsoever they could lay hands on, a watchman was observed passing by 'with his lantern in his hand, calling the hours as if in time of profound tranquillity'. In the circumstances there was no alternative to calling in the army, and more than 200 people had been shot dead before order was restored.

Even a disaster on the scale of the Gordon Riots, however, was not enough to persuade the government that a regular police force was necessary. Ministers explained their reluctance to create one by reference to their devotion to liberty. But the real cause of inaction was the old problem, the root of so many of London's ills, that no single authority existed within the capital to which control of police, or health, or drainage, or roads, or anything, could be entrusted. Outside the City, London's administration was in the hands of a host of separate parish committees called vestries, whose activities were supervised to a greater or lesser extent by Justices of the Peace for the county of Middlesex. As has been observed, men of the Fieldings' quality were very

much the exception: Edmund Burke, admittedly a somewhat jaundiced authority, considered that the Middlesex
justices were 'the scum of the earth – carpenters, brick-
makers and shoemakers; some of them were notoriously
men of such infamous characters that they were unworthy of
any employ whatever and others so ignorant that they could
scarcely write their own names'.

Perhaps it was as well, then, that the powers of the justices
and vestries were in fact so limited. Almost any improvement involving the raising of local taxes required the sanction of an Act of Parliament which established the necessary
authority (e.g. the Westminster Paving Commissioners)
within a particular area. The result was that by 1800 London
was being administered by over 300 different bodies. At the
heart of this chaos was the City, the only authority with
comprehensive and effective control of its area, but far too
jealous of these rights to countenance the idea of a rival
institution with powers over the whole of London.

THE CITY IN OPPOSITION

The City also continued to regard the national government
with intense hostility, treating Parliament with the same
wariness that it had once shown to medieval kings. The
great financiers and aldermen were now too closely involved
with matters of state to lead this opposition, but they were
losing power within the City to the larger and more
democratic Common Council, a body descended from the
assembly of advisers which John of Northampton had
consulted in the fourteenth century (see pp. 117–18) and now
elected by all rate-paying citizens. The Common Council
was at odds with nearly all eighteenth-century governments.
Even the City's loyalty to the Crown seemed to some contemporaries to be suspect: When the Young Pretender

tried to win back the throne for the House of Stuart in 1745, and flung London into a panic with his march south from Scotland, there were rumours that he did not lack support within the City.

Since a greater proportion of the inhabitants of the City and Westminster than in most other towns was qualified to vote, these constituencies often returned radical members of Parliament. Only from 1757 to 1763 and from 1783 to 1801, when Pitt the Elder and Pitt the Younger were in power and the country's commercial future was at stake in wars with France, did the City wholeheartedly support the government. Its opposition reached a peak during the years after Pitt's resignation in 1763, when the merchants shared his desire for a more lenient policy towards the American colonies. In 1770 Pitt's henchman, Mayor Beckford, flaunted convention by using a formal interview as an occasion to lecture the king to the effect that those who had poisoned his mind against the City were enemies of the people. This performance won Beckford the statue in the Guildhall on which his speech is imprinted, but his predecessor, Mayor Crosby, had behaved with even greater daring when he seized a House of Commons messenger who had been sent to the City to arrest some printers accused of publishing Commons debates. For this impertinence the Lord Mayor was cast into the Tower – and accorded a triumphal procession through the streets on his release. The mayor was now chosen by the freemen of all the Livery Companies, and in 1774 the City set the seal on this period of opposition by electing the notorious John Wilkes, who had plagued the king and governments alike during the previous decade.

But a glimpse of the City in the role of gallant underdog should not obscure the fact that the petty manner in which it asserted its independence and privilege, combined with its continued uncompromising refusal to take responsibility for the rest of the town, constituted a serious obstacle to progress. By 1800 nine-tenths of Londoners were living outside the City, the government of which still persisted in regarding itself as London's sole authority, offering pig-headed resistance to reforms which appeared to infringe this claim. It was as though the vast metropolis that now stretched two miles and more from the bars on either side of the City, east as far as Limehouse and west to the Portman estate on the north side of Oxford Street, had entirely escaped the notice of the Common Councilmen.

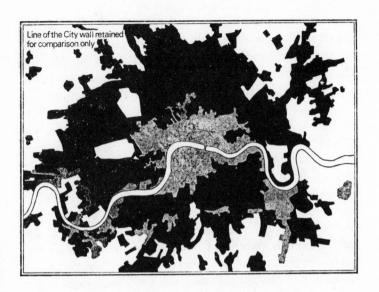

Line of the City wall retained for comparison only

7. 'This monster London is really a new city'
[1800–89]

BUILDING THE DOCKS

There was no right, privilege or possession which the City treasured more dearly or guarded more jealously than the crush of shipping in its midst. Although after 1663 various concessions had allowed imports, restricted to the 'legal quays' in 1558, to be landed at a further 3700 feet of wharves to the east of the Tower and on the south bank of the Thames, the main part of the port's activity had remained still very much within the City's sphere. Inevitably this concentration meant chaos. The Pool of London had always been crowded, yet in the eighteenth century both the average size of the ships and the number handled there had doubled. The problem of congestion was worse because the vessels were all subject to the same wind and weather, and therefore tended to arrive in seasonal batches. Sometimes they had to wait for as long as three months for quay space at which to unload.

The attainment of a berth could be the beginning of a new series of troubles. As there was pitifully little warehousing available, perishable items like sugar often had to be left on the quayside to the mercy of the elements. And nowhere was cargo safe from the thieves who made off with half-a-million-pounds' worth of goods every year. As if these hazards were not enough, the whole port was constantly enveloped in coal dust. During the Civil War John Evelyn had noticed that City gardens did better when the 'hellish and dismal cloud of sea-coal' disappeared as a result of the siege of Newcastle; he would not have appreciated conditions 150 years later when there were often as many as ninety colliers unloading at one time. Altogether, it is a measure of London's commercial stranglehold that the port retained its supremacy in such circumstances.

The need to build docks could scarcely have been more glaringly obvious, especially as the possibilities of man-made basins – albeit only used for fitting-out ships – had already been demonstrated in the seventeenth century. But nothing further had been done. Understandably enough the City would not countenance the destruction that would be involved in making proper docks between London Bridge and the Tower; but nor would it accept that docks must therefore be built elsewhere, outside its ambit. A critic once superciliously remarked of the Common Councilmen that 'counter transactions in small coins have no tendency to give a man an enlarged view'; and certainly the manner in which, throughout the eighteenth century, they bristled at any mention of improvements in the port, justifies this judgement. Even the outbreak of war with France in 1793, imparting all the urgency of national crisis, did not prevent the City from objecting strenuously to a plan put forward in the Parliament of 1796 for the building of docks at Wapping. But the climate of opinion was now such that the City felt obliged to produce an alternative scheme of its own, which won general acceptance.

The result was the opening in August 1802 of the West India dock, which was built across the north side of the Isle of Dogs. It provided berths for 600 ships with warehousing to match, the whole complex being surrounded by a twenty-foot-high brick wall as a protection against theft. Further docks soon followed – the London dock at Wapping, which opened in 1805; the East India at Blackwall (1806); and others on the south bank. By 1811 more than £5 million had been spent in the port and not a penny had come from the government. The money had all been privately invested in the separate companies formed to build each dock, just as the railways were later financed.

To convert so many areas of pastureland into shipping channels at a time when picks and shovels were still the main excavating tools was a tremendous feat of muscle-power. In their early days the docks and their contents were one of the sights of London for tourists. 'Nothing', considered the nineteenth-century Baedeker guide, 'will convey to the stranger a better idea of the vast activity and stupendous wealth of London than a visit to the ware-houses, filled to overflowing with interminable stores of every kind of foreign and commercial products.'

There was certainly no doubt of the docks' success from the point of view of shipping: the costs of loading and unloading were reduced by a fifth. Nevertheless, investors were compelled to watch their dividends dwindle. The dock companies prospered for a while because, in order to attract capital, those on the north bank had each been granted a twenty-one-year monopoly over specified trades. On the expiry of these exclusive rights, however, they were plunged into a chronic financial crisis from which they never really managed to extricate themselves.

Part of the trouble was that Parliament, in order to satisfy owners of river craft, had stipulated that their barges should be allowed into the docks free of charge: there was thus nothing to prevent ships avoiding docking fees by unloading into lighters in midstream. This 'free water clause' was an uncharacteristic and illogical exemption in an age which generally showed as much faith in unlimited private competition as the twentieth century does in un-limited public expenditure. Both dogmas have produced their share of the ridiculous. In the case of private enterprise

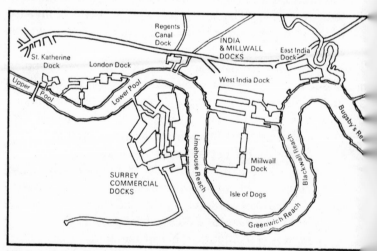

The London dock systems.

and the port, it was not merely that price-cutting between the different companies diminished the profits of all. The docks also suffered because they originated and were run as isolated ventures instead of being co-ordinated to complement each other in layout and purpose. Before 1811, for instance, four separate concerns were running docks in Rotherhithe on the south bank.

Absurdity assumed a more destructive guise after 1824 when, with the expiry of the West India monopoly in mind, proposals were made to build a small dock by the Tower. For a while the 600-year-old St Katherine's Hospital presented a tiresome obstruction to the disciples of progress, but the hospital governor's objections began to waver when he discovered that the projected new site in Regent's Park included a villa with stables for his own use. The greatest care was taken with the coffins found during the demolition of the old church, but the living fared less well. 'In clearing the ground for this magnificent speculation', *The Times*

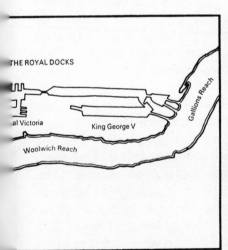

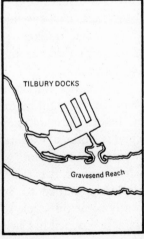

proudly declared, '1250 houses and tenements were purchased and pulled down – no less than 11,300 inhabitants
having to seek accommodation elsewhere.'

Alas, the 'magnificent speculation' produced precious few
returns, and St Katherine's was eventually compelled to
amalgamate with the London dock (1864), just as the East
and West India Companies had united in 1838. In the later
nineteenth century these two combines extended their
futile rivalry to docks built further downstream to accommodate the larger steamships: not until 1909 were the
various parts of the port united under a single authority.
The migration of the port's traffic downstream has continued, and although London still handles more goods than
any other British port (with the exception of the oil terminal at Milford Haven) the centre of the port's activity is
now twenty-five miles from the City, at Tilbury. Of the
original group of docks only the first, the West India,
remains in use. St Katherine's, the London, and the Surrey
docks were closed in the late 1960s and early 1970s; and
now lie derelict and forlorn behind their walls while
developers, councils, local organizations and government
all press their different plans with a blind disregard of each
other which recalls the old rivalries between the dock
companies.

Only at St Katherine's has anything been achieved, since
its prime site, right by the Tower, attracted private developers before the paralysing hands of the planners were laid
upon it. Some of Telford's handsome warehouses have been
retained in a scheme which comprehends an hotel, conference centre, flats and marina. (Incidentally St Katherine's
Hospital returned to Stepney in 1948, so the wheel has
nearly come full circle.) At the neighbouring London dock
the local council has at last begun to work with a property
company and the Port of London Authority on a project
which envisages houses, factories, offices and parks, a whole

new Wapping village in fact. A present there are no takers for the Surrey docks, which have proved too far away from the City to tempt developers. It remains to be seen whether the trend of centuries, whereby the wealth which has poured into the port has been spirited away to the West End, can be reversed. At present a visitor's impression must be far removed from that of the German who looked at the 'immeasurable work' of the West India dock in 1826 and reflected that 'the spectator must feel astonishment, and a sort of awe at the greatness and might of England'.

REGENT'S PARK AND REGENT STREET: JOHN NASH

Such grandeur as London now possesses derives in great measure from a happy coincidence of events roughly contemporary with the building of the docks. In 1811 the Prince of Wales, later George IV (1820–30), became Regent for his mad father, at the same time as the leases of the Crown land of Marylebone Park expired. The Prince, who never shared his subjects' scepticism about his glory, determined to render the capital worthy of his illustrious personage. But although he was more aesthetically conscious than any monarch since Charles I the form of the Marylebone Park development possibly owed something to his other tastes.

In 1798 a girl associated with the Prince called Mary Ann Bradley, the ravishing daughter of an impecunious coal merchant, married John Nash (1752–1835). Miss Bradley was pregnant; Nash was an exceedingly ambitious architect who suddenly found himself able to afford an estate in the Isle of Wight and a huge town house of his own design (now demolished) in Dover Street. Thus far fact: *honi soit qui mal y pense*. Nash never acknowledged any of his wife's five children as his own, but he did secure a working relationship with the Prince that was responsible for the greatest scheme of town planning in London's history. The results, as a contemporary predicted, have been 'more felt by posterity than the victories of Trafalgar or Waterloo', praise which would have delighted a monarch who keenly resented being robbed of military glory merely because he happened to be a coward.

Some plans had been drawn up for developing Marylebone Park in much the same way as Bloomsbury, with well-ordered streets and squares covering the whole territory. Nash swept such pedestrian ideas from the Regent's mind. The Park, which was then bare heathland, should be retained, landscaped to provide vistas for twenty-six aristocratic villas, and encircled with great terraces. To attract residents to the area a magnificent new thoroughfare should be constructed, which would link the new scheme to the Prince's residence at Carlton House at the north-east corner of St James's Park. This new street, Nash argued, would also have the advantage of running between Mayfair and Soho (from the latter of which access would be strictly limited), thus providing 'a boundary and complete separation between the streets and squares occupied by the Nobility and Gentry, and the narrow streets and meaner houses occupied by mechanics and the trading part of the community'.

Such was the first outline of Regent Street and Regent's Park. Of course it did not all become reality. In the park only eight of the twenty-six villas proposed were built and projects for a royal pleasure garden, a central circus, and crescents on the west side were all abandoned. The story of Regent Street's construction, moreover, was a prolonged struggle between the ideal and the possible. On the whole, however, it is remarkable to what extent Nash was able to achieve his original scheme. Much was owed to the Regent, who signalled his delight with the plan by exclaiming, 'It

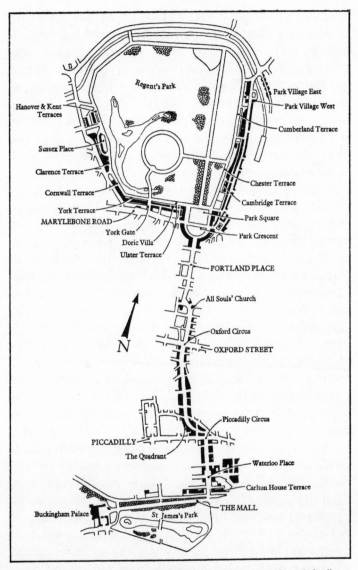

Nash's Regent Street, with his buildings (many are now demolished) shown in black.

will quite eclipse Napoleon', and whose enthusiasm for that worthy aim caused him to support his architect with a constancy that entirely belied his normal reputation for treachery. (Not that London returned any gratitude. While the Bill to rid the king of his unseemly queen was before the House of Lords, popular feeling against him ran so high that, a biographer records, 'He was as effectually barred from entering his capital as ever Charles I was in the Civil War.' Radical sentiment was always more widespread than architectural appreciation in the capital.)

In England no amount of royal patronage could convey a right to override the laws of property. The creation of Regent Street caused chaos, and it was Nash who had to handle the endless wearisome negotiations with builders, to deal with owners of adjoining land, and to endure the carpings of other architects, beside which the task of actually designing the buildings must have been light and welcome relief. Work began on Park Crescent, just west of Great Portland Street tube station, in 1813, and for the next fifteen years all Nash's boundless optimism, energy and determination, together with his remarkable improvisatory skills, were needed to keep the project alive. A straight Regent Street proved impossible: Nash was obliged to adjust its line to whatsoever property was either owned by the Crown or easily acquired. Yet he generally contrived to make a virtue out of necessity. Thus the circular portico of All Souls' Langham Place lent naturalness to a sudden and enforced change of axis at the bottom of Portland Place. Similarly, Piccadilly Circus and the quarter circle (or Quadrant) described by the street to reach it were created as a means of taking the line through Crown land. When no builder could be found to take the risk of financing the Quadrant Nash sank his own fortune into its building, achieving a fine effect with his sweep of colonnades which were not, however, appreciated by the endarkened shopkeepers, nor indeed by Victorian moralists who objected to the characters that loitered thereunder. The colonnades were demolished in 1848, though without (as the *Builder* tartly commented) 'the beneficial effect on public morals which was supposed to justify its destruction'. It was left to the twentieth century to tear down Nash's great street for unvarnished motives of commercial greed. All that now remains of the original Regent Street, which consisted not of uniform and unbroken terraces but of a great variety of building in all manner of styles, is its line. Only in Suffolk Place, off the east of the Haymarket, does anything survive of Nash's street architecture, though on a less grand scale than his conception of Regent Street.

But the Park is still ringed with Nash terraces, and very splendid they look. Their survival is fortunate because they incurred the deepest disapproval of the Victorians. What business had narrow town houses to masquerade as gorgeous country palaces? And what was the stucco covering but another gross deception? Magnificent façades like Hanover Terrace on the west and Cumberland Terrace on the east side of the park struck those earnest spirits as a meretricious and tawdry imposture: the present age is delighted with the illusion, especially as in some places it now conceals government offices.

Certainly Nash's genius was essentially theatrical: behind the glittering frontage the construction was sometimes as flimsy as stage scenery. In fact Nash often contented himself with a rough sketch and left his assistants to work out the details. But he was not simply concerned with producing those grand effects which made the terraces a natural lure for 'the happy freeborn sons of commerce', as the *Builder* described them. To the east of the park he created a working-class 'service' area, although that is now destroyed. And at the very end of his career, in 1830, Nash designed two 'villages' at the north end of Albany Street. These, Park East and Park West, are still partly preserved and, with their detached and individually styled villas, have been described by Sir John Summerson as 'the ancestors of all picturesque suburbia'.

BUCKINGHAM PALACE

Regent's Park and Regent Street were handsome financial, as well as architectural, successes, but unfortunately neither Nash's temperament nor George IV's caprice allowed them to rest on their laurels. No sooner was Regent Street complete than the king tired of its starting point. 'I do not like Carlton House standing in a street', he complained, although Nash had designed Waterloo Place as a splendid frontispiece. The real reason for George IV's dissatisfaction was that the Hanoverian whim had lighted on Buckingham House, then a building of moderate size which his father had purchased when it was conveniently discovered that, due to a faulty seventeenth-century lease, the house stood partly on Crown land. George IV insisted that he intended only a *pied-à-terre*, but the plans for 'improving' the house, which Nash concocted on his instructions, were on the grandest scale. As work proceeded it became evident that Nash's original estimate of £252690 had only been a blind to dupe the Treasury. The old operator had got away with so much in his life through sheer nerve that he must have believed himself beyond retribution. In what was conceived as an economy measure, Carlton House, on which the king had lavished thousands, was pulled down so that its fittings could be re-used at Buckingham House and the site redeveloped. To this end Nash designed Carlton House Terrace, his last great essay in this genre, but the income therefrom could never match the soaring costs at the new palace. Worse still, as the building rose, Nash's plan – a great open court facing down the Mall and flanked with colonnaded

wings – attracted universal derision, which scarcely seems
justified by the illustrations which survive. The critical
venom may have been in large part due to the king's un-
popularity and to the jealousy aroused by Nash's prolonged
run of success. But there was a deeper cause at work. Nash
had conceived the palace as a glorified terrace composition,
light and gay in spirit, and even under George IV the English
took their monarchy more solemnly than that. 'The Crown
of England does not require such splendour', one journal
pronounced in patent disregard of the king's tastes. 'Foreign
countries might indulge in frippery, but England ought to
pride herself on plainness and simplicity.'

Matters were not improved when Nash, who was always
alarmingly prone to express surprise at the effect of his own
buildings, admitted to misjudgements over the proportions
of the wings, which he began to rebuild with a Marble Arch
as the centrepiece between them. Unhappily the Duke of
Wellington, who became prime minister in 1828, did not
treat the second thoughts of architects, even those employed
by the king, with indulgence. 'If you expect me to put my
hand to any additional expense', he told Nash, 'I'll be
damned if I will.' Suddenly expenditure was reduced from
£10000 to £2500 a week, and Nash found himself called
upon to defend his financial arrangments before a House of
Commons committee. He emerged unscathed, much to
the joy of the king, who wanted to make him a baronet.
Wellington refused this request point-blank.

When his royal protector died in 1830, the seventy-eight-
year-old architect was summarily dismissed. Seven years
later, Queen Victoria, the first monarch to live in the
palace, discovered it to be 'a disgrace to the country'. To
accommodate her swelling brood the forecourt was enclosed in 1847 by an east front built between the projecting
wings. This façade was itself remodelled in its present form

in 1911-12, when the Victoria Monument was set up in the Mall. The 1847 work occasioned the removal of Marble Arch to its present site: there was a story, probably apocryphal but indicative of Nash's reputation for slapdash decisions, that the arch had proved too narrow to take the state coach. Little of Nash's work at the palace is visible to the public today, although anyone favoured with an invitation might still see his gaudily ornate staterooms. Of the exterior, the garden front is still much as he left it, while the portico which once faced down the Mall now lurks within the courtyard.

NASH AND HIS CONTEMPORARIES

Nash's fellow architects would have been more than human if they had not felt secret delight at his fall. In particular Sir John Soane (1753-1837), who possessed a more substantial talent, must have borne with fortitude the disgrace of a man who had treated him with breezy patronage. Soane had in fact prepared a magnificent design for a palace in Green Park (which can be seen at his house, Number 16 Lincoln's Inn Fields, now the Sir John Soane Museum), only to have the commission snatched away by George IV.

Architects could hardly differ more in temperament than Nash and Soane: the one improvisatory, sanguine and light-spirited; the other painstaking, neurotic and deeply serious. Connoisseurs of irony are likely to derive more pleasure from their respective fortunes than connoisseurs of architecture. Soane's bad luck has dogged him beyond the grave, for few of his buildings survive in London. Whereas Nash's hastily sketched terraces have been carefully (and quite properly) preserved, Soane's masterpiece, the Bank of England, on which he lavished twenty years' labour, was, with the exception of the outer screen wall on the south and west sides, taken down in the 1920s because the Bank of England needed more space. (The Bank might just as well have acquired other premises since a few years later it was forced to do this anyway.) The best of Soane's work remaining in London is the art gallery in Dulwich, and even that was struck by a flying bomb in the war, although now rebuilt.

There were several other distinguished architects amongst Nash's contemporaries, whose work includes many familiar London landmarks. Robert Smirke built the British Museum (1823–47) on the site of Montagu House, in the first instance to house the royal library which, in return for a handsome fee, George IV had graciously 'presented' to the nation. The king was also responsible for the government's purchase of Sir John Angerstein's collection of pictures; it eventually formed the basis of the National Gallery (1832–8), which was designed by William Wilkins on the site of the old royal mews. Another of Wilkins's buildings is University College (1827–9) in Gower Street, an institution founded by Jeremy Bentham to provide higher education without religious bias: it is presumably in accord with these secularist principles that Bentham's corpse sits fully dressed in a glass case in the lobby. But the benighted Anglicans would keep building churches, especially after another Parliamentary grant for that purpose in 1818. St Pancras parish church, in Woburn Place (1822), and St Mary Marylebone (1818) at York Gate are both, with their porticoed fronts, fine examples of the classical style that was still in vogue: St Luke's (1824), off Sydney Street in Chelsea, prefigured a Gothic future which was itself to be transmuted into a specialized brand of High Victorianism displayed in full vigour at All Saints Margaret Street (1849–59). Exclusively male temples began to rise along Pall Mall, which was soon established as the heart of clubland. Charles Barry (1795–1860), who later designed the Houses of Parliament, built the Travellers' Club (1832) on the lines of an Italian palazzo, while Decimus Burton matched Nash's United Services Club with the solid grandeur of the Athenaeum on the opposite side of Waterloo Place. Burton's talent for the ornamental is also evident at Hyde Park Corner, where he was responsible for the grand arch and for the screen leading into the park alongside Wellington's Apsley House. The ensemble was created as part of the ceremonial approach to Buckingham Palace.

So there was no lack of talent among Nash's contemporaries. Yet it is doubtful whether any of these architects, even given his opportunities, could have accomplished so much. Nash's buoyancy and flair perfectly matched the Regent's fitful aesthetic enthusiasms; he possessed, moreover, the drive and resilience to realize projects that must have failed under the guidance of a man of Soane's delicate sensibility. Nash had a stroke in 1830, but up till then his vitality ensured a bubbling stream of ideas. It was typical of him that all his worries over Buckingham Palace did not prevent him embarking an another grand piece of town planning after the completion of Regent Street, this time for an avenue to link Whitehall with the British Museum. But there was no question of a by now understandably suspicious Treasury providing funds to carry out this scheme; and Charing Cross and Tottenham Court roads, developed in the 1880s, were to be a poor substitute for Nash's ideas. His plan did, however, bring forth Trafalgar Square, although the actual buildings were all the work of other men.

By the time Nash died, in 1835, fashionable aesthetic opinion, always as prone to error as to arrogance, had decreed that he was a figure of no account whatever. But his achievements were more obvious to foreign visitors. Prince Puckler-Muskau, that same German who had gazed in wonder at the docks, was equally impressed by recent developments in the West End. 'Now for the first time', he wrote, 'it has the appearance of a seat of government, and not an immeasurable metropolis of shopkeepers.'

PADDINGTON, BAYSWATER AND NORTH KENSINGTON

Yet, the point needs emphasizing again, this sudden imposition of grandeur from on high across a large area in the heart of town was a unique event in London's history. Even while Nash was at work the capital was still expanding according to the well-established Georgian pattern, as owners of estates hitherto far removed from London suddenly found their land ripe for development on the edge of town. In 1752 Henry Fielding had noted how the 'people of fascination' were forever establishing new frontiers to the west: 'had they not been stopped by the walls of Hyde Park', he considered, 'they would by this time have arrived at Kensington.' Now, with the removal of the gallows from Tyburn (Marble Arch) in 1825, respectability was on its way towards Paddington, hitherto only a cluster of houses around the village green where the eighteenth-century church still stands.

The land to the west of the Edgware Road belonged to the bishop of London and was developed in handsome style from the 1820s. But fashion can be capricious: when the tide of gentility receded from the Sussex Gardens area at the end of the nineteenth century the Anglican church was left with some embarrassing offscourings in the seedy crumbling terraces. Bayswater was to enjoy an even shorter period of smartness: Westbourne Grove was described in

1879 as 'the centre of a new, prosperous and refined district', but by the turn of the century it was already passé.

Well before Bayswater was built, however, the expanding town had already leap-frogged further west to North Kensington. From Notting Gate a cart track ran north to a 'very valuable grass farm' which had been named Portobello by its patriotic owner after Admiral Vernon had captured that town from the Spanish in 1739. The track, now the Portobello Road, apparently afforded 'one of the most rural and pleasant walks in the summer in the vicinity of London'; it also formed the eastern boundary of the Ladbroke estate, which had been given over to the Hippodrome Racecourse between 1837 and 1841. After the failure of this venture, one of the most imaginative of all Victorian building developments took place on the site. A church replaced the Hippodrome grandstand at the summit of Ladbroke Grove, and from this central point crescents spread out in ripples to the west, with spacious communal gardens between them. Yet this scheme was a financial disaster for its promoters; it is only since the Second World War that the Ladbroke estate has become a natural habitat for the beautiful people.

BELGRAVIA AND PIMLICO

Meanwhile, the town had also been expanding to the south of Hyde Park. Already in the 1780s Knightsbridge had been joined to Chelsea by the Hans Town development, with Sloane Street as its spine. (The name was derived from the wealthy Sir Hans Sloane (1660–1753), whose daughter married into the Cadogan family, from whom the architect, Henry Holland, had leased the land.) The ground to the east of Sloane Street, where there is no underlying gravel, had hitherto been regarded as too marshy for building. It was part of the Grosvenors' estate; and just as they had turned the north section of Ebury Manor to such good account in the eighteenth century, so now in the nineteenth they exploited the southern portion to such effect that in 1874 the family attained a dukedom (of West-minster), a distinction still unsurpassed among property developers.

The Grosvenors employed building leases in Belgravia in much the same way as they had done in Mayfair, with one important difference. In Mayfair they had negotiated agreements with a number of different builders; in Belgravia and Pimlico they entrusted almost the entire development to one great contractor, Thomas Cubitt (1788-1855), so that this part of the estate became popularly known as 'Cubittopolis'. In similar fashion, the Bedford estate had, from the 1790s, depended on one builder, James Burton, for the development of Russell Square and its environs.

Cubitt had succeeded Burton in Bloomsbury, extending the building north through Tavistock and Gordon squares to the New Road, but he was an entirely new phenomenon. His early success had been conventional enough; in gradua-ting from craftsman (in his case, a carpenter) to building speculator he was following a well-established eighteenth-century pattern. But whereas Burton had stuck to the traditional speculator's practice of subcontracting work to independent specialist craftsmen, Cubitt was so frustrated by the unreliability of this method that he brought the entire operation under his own control. He became the first speculator to employ the whole range of craftsmen, from bricklayers to plumbers, from masons to plasterers, on a permanent wage-earning basis. In short, Cubitt organized the first large-scale building firm. As a result he was able to guarantee high standards, but he needed a continuous supply of work to keep his set-up in business. Thus necessity as much as nerve led him to sign agreements with the Grosvenors in 1827 on such a scale that the work was still incomplete at his death thirty years later. Once these contracts had assured his future, he established a huge depot by the Thames at Pimlico and expanded his work-force to 1000. Perhaps only a man with Cubitt's vast resources could have developed Belgravia: the problem of marshy ground, for example, he solved by bringing earth from the excavation at St Katherine's docks, another project in which he was involved.

The new building north and south of Hyde Park was too much in the traditional Georgian vein to win favour from contemporary judges. Although entrance porches had been introduced to emphasize the separateness of individual houses in the terraces, Belgrave and Eaton Squares were pronounced 'only a very few degrees less insipid and interesting than Baker, Harley and Gower Streets'. Far more to high Victorian taste was the Cadogan Square region, built later (c. 1880) in plain red brick instead of that 'lying' stucco. Although the houses betray a common indebtedness to a 'semi-Dutch, semi-Queen Anne' style, they were deliberately designed differently from each other in order to produce what was felt to be 'that charming individuality of architectural effect'. Only the *Building News* struck a sour note with the comment that 'the old builder of Queen Anne's date was never so ridiculous as to use the same features in a street row of houses as he did in a country villa'.

All the same, Cadogan Square was sufficiently approved of to give a fillip to 'impoverished' Chelsea; and none of the critical strictures on Belgravia prevented it from becoming the most expensive and aristocratic part of town. It is still expensive. Yet Pimlico, in spite of the excellence of

Cubitt's work, was deserted by fashion as quickly as Bayswater. Described as an 'abode of gentility' in 1870, it had degenerated into a seedy slum by the turn of the century. The reason was that terraces and squares no longer met the requirements of middle-class respectability. What was the point in leaving the town centre for exactly the same kind of development elsewhere?

THE GROWTH OF SUBURBIA

The Victorians had fallen for the attractions of suburban life and, although Pimlico and Bayswater had been suburbs in the sense that they were originally built on the edge of town, they did not conform to the new ideal which had been born in St John's Wood early in the nineteenth century. Here, on the Eyre estate, in roads like Clifton Hill and Carlton Hill (1820–30), detached and semi-detached houses, each with its own walled garden, had been built instead of the usual terraced rows. These villas, the Victorians whispered, were 'once resorted to by dissipated men of affluence for the indulgence of one of their worst vices', which, being translated, meant that rich men installed their mistresses there. This reputation was ironic since the kind of suburbia for which St John's Wood served as a model was first and foremost a refuge for family life. Whereas in the West End the most circumspect eye could hardly avoid the spectacle of prostitution, poverty and disease, in the salubrious suburb the delights of domesticity might be indulged in hermetic isolation from the vulgar throng and far away from the corruptions and crush of the town. By living in this way, the Victorians triumphantly concluded, 'our habits are improved and our morals are improved'.

The retreat to the suburbs, then, began as an essentially

upper-middle-class phenomenon. In the eighteenth century
a man might signalize his prosperity by purchasing a house
in one of the villages around London; in the early nineteenth century it was again the wealthy who first created the
suburban way of life. The great revolution of the Victorian
age was that the escape from the centre, hitherto a luxury
for the privileged, became a necessity for the masses. In the
course of the nineteenth century the capital's population
quadrupled to more than four million: as Baedeker's guide
tellingly put the matter, London came to shelter more
Scotsmen than Aberdeen, more Irishmen than Dublin and
more Roman Catholics than Rome. Such a vast increase in
numbers could never be accommodated within the bounds
of the Georgian town, although, as the 1774 Building Act
had not limited height, houses could now be built taller. A
vast outward expansion was inevitable. Since the building
trade was one of London's largest industries, and house-
building was reckoned the best possible investment,
suburbs fairly shot up to meet a demand that remained so
lively that houses could often be rented before they were
completed.

Of course separate villas on the St John's Wood model
were confined to the privileged rich: as different suburbs
appeared for different classes so every kind of housing
proliferated, including the back-to-back terraces from which
the original suburbia had offered an escape. Yet at every
level, whether one is thinking of a large mansion standing
in its own grounds on Denmark Hill, 'the Belgravia of the
South', or of a Holloway terrace house that a City clerk
could rent for £28 a year, or of the lowly 'artisan' cottages
on the Shaftesbury estate in Battersea, the suburban house
proved more attractive than its central equivalent, always
assuming that such an equivalent existed. It is beyond the
scope of this book to chart the progress of suburbia: the

table on pp. 258-9 shows how many moved where, and when. The result of this process, however, was that nineteenth century London became surrounded by rings which gradually sucked population from its heart.

TRANSPORT AND THE GROWTH OF LONDON

Obviously the growth of suburbia would never have extended so far without the advent of buses and railways. Yet the connection between improved transport and the capital's expansion was initially by no means as close as might be supposed. The classes responsible for the early suburbs had long since shown themselves willing to face frequent and considerable journeys by coach. Indeed, not merely suburbia but also commuting from afar preceded the railways. 'The town of Brighton, in Sussex, fifty miles from the Wen, is on the sea-side', noted William Cobbett in 1823, 'and is thought by the stock-jobbers, to afford a salubrious air. It is so situated that a coach, which leaves it not very early in the morning, reaches London by noon; and, starting to go back in two hours and a half afterwards, reaches Brighton not very late at night. Great parcels of stock-jobbers stay at Brighton with the women and children. They skip backward and forward on the coaches, and actually carry on stock-jobbing in 'Change Alley, though they reside at Brighton.'

The first regular horse-drawn bus service in London appeared along the Marylebone Road in 1829; and there were soon routes to such distant parts as Hammersmith, Greenwich, Camberwell and Kennington. Until the 1840s, however, the minimum fare was usually sixpence, which put the new conveyance well beyond the pockets of the masses. (The only cheap transport at this time was provided by steamboats on the river.) Indeed, far from taking

The expanding suburbs : LCC boroughs (created 1889)

	Population in thousands								
	1801	1821	1841	1861	1881	1901	1921	1931	1951
CENTRAL AREA									
City	128	124	123	112	51	27	14	11	5
Westminster	161	190	229	257	230	183	142	130	99
Bermondsey	46	57	69	102	135	131	119	112	61
Bethnal Green	22	46	74	105	127	130	117	108	58
Finsbury	55	86	113	129	119	101	76	70	35
Holborn	67	88	94	94	79	59	43	39	25
St Marylebone	64	96	138	162	155	133	104	98	76
St Pancras	32	72	130	199	236	235	211	198	138
Shoreditch	35	53	83	129	127	119	104	97	45
Southwark	63	100	134	174	195	206	184	172	97
Stepney	114	154	204	257	282	299	250	225	99
	787	1066	1391	1720	1743	1623	1364	1260	738
INNER RING									
Battersea	3	5	7	20	107	169	168	160	117
Chelsea	12	27	40	60	73	74	64	59	51
Islington	10	22	56	155	283	335	331	322	236
						177	176	181	168

	2	6	25	79	126	144	144	145	125
(partial, top of page cut)						303	305	290	230
Paddington	64	132	271	546	1008	1201	1186	1163	927
SECOND RING									
Camberwell	7	18	40	71	187	259	267	251	180
Deptford	11	14	19	38	77	110	113	107	76
Fulham	4	6	9	16	43	137	158	151	122
Greenwich	22	29	40	57	65	96	100	101	91
Hackney	13	22	38	77	164	219	222	215	171
Hammersmith	6	9	13	25	72	112	130	136	119
Hampstead	4	7	10	19	45	82	86	89	95
Lewisham	4	9	15	29	67	127	174	220	228
Poplar	8	19	31	79	157	169	163	155	74
Stoke Newington	2	3	6	11	38	51	52	51	49
Wandsworth	14	23	33	51	103	232	328	353	330
Woolwich	13	21	31	69	75	117	140	147	148
	108	180	285	542	1093	1601	1933	1976	1683
TOTAL	959	1378	1947	2808	3844	4425	4483	4399	3348

SOURCE: N. Pevsner, *The Buildings of England: London II* (Penguin, 1952)

workers to the suburbs, the effect of the early buses was rather to exclude them therefrom. As long as each respectable family kept its own horses the smartest areas had perforce to accommodate grooms and coachmen in nearby mews, but now, with the advent of the bus, it became possible to build substantial houses without stabling and its attendant work-force. For the first time a neighbourhood could be exclusively (always excepting the servants, who lived in) middle-class, and the pattern was set for the division of the suburbs into socially distinct sections.

Even the railways did not at first have any positive effect on the way in which London grew. The capital's first steam-powered railway, from London Bridge to Deptford (later extended to Greenwich) opened in 1836; the London to Birmingham followed in the next year; and within two decades the various railway companies had put London at the heart of a network of lines stretching over most of the country. Yet the early railway promoters were mainly concerned with long-distance traffic. The first stop on the London–Birmingham line was at Harrow (eleven miles from Euston), on the Great Western at Ealing (five and three-quarter miles from Paddington) and on the Great Northern at Hornsey (four and a half miles from King's Cross). Moreover, only Fenchurch Street and London Bridge of the early termini were near work centres. So before the 1860s very few people went to work by train, and the prospect of relieving congestion in the centre by creating working-class suburbs served by the railway simply did not exist outside the minds of a few idealistic planners.

In fact, the early railways certainly worsened crowded living conditions, because so many houses were torn down to make way for the tracery of lines which criss-crossed their way into the capital. Over 5 per cent of London's built-up area was appropriated by the railways in the nineteenth century; and over 100000 people – most of them poor, as the railway companies found it cheaper to construct their lines through slums – lost their homes in this way. Whatever an area's status might have been before the arrival of the railway, it was bound to be lower afterwards. North of King's Cross, St Pancras and Euston, for example, the railways created the wasteland which separates the respectable districts of Regent's Park and Islington, while even Bloomsbury, to the south of these termini, declined in reputation as a result of their presence. Likewise, much of southern London was permanently debased by the tangle of lines which the competing companies built, only the higher ground at Dulwich, Sydenham and Norwood retaining much claim to smartness.

Far from finding refuge in some distant and spacious suburb, those displaced by the railway crammed into such run-down property as remained beside the devastation. Not until the 1860s, when some companies began to run workmen's trains at specially reduced prices, was any attempt made to redress the havoc caused by railway building. Only then, towards the end of the nineteenth century, did working-class railway suburbs, like those at Edmonton and Walthamstow along the Great Eastern's line, become a reality – and a fairly harsh reality at that, since the workmen's trains from these places arrived at Liverpool Street station between five and six every morning. By contrast, the north-west sector of London's suburbs was more middle-class in tone, partly owing to the fact that the Great Western and the London–Birmingham lines had been built before Parliament began to insist on workmen's tickets as a condition of granting railway companies the powers which they required. Nevertheless the north-west became a commuter belt in the late nineteenth century, due to the

North London line which stretched in a great arc from the City, through Hampstead and Finchley and down to Richmond. The City terminus of this line, the now almost deserted Broad Street station, once handled more trains than Euston and Paddington together. But this happened almost by accident: it is typical of the railway companies' lack of foresight about commuting that the North London had originated as a line for carrying freight between the docks and the London–Birmingham railway. Although suburban traffic did multiply in the last quarter of the nineteenth century the majority of Londoners were still walking to work in 1900.

RIVALRY OF THE RAILWAY COMPANIES: THE TERMINI

Still, no one could complain of a shortage of stations. In the 1840s the idea of bringing all subsequent lines to one great terminal was mooted and rejected: thereafter it was inevitable that the number of termini would proliferate as the various companies competed against each other to establish railheads as close to the centre as was permitted. Since lines from the north had been forbidden south of the Euston Road, the main rivalry over termini was between those companies operating trains from the south.

Between 1860 and 1866 four railway bridges were built over the Thames to bring trains to the heart of the West End and the City. In 1860 the London, Chatham and Dover railway extended its line across the river to Victoria, which it shared with a company running trains to Brighton: this ancient partition is still represented by a wall down the centre of the station. The rival South East Company, which also had a route to Dover, countered by opening Charing Cross (1864), only to have this ace trumped by the London,

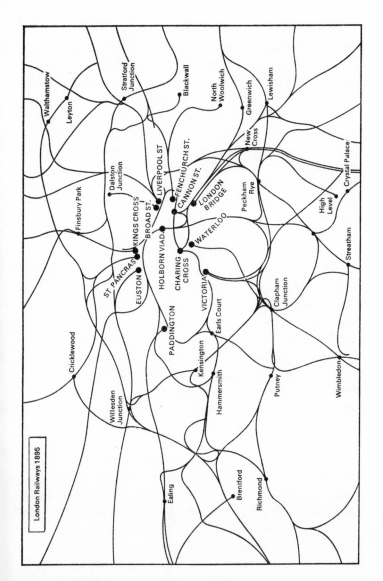

London's railways at the end of the nineteenth century, showing the
complex of lines which wrought such destruction.

Chatham and Dover's scheme to bring a line across the
river at Blackfriars. From there this route ran northwards
(by way of the viaduct across Ludgate Hill that ruins the
vista of St Paul's) to Farringdon Street, making possible a
link with the Metropolitan that enabled trains to travel right
through London. For good measure no less than three
stations were built along this mile of track to the north of
the river: Ludgate Hill (1865), Holborn Viaduct (1874) and
Blackfriars (1886). But the South East company was still
fighting: in 1866 it crossed the Thames again to Cannon
Street station in the heart of the City. So the competition
between these two companies had resulted not only in six
stations when surely two would have served, but also in
unnecessary trails of devastation where the various lines
had cut through south London. The story is not an impressive vindication of private enterprise. On the other hand
the energy generated by unfettered capitalism is well
attested by the sixteen termini that were in use in London
at the end of the century.

As *Building News* acutely observed in 1875, 'railway
termini and hotels are to the nineteenth century what
monasteries and cathedrals were to the thirteenth century.
They are truly the only real representative kind of building
we possess. Our churches, scholastic establishments and
domestic structures are more or less copies of medieval
buildings. If we want to see our representative buildings we
must turn to our railway stations. . . .' A hundred years
after that was written most of the termini still proclaim an
uncompromising Victorianism. Looking at the great vault
of iron and glass which roofs over the platforms at St
Pancras, it hardly seems far-fetched to think in terms of a
great secular cathedral from which, in Dickens's phrase,
the railroad 'trailed smoothly away on its mighty course of
civilisation and improvement'.

Like cathedrals, the termini maintain their own character while all serving a similar purpose. The grandest was Euston (1837), where a triumphal entrance arch, unfortunately demolished when the station was rebuilt in the early 1960s, symbolized the justifiable pride felt at the completion of the London to Birmingham line, 'probably then the largest work ever to be undertaken in the whole history of man, with the possible exception of the Great Wall of China'. King's Cross (1852), by contrast, impresses with its starkly functional façade, while the hotel in front of St Pancras is a Gothic fantasy with ornamentation deriving, if you please, from sources which include the cathedrals at Winchester, Salisbury, Amiens and Caen. The termini provided London with its first large hotels, much to the joy of overseas visitors who had long been grousing about the lack of accommodation. Several railway hotels – for example the Great Western Royal at Paddington, the Great Northern (King's Cross), the Grosvenor (Victoria) and the Great Eastern (Liverpool Street) are still in use.

THE UNDERGROUND

The dispersal of London's termini soon prompted demands for a link between them, and the result was the world's first underground system, of which the inaugural section between Paddington and Farringdon opened in 1863. The term 'underground' is used in distinction to 'tube': the techniques of deep tunnelling were not adequately developed until 1889 when Greathead built a subway (now used to carry water mains) under the Thames at the Tower. The Metropolitan was constructed simply by cutting a channel in the surface and then covering it over. Such a method obviously entailed great difficulties with sewers, water mains and gas pipes (London had been gas-lit since the beginning of the nineteenth century). At least, though, the route along the Marylebone Road meant that little housing had to be demolished on the opening stretch. By contrast the extension through Bayswater to Kensington High Street, which was opened in 1868, ran under squares and terraces, as the dummy houses at 23/24 Leinster Gardens, built to maintain the façade after the railway had been cut underneath, bear witness.

Another difficulty was ridding the tunnels of smoke from the steam engines which were used before the introduction of electric locomotion at the end of the century. Special engines were developed to condense the smoke, but the Metropolitan's cheery statement that the atmosphere in the tunnels was usually clear enough to enable the drivers to see the signals cannot have been entirely reassuring. Nor did the general manager's suggestion that a visit to Great Portland Street station would bring instant relief to bronchitis sufferers carry much conviction. Still, the Metropolitan was an instant success and the extension to Kensington was continued, at immense cost, to Westminster (1868) and Mansion House (1871), until the Inner Circle was finally complete in 1884. By that time a number of other underground lines had been built, like that to Earls Court (1868), which had been farmland in the early 1860s but was now quickly covered by bricks and mortar.

FLATS, AND THE SEGREGATION OF CLASSES

At the end of the nineteenth century, large mansions of flats were built in Earls Court and around Victoria Street, an uncommon type of development for London even at that late date. For though flats had begun to appear in the 1850s, they had only slowly become acceptable to the middle classes, being too readily associated with the massive blocks of dwellings that charity provided for the poor. Besides, the very nature of flats threatened the ever active Victorian sense of propriety. It just could not be right that bedrooms should be so close to sitting rooms, sometimes even interconnecting with them; and anxieties on this score were in no way allayed by the easy acceptance of this layout in the immoral city of Paris. 'We need not be reminded', reminded *Building News* in 1857, 'that French ideas of comfort differ from English ones. . . . Of course they do not feel incommoded, or they would not put up with such highly objectionable arrangement of plan. Put up with it, however, they do; and their doing so does not say much for their refinement.' There was also the insufferable embarrassment of meeting members of other classes on the stairs. This was bad enough for gentlemen; 'and as for the ladies', considered the *Architect*, 'it is difficult to assign a limit to the distress and shame that would be occasioned by an habitual encounter on mutual steps and risers between one caste and another'. So when the Grosvenor estate, as part of its great plan for linking the new rail terminal at Victoria with Hyde Park Corner, built a very French block of flats in Grosvenor Gardens (1868), it was careful to provide several entrances so that the tenants might enjoy complete privacy. But smart flats were rare in London before the 1890s, and only Albert Hall Mansions (1881), by Norman Shaw, was an original contribution to the genre.

Nevertheless, one massively undistinguished block exercised considerable influence on London's future appearance. There was an obvious temptation, not unknown to today's developers, to maximize a site's potential by piling storeys on top of each other. The hideous Queen Anne's Mansions (1873–89, demolished 1971–2) near St James's Park station in Broadway overstepped the mark not just by its height, which was over 150 feet, but also by overlooking Buckingham Palace gardens, to Queen Victoria's considerable chagrin. The result was an Act of 1888 which limited the height of buildings to eighty feet or to the width of the street in which they stood. The regulation remained an effective curb until the Second World War, when towers like those of the Imperial Institute (1893) and London University's Senate House (1932) were still exceptionally tall structures by London standards.

However careful the Victorians might be to keep the classes segregated in their own developments, they were obliged to accept the proximity of rich and poor in the London which they had inherited. Even a parish like St George's Hanover Square, in the heart of fashionable Mayfair, contained a ward where 1465 families were crowded into 2174 rooms with only 2510 beds. Yet if, as Charles Dickens observed, 'repletion and starvation laid them down together', the Victorians earnestly strove to separate the two states. Charity could not afford to fail if property values were to be maintained in such a socially sensitive society. Few landlords had the means to secure an area's smartness in the manner of the Duke of Westminster, who rebuilt the seedy streets around Grosvenor Square in fashionable brick and terracotta, and rehoused the poor in carefully segregated 'artisan dwellings' behind Duke street. For all property owners, however, the price of profit was eternal vigilance.

The penalties of careless adminstration were (and remain) evident on the Northampton estate in Clerkenwell, where the original leases had not adequately guarded against multiple occupation, and the landlords lacked the will, resources and lawyers to reverse the inevitable consequent decline into slumland. If the Marquess of Northampton failed, how could lesser mortals hope to rescue a district?

There was no chance of redemption for the industrial ring which had hemmed in the City since the seventeenth century: a great arc of squalor stretched from Finsbury through Shoreditch and Stepney, spilling over the river into Bermondsey and Southwark. 'A Polynesian savage in his most primitive condition', reckoned one nineteenth-century critic, did not endure conditions 'half so savage, so unclean and so irreclaimable as the tenant of a tenement in an East London slum.'

THE REVOLUTION THAT NEVER WAS

Yet if life was undeniably nasty, brutish and short in the slums the sufferers themselves were rarely given to self-pity; indeed they exhibited more vitality than those committed to the genteel refinements of middle-class suburbia. The preferential reference to the Polynesian savage may be explained by that gentleman's more favourable reception of missionary activity. Despite the Victorian reputation for piety, the urban working class remained unrepentantly pagan, marriage being chief among the sacraments which they preferred to eschew. Not that the attempt to convert them was hopeless. 'If a missonary came among us with plenty of money', a coster kindly explained, 'he might make us all Christians or Turks or anything he liked.' Missionaries without money, though, were apt to find themselves in trouble, as one unfortunate discovered when he visited the St Giles Holborn rookery. His clothes were ripped off, his mouth stuffed with powdered pepper and his treatment rounded off with a spell in a water butt. Small wonder that the respectable denizens of Bloomsbury showed little enthusiasm for the walk to the church of St Giles-in-the-Fields.

Granted the intensity and extent of misery it seems extra-ordinary that such outbreaks of violence as occurred were confined to isolated incidents in particular places. Early nineteenth-century politicians felt that they were living on the edge of a volcano and spent much time worrying about the consequences of a general eruption. 'What can be stable with these enormous cities', wondered the Earl of Liverpool, prime minister between 1812 and 1827. 'One insurrection in London and all is lost.' The appalling example of Paris (with only half London's population) during the French Revolution lent credence to these fears, the comforting notion that 'it couldn't happen here' not yet having occurred to the English. When the Houses of Parliament burnt down in 1834 the freeborn London citizenry expressed its natural affection for the parliamentary process by gathering in joyful crowds to admire the blaze. 'A judgement on the Poor Law Bill', they yelled, and 'There go their *hacts* [acts]'. One observer found the feeling among the people 'extraordinary – jokes and radicalism universal. If ministers had heard the shrewd sense and intelligence of these drunken remarks! I hurried Mary away.' When plans for the new Houses of Parliament were under discussion, the Duke of Wellington stressed the importance of one side being on the river in order to prevent the building being completely surrounded by angry mobs. No doubt about it, the ruling classes were scared.

But the decisive blow was never struck; the several springs of violence in London never coalesced into one overwhelming flood. The capital was dangerous in parts but indifferent in the mass. Even in the years of depression after Waterloo when a crazed conspirator called Arthur Thistlewood noised abroad his intention variously to seize the Tower, blow up the Bank of England and assassinate the entire cabinet, he recruited as many government spies as genuine revolutionaries. Being unable to distinguish these two categories, Thistlewood ended on the gallows after his

gang had been surprised by the Bow Street Runners at
their hideout in Cato Street near Marble Arch (1820). There
were more dangerous riots during the Reform Bill crisis
(1830-2), when the Duke of Wellington, who led the
opposition to any extension of the vote, was the principal
target. Apsley House, his home at Hyde Park Corner, was
surrounded and pelted by angry mobs, but he treated their
hostility with the same disdain as he was wont to accept
their plaudits. When out riding, and crowded by a threatening rabble, he quickly discovered that a flick of his whip
sufficed to disperse the danger. Wellington was also to the
fore in meeting what was perhaps the greatest scare that
ministers had to face in the nineteenth century.

In 1848, Europe's year of revolutions, the Chartists, a
predominantly working-class movement pressing for universal suffrage and other constitutional reforms, decided to
march *en masse* from Kennington Common to Parliament
in order to present a monster petition which they claimed
had been signed by six million people. The government
took fright and called in the Duke, now close on eighty, to
organize the capital's defences. No fewer than 170000
special constables, outnumbering the Chartists by six to one,
were enrolled; among them was Louis Napoleon, who thus
became the only member of his family to serve under
Wellington. But the event proved a damp squib: the
Chartists meekly dispersed when told that their crossing
of the river would be contested. 'My poor friends', commented the French composer Hector Berlioz, who was
present, 'you know as much about starting a riot as the
Italians about writing a symphony.' The Chartists' weakness in London had proved a fatal handicap, and with their
failure the spectre of mob rule receded. In the later nineteenth century the capital's radical tradition would be more
effectively represented by middle-class intellectuals like

the Fabians, the brains behind the emerging Labour Party, than by sporadic and localized outbursts of violence.

The truth was that London had grown too big and diverse to allow any easy concentration of dissidence. Moreover in 1829 the town had finally acquired an effective police force. Sir Robert Peel was the minister responsible for this daring assault on liberty, and the police are still nicknamed 'bobbies' after him. The first idea had been to dress them in red and gold uniforms, but in the end dark blue and black were preferred as smacking less of the dreaded military. A constable was enjoined to be 'civil and attentive to all persons, of every rank and class; insolence and incivility will not be lightly passed over'. In addition he should display 'a perfect command of temper, never suffering himself to be moved, in the slightest degree, by any language or threats that may be used; if he do his duty in a quiet and determined manner, such conduct will probably induce well-disposed by-standers to assist him should he require it'.

THE ADMINISTRATIVE VACUUM

The City, true to form, refused to be associated with any general scheme for the organization of police over the entire capital, and formed its own force a few years later. As an alternative London authority simply did not exist, the Home Office, a department of state, had to assume ultimate responsibility for Peel's 'bobbies': Incredibly, London continued without a government for almost the entire nineteenth century. Other English towns received elected councils in 1834, but the City exercised pressure to ensure that this measure did not apply to the capital. By 1843 Lord Brougham was declaring it to be 'utterly impossible that many months should elapse before municipal reform should be extended to the City of London'. The impossibility duly extended itself for months, years and decades; and although the Metropolitan Board of Works was created with limited powers to build sewers and effect street improvements in 1855, it was not until 1889 – after the town's population had reached four million – that the London County Council came into being. Even then the City was left supreme in its own area. Indeed, in practice it only lost one of its ancient powers during the nineteenth century. In 1857 the control of the Thames below Staines, which had been vested absolutely in the Corporation for the previous 700 years, was forfeited to the Thames Conservancy, on which, however, the Mayor and aldermen were well represented.

Parliament did not appear much keener than the City to see London given a proper government. Perhaps ministers feared that a London Council would prove as unruly and dangerous an institution as medieval kings had found the City. The eighteenth-century system of parish vestries supplemented by thousands of special commissioners endowed with responsibilities for paving, lighting, street-cleaning and the like, achieved nothing but paralysing confusion, but for that very reason it presented no threat to anyone's power. One monster authority for the whole town might be a different matter. Besides, the absence of any proper means for governing London provided ministers with a splendid excuse for doing nothing for the capital, in accordance with the fashionable doctrine of *laissez-faire*. The routine response of governments when faced with an obvious abuse was to set up a committee to investigate, ponder its conclusions with suitable gravity, and then forget about the whole affair. Generally the only chance of inducing the Victorian Treasury to spend money in London was to show that disease, starvation and death in the slums were uneconomic and wasteful. Otherwise the compassion of Chancellors was not easily engaged.

Considering that up to 1855 the City and the government were the only agencies capable of tackling the appalling slums, neither of them achieved very much. The City's main work during the first part of the nineteenth century was the construction of King William Street, Princes Street and Moorgate as a route to the new London Bridge which had been completed in 1831. This was one of several bridges built by John Rennie and his son George in the capital; others were Vauxhall (1816), Waterloo (1816), Southwark (1819) and, the only one still standing, that across the Serpentine in Hyde Park (1826).

The government's attitude to London improvements is best gauged from the fact that this responsibility was delegated to the Commissioner for Woods and Forests. The creation of Victoria Street (1851) and the formation of Battersea Park (1853–8) were among the projects carried out by this department. It also attacked the slum at St Giles Holborn in 1845–7 by the simple expedient of driving a clearing, New Oxford Street, straight through the middle, no doubt a satisfactory enough technique when applied to woods and forests, but a trifle crude in the urban context.

HOUSING FOR THE POOR

The unlucky inhabitants of the St Giles rookery, having nowhere else to go, stayed put even after their roofs had been pulled off. 'The poor are displaced but they are not removed', *The Times* noted in 1861: 'They are shovelled out of one side of the parish, only to render more overcrowded the stifling apartments in another part. . . . But the dock and wharf labourer, the porter and the costermonger cannot remove. You may pull down their wretched homes; they must find others, and make their new dwellings more wretched than their old ones. The tailor, shoemaker and other workmen are in much the same position. It is a mockery to speak of the suburbs to them.'

So conditions in what remained of St Giles rookery became more ghastly than ever until finally tackled by the London County Council at the beginning of this century. The area became a favourite horror spot for literary-minded reformers. 'Go, scented Belgravian, and see what London is', urged Charles Kingsley, as though the place were not crowded enough already. Charles Dickens, who could scarcely write without the stimulus of nocturnal prowls around London, was another to feel the 'attraction of repulsion' for St Giles which, under the name of Tom All Alone's, he described with magnificent indignation in *Bleak House*.

One or two scented Belgravians responded nobly to such protests. George Peabody (1795–1869), an American millionaire, and Baroness Burdett-Coutts (1814–1906), of banking stock, each poured hundreds of thousands of pounds into buildings for the poor. The Victorian social conscience was much preoccupied with designing model homes for the working classes; and the first of all the queen's subjects, Prince Albert, included two such houses, which now serve as a lodge at the entrance to Kennington Park, in the Great Exhibition of 1851.

For the most part, however, Victorians clung to the conviction that charitable impulses, being quite as virtuous as commercial ones, should also yield a steady 5 per cent. This principle was even applied to church-building. Remarking that some land in Onslow Square and Earls Court had been set aside for churches, the *Builder* expressed its satisfaction that such liberality had often proved 'not prejudicial to worldly interests'. Naturally the provision of housing encouraged hopes of more positive returns. Thus the Metropolitan Association for Improving the Dwellings of the Industrious Classes (1841) aimed to supply 'the labouring man with an increase of the comforts and conveniences of life, *with full compensation to the capitalist*'. The Association was actually to accuse Peabody's trustees of being 'unfair traders' because they charged only five shillings a week rent for flats valued at nine shillings by its own inflexible law of 5 per cent.

The buildings to which Victorian charity condemned the poor – for example the Peabody estates in Pimlico and Clerkenwell – are so prison-like that one wonders how judges such as Charles Dickens could have welcomed their appearance with enthusiasm. The answer, of course, is that they knew the full horror of Victorian slums that have now generally been destroyed or renovated into respectability. The way in which the relative status of nineteenth-century buildings can be reversed is evident in Peel Street, on Campden Hill by Notting Hill Gate. Thanks to the street's prime position, the original houses which were built, and none too solidly, for working-class occupation have been turned into much sought-after bijou residences. At the top of the street, however, Campden Buildings, a block of artisan flats put up in 1877-8 by the National Dwellings Society Limited, obtrude in massive disproportion and bleak contrast to their surroundings. The mind has to be jerked into the realization that 100 years ago it was the terraced cottages that were slums (in 1856 there were complaints of a man keeping pigs there), whereas Campden Buildings represented the spirit of improvement.

In their contemporary context the main fault of Victorian associations for housing the poor was simply that there were never enough of them to do more than scratch the surface of the problem. They concentrated, moreover, on the deserving poor although, as Mr Alfred Doolittle, the dustman in Bernard Shaw's *Pygmalion*, correctly insisted, it was the undeserving that most needed help. Thousands were completely homeless, like the little boy who was discovered to have spent the winter inside a roller in Regent's Park. There was no hope of relief for destitution on such a scale save in the ministrations of a benevolent state. But Victorian governments did not minister, nor were they especially benevolent.

THE REIGN OF 'KING CHOLERA'

Even the onset of deadly disease failed to shake Parliament's complacency. When cholera threatened in 1831 nothing was done beyond setting up local health boards, which proved utterly ineffectual and soon disappeared into oblivion. Government preparations also included a day of national prayer and fasting, a gesture which the Almighty acknowledged with the first cholera victim in the capital four days later (10 February 1832). By autumn 5000 had died from the disease, but still no counter-measures were taken. Cholera showed an alarming tendency to jump unpredictably from area to area, not even disdaining the habitations of the rich, but its preference for slums like Whitechapel was always sufficiently pronounced to allow the Belgravians to live with their concern.

Ten years later, in 1842, an *Inquiry into the Sanitary Condition of the Labouring Population of Great Britain* described conditions in the slums in horrifying detail, establishing the connection between squalor and disease beyond all reasonable doubt. The *Inquiry*, largely the work of Edwin Chadwick (1800–90), a fanatic for sanitary reform, was a bestseller, but it failed to generate any action. Two of Chadwick's campaigns, however, did produce reforms. His

report on the dangers arising from overcrowded churchyards was full of gruesome details, like those submitted by a
Bermondsey woman who had seen four green and putrefy-
ing heads sticking up from the churchyard at St Olave's.
In 1850 and 1852 legislation was passed to prevent further
burials in such places; by that time the large cemeteries at
Brompton (1831), Kensal Green (1833) and Highgate
(1838) were already in use. The other success was the removal of Smithfield live cattle market, 'that sink of cruelty,
drunkenness and filth', from the City in 1855. Henceforth
only dead meat was sold at Smithfield: the present building
used for this purpose dates from 1866-7.

'Had he killed in battle as many as he saved by sanitation',
one of Chadwick's obituaries observed, 'he would have had
equestrian statues by the dozen put up in his memory.' Yet
he achieved none of his wider aims and the death rate in
London actually increased during the period 1850–70.
The trouble was partly – but only partly, for his personality
was also at fault – that Chadwick's ideas were out of tune
with his age. He wanted one centralized authority to control
all sewage and water services in London, a scheme which
never had any hope of realization in a Victorian Parliament
where the interests of the water companies were well
represented, and where threats to freedom were always
likely to stir more concern than threats to life. In 1848, with
the shadow of cholera again looming, the government
created central and local health authorities, but it dared not
apply this measure to London. 'The principles of this Bill,
the opposition thundered, 'would breed a revolution even in
Russia, if attempted there.' So London gained nothing
except a single Commission of Sewers, with Chadwick in
charge, to replace the eight separate commissions which had
previously existed.

Needless to say, the City was at the root of the opposition

to this Public Health Act. One could scarcely have faulted the workings of divine justice had its inhabitants been punished by a plague of Old Testament proportions. Many City dwellers did in fact die of cholera in 1849 but, more by luck than by judgement, the Corporation had in October 1848 appointed as Medical Officer Dr John Simon. Under the care of this brilliant administrator the City became one of the healthiest parts of the capital. The next cholera outbreak, in 1854, claimed 10000 victims, but only 211 of them in the City.

Even Simon, however, had unwittingly made a fatal mistake in 1849, when he ordered the City's sewers to be flushed out. That same year Dr John Snow published a pamphlet arguing that the cholera germ was carried in water. This explanation, which accounted for the disease's habit of leap-frogging to new districts, was in fact correct, as Snow dramatically confirmed in 1859 when he was able to show that all the cholera victims in a certain part of Soho had taken water from the same pump. So the dire consequences of flushing the sewers into the Thames, from which all London's water companies save the New River drew their supplies, may readily be imagined. With Chadwick, at the Metropolitan Commission of Sewers, following the same policy, it was probably no coincidence that the 1849 cholera outbreak, which killed 14000 in London, was the most deadly of all. But whereas the death toll did not prevent Simon from winning the confidence of the City authorities, Chadwick was not the kind of man opponents were inclined to let off lightly. Narrow, opinionated (to the end of his days he clung to his belief that disease was inhaled from the atmosphere), authoritarian and utterly without tact, he had appeared insufferable enough with right on his side. Now that he had proved ineffective he was suffered no longer but unceremoniously booted off the Metropolitan Commission of Sewers (October 1849). London, it seemed, would be condemned to eternal fever.

Fortunately, members of Parliament possessed nostrils which proved more sensitive than their reaction to mortality figures from the East End. In the 1850s the stench from the Thames became unbearable. Of course the river had been polluted since Roman times, but at the beginning of the nineteenth century it had been clean enough for salmon to be plentifully caught in central London, and for Byron to commit his lordly limbs to the stretch between Westminster and Waterloo bridges. Not only was swimming out of the question fifty years later: the House of Commons showed itself none too partial even to debating when the stench reached its peak of foulness during the summer months. Ironically, the cause of this deterioration was a sanitary breakthrough, the flushing lavatory, which first appeared in London around 1810, became increasingly popular after 1830, and was rendered compulsory in 1848 when the use of cesspools was forbidden. The Thames thus received direct that which had previously been deposited in countless cesspools, and the gentle reader is requested to imagine the state of the foreshore at low tide. Not surprisingly, a report on water supplies found them abounding in animal life, unfit even for washing, and so repellent for drinking that the working classes were being driven to alcohol. The result was an Act which forbade the water companies to draw supplies from the Thames below Teddington after 1856. But this prohibition was laxly enforced, and even in 1868, long after the cholera's water-borne nature had been definitely established, one company was still blithely drawing water at Battersea.

It was primarily to deal with the problem of sewage passing into the Thames that the Metropolitan Board of Works was set up in 1835. Its powers were wholly inadequate, and for three years nothing effective was done. Then, on 30 June 1858, members of a House of Commons committee suddenly rushed out of their room in the greatest haste and confusion; 'foremost among them', reported The Times, 'being the Chancellor of the Exchequer [Disraeli], who, with a mass of papers in one hand and with his pocket handkerchief clutched in the other, and applied closely to his nose, hastened in dismay from the pestilential odour . . .; Mr Gladstone also paid particular attention to his nose. . . .' That settled matters. Strong men whose laissez-faire principles had not flinched in the face of 10000 cholera deaths in the remote regions of Whitechapel and Bethnal Green now wilted before this savage attack, and rushed a Bill through Parliament to provide the Metropolitan Board of Works with the powers it needed to abate the nuisance. Within the next seven years London acquired an eighty-two-mile complex of sewers running west to east in five lines (three on the north, two on the south of the river) which intercepted all flow into the Thames in central London. The sewage was carried off via two magnificent pumping stations at Abbey Mills (north) and Deptford (south) to the wastes of Barking and Crossness, where it was discharged on the ebb tide. The unsung hero of this achievement was the Board's chief engineer, Sir Joseph Bazalgette (1819–91), who deserves to be remembered among London's greatest benefactors. His system is out of sight underground, but would not be out of mind had it proved less efficient. The greater part is still in use and surely its rare manifestations, such as the aqueduct which carries a sewer over the Metropolitan line at Sloane Square, deserve a sniff of acknowledgement.

A more impressive visual memorial to Bazalgette's work is the Victoria Embankment between Westminster and

Blackfriars, which reclaimed thirty-seven acres from the Thames. The river had been embanked between Chelsea and Millbank in 1854, and from 1839 the new Houses of Parliament were being built on ground that had been partially stolen from the river. But the Victoria Embankment (1864–70), incorporating the District railway and the new sewers underneath a fine highway represented a greater engineering triumph. It was soon lined with impressive buildings, including New Scotland Yard where the basement contains the dressing room of a National Theatre that was never finished. For years the headquarters of the Metropolitan police, New Scotland Yard now provides extra accommodation for Members of the House of Commons, who have been grousing about their working conditions at Westminster ever since the present Parliament building was under construction. At that time Disraeli suggested that nothing sensible would ever be accomplished until an architect was hung *pour encourager les autres*.

THE PALACE OF WESTMINSTER AND OTHER WORKS

The architect of the new Palace of Westminster (1839–60), Charles Barry, escaped hanging, but had to endure harassment over every detail. 'All the arrangements of the new House of Commons', he wrote to his collaborator Pugin, 'including the form, size, proportions, taste and everything else concerning it are in abeyance, and awaiting the fiat of a Committee of the House of Commons, of all tribunals the most unfit to decide.' Barry and Pugin apparently worked together harmoniously enough, although after Pugin's tragic end in the public madhouse at Bedlam (1852) his son was to accuse Barry (now Sir Charles) of taking credit for what was principally another's work. In fact

Barry was responsible for the main plan and Pugin for the abundant ornamental detail. Few except members of Parliament have questioned the building's success: even that celebrated architectural critic Adolf Hitler referred to it as 'Barry's masterpiece', adding the phrase 'its windows reflected in the waters of the river Thames' to show what a beautiful and sensitive nature he possessed. Unluckily his admiration did not extend to any determined effort at conservation, and on 10 May 1941 German bombing demolished the House of Commons. The chamber was rebuilt in a plain Gothic style, with Pugin's decorative skills as conspicuous by their absence as by their presence in the House of Lords. Still, the palace as a whole survived the war; and its great outline, framed with calculated asymmetry by the Victoria and clock towers, is probably the first image of London in the majority of minds.

The clock tower, or rather its bell, was named after Sir Benjamin Hall, 'Big Ben', the man who had been responsible for the Act setting up the Metropolitan Board of Works. 'A huge impostor of a man', Chadwick called him, but then Hall had led the movement which secured Chadwick's dismissal. Having crusaded against the great sanitarian's centralizing methods, Hall was consistent enough to create a Board which, as we have seen, initially lacked means to do anything at all. Nevertheless, the Metropolitan Board of Works, London's first authority covering the entire town beyond the City, did not exist by sewers alone. Although the Board's innate powers were always limited, Parliament sometimes bestowed additional rights to enable it to make particular street improvements.

So Northumberland House, the last great private house remaining along the Strand, was knocked down in 1874–5 to make way for Northumberland Avenue, which began as a line of great hotels. Other Board schemes included the

construction of Queen Victoria Street (1870–1), Shaftesbury Avenue (1877–86) and the Charing Cross Road (1887).
The last two projects had the merit of destroying more of
St Giles rookery and other slums, but the Board was unable
to buy enough land beside the new route to tempt developers
into erecting first-class buildings. It might have done better
with more honest officials. In the case of Shaftesbury
Avenue the Board Valuer was discovered to have disposed
of the London Pavilion site on favourable terms to the
existing leaseholder, in return for personally receiving a
£6000 cut out of the subsequent profit. Truly the twentieth
century was not far away.

Meanwhile the City Corporation, with powers untouched
by this feeble newcomer to London government, had been
busy with works of its own. The Fleet valley was spanned
by the costly Holborn viaduct in 1869, and its higher reaches
followed by the line of the Farringdon Road, which cut
through the slums of Clerkenwell in the 1850s. A new
Blackfriars Bridge appeared in 1869, while further down the
Thames Tower Bridge (1886–94) became another familiar
London landmark. Such municipal works, however, did
not match those carried out in the City by individual
landowners. Before 1840 the office block, as such, hardly
existed: by 1900 almost the entire City had been rebuilt
in order to accommodate this new phenomenon. After
eighteen centuries the square mile lost its residents. Of course,
as a centre of commerce, it had long been avoided by the
sensitive sparks of fashion. When, around 1800, the celebrated Beau Brummell bumped into Sheridan in the Strand
he felt obliged to claim that he had lost his way in straying
so far to the east of town. Nevertheless, there were still over
100000 people living in the City in 1850, a number which
dwindled to 27000 by the end of the century as offices
proliferated and commuting became the rule.

AN AGE OF CHANGE: THE GREAT EXHIBITION OF 1851

After 1881 not merely the City but the whole central area of London was losing population, a decline that has continued without a break right up to the present as the town spread itself ever further over the Home Counties. But the builders have been kept busy in the centre, for the renewal of old London has always gone together with the development of new London. So much Victorian building – the Houses of Parliament, Tower Bridge, Whitehall, the Embankment, the Albert Memorial – has become fixed in our minds as part of London's traditional image that it has became fatally easy to incorporate this same monumental character into our conception of the age in which these landmarks first appeared. Nothing could be further from the truth: the Victorians were bewildered by the transformation of the capital. 'Old London, London of our youth', observed *Building News* in 1873, 'is becoming obliterated by another city which seems rising up through it as mushrooms do in a sward.'

The character of the age had been caught, even to some extent set, by the Great Exhibition of 1851 which was held in Hyde Park. The exhibition aimed to show how developments in technology and the arts could be harnessed to the service of industry, a theme which was illustrated by products from all over the world. The whole occasion was a triumphant success, visited by one in six of Great Britain's population, which shows how the railways had integrated London into the life of the entire country. The most remarkable exhibit of all was the immense building in which the event was held. Joseph Paxton's Crystal Palace was, as befitted a gardener's design, a gigantic greenhouse, three times the size of St Paul's and enclosing great trees. It was set down on the south side of the park, with the main entrance facing Ennismore Gardens, and the glass and iron construction enabled the builders to anticipate the techniques of prefabrication. Such modernity was a portent. Although the Great Exhibition is often regarded as a symbol of the wealth and stability of mid-Victorian Britain, for millions of Londoners it heralded a period of change that had given the life of the town a recognizably modern cast by the turn of the century. Where one lived, how one travelled, how one amused oneself, where one shopped: all such questions, great and small, were receiving new answers.

Not that the exhibition should be taken as a clean break between two worlds. Just as suburban life had existed before the main suburban explosion, so other, more trivial changes also had roots in the past. For example restaurants, where 100 might eat at a sitting and where women might go unaccompanied, 'care always being taken to avoid passing through a drinking bar', were certainly a new development, yet obviously there had always been eating houses of a kind. It was the same with shops. Dickins and Jones (1803), Swan and Edgar (1812) and Marshall and Snelgrove (1837), all of which began as drapers in the fashionable centre of Regent Street and Oxford Street, were soon offering a wide variety of merchandise. Nevertheless, William Whiteley's store in Bayswater, which also opened (1863) as a draper, soon extended to an altogether grander style of retailing, with nineteen different departments under one roof by the end of the century. The Army and Navy Stores (opened 1871, present building 1977) in Victoria Street, Harrods (a department store from 1869, present building 1901–5) in Knightsbridge, Barkers (from 1870, present building 1937 and 1957) in Kensington High Street, and Selfridges (1908) in Oxford Street also exemplified this trend.

Similarly, the many pubs built in the late nineteenth century – 'the modern plague of London', the National Temperance Society called them – were descendants of the taverns that had existed in every age, but their character was distinctly Victorian and they bred their own traditions. One of them was the music hall, which grew out of sing-songs in the bar and only became a separate institution with its own theatres in the second half of the century. The sum of such innovations was a revolution in town life. As a contemporary wrote in 1888: '. . . This monster London is really a new city . . . new as to its life, its streets, and the social condition of the millions who dwell in them, whose very manners, habits, occupations and even amusements have undergone as complete change within the past half century as the great city itself. . . .'

Perhaps it was inevitable that architecture should fail to settle into any distinct style in such times. 'The student may be fitted with his favourite style of architecture anywhere between St Paul's and Aldgate Pump', a commentator noted in reference to the astonishingly diverse types of office block that appeared in the City during the 1860s. In the last quarter of the century the Gothic revival was ebbing: the Law Courts in the Strand, completed in 1882 but designed in the 1860s, represented its last great flowering in London. Thereafter no new style emerged as a dominating influence. The rebuilding of Oxford Street at the end of the century produced a totally anonymous and undistinguished effect, although the use of brick and terracotta sometimes suggests an attempt at the ideals practised on the Cadogan estate.

More interesting were developments in South Kensington, the one place where the Great Exhibition certainly did represent an entirely new departure. The Exhibition's profits were used to buy eighty-eight acres facing the park, roughly between where Queensgate and Exhibition Road now run.

Here Prince Albert sought to found institutions which would permanently further the Exhibition's aims. Today his ideals are represented in South Kensington by the Royal Colleges of Art, Organists and Music, various learned societies such as the Royal Geographical Society, the Imperial College of Science and Technology, and the four great museums. The Victoria and Albert, begun in the 1850s (though the present façade dates from the turn of the century), was the first to appear, followed by the Natural History (1873–81), Science (1907) and Geological (1933–5) museums. The Imperial Institute, built in 1887–93, has now decamped to Kensington High Street under the more contemporary guise of the Royal Commonwealth Institute; of its original buildings off Exhibition Road only one of the towers, which has been incorporated into Imperial College, still survives.

From its elevated position under the canopy of the Albert Memorial, a little to the west of where the Crystal Palace once stood, a huge seated statue of the Prince Consort gazes south towards the complex of institutions which his endeavours directly or indirectly brought into being, while at the monument's base galaxies of genius are assembled in relief to do him honour. The Prince was never lucky; in rejecting a proposal for a memorial in his lifetime he came remarkably close to anticipating his fate. 'It would disturb my quiet rides in Rotten Row to see my own face staring at me, and if (as is very likely) it became an artistic monstrosity, like most of our monuments, it would upset my equanimity to be permanently ridiculed and laughed at in effigy.' We must hope that the grave has removed him from such concerns, especially as his equanimity would also be ruffled by the presence of the Albert Hall (1867–71) on the ground that he had specifically reserved for one of his most cherished projects, a new National Gallery.

The transformation of rural South Kensington into a centre of arts and learning proved a mighty encouragement to housebuilders, who now bent themselves to provide 'suitable residences for the more aristocratic stream of our London population' in the area. This new housing, and the coming of the Metropolitan and District railway, integrated Kensington with central London. The High Street, a village lane before 1851, was being described as 'one of the most popular and fashionable promenades in London' thirty years later. Yet the grand terrace houses of Kensington belonged to a phase that was already passing when they were built. The Crystal Palace provided a better symbol of the times. After the last visitors had departed it was dismantled and set up again at Sydenham, in the suburbs.

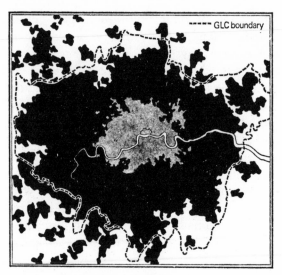

8. 'A tide of mean, ugly, unplanned building'
[1889 to the present]

THE PRIVATE DEVELOPER SURVIVES

At last, in 1889, London acquired a directly elected government of its own, with authority over the entire town as it
then existed except for the City, which still retained its
privileges. The London County Council's powers were
limited, but the mere existence of such a body was enough
to encourage the idea that a new chapter in the capital's
history had opened.

London had hitherto, with only a few exceptions like
Nash's Regent Street and the Metropolitan Board of

Works improvements, been created piecemeal by private enterprise and capital, without any overall plan. The energies thus generated had produced a truly astonishing rate of growth, though the social consequences had been terrible. London town was brimming with a vitality that spilt over into ever more distant suburbs; London inhabitants often found themselves stranded by the outward surge in conditions that afforded but a wretched and short-lived existence. Instead of being reformed, the slums were avoided, bypassed, leap-frogged by newer developments, and forgotten. As a result the town presented a series of startling contrasts. In west London, for example, every other child born in the derelict slum of Notting Dale, even as late as 1900, was dead by the age of one, yet Hammersmith, only a mile or so away, was a flourishing suburb which absorbed 40000 newcomers in the last two decades of the nineteenth century. Now, though, the London County Council had appeared as the instrument through which a more rational order might gradually be established. The first councillors to be elected included a number of Fabian socialists, who were not at all short of prescriptions for mortal ills, and did not doubt that London could be governed in the communal interest.

In many ways their hopes have not been disappointed. Today's local authorities are by far the largest landholders in London, and one in every four Londoners now lives in a home rented from the Council. The desirability of community ownership on such a scale is arguable, but it would be churlish to dismiss out of hand a process that has provided more than half a million new council houses in London since the Second World War. One must also acknowledge that huge sums of money have been spent on education. Indeed, as far as the provision of services is concerned (and it concerns millions) the record of municipal achievement has probably exceeded all but the wildest dreams of those first members of the London County Council. The extremes of poverty and distress, which formed a running accompaniment to the first eighteen centuries of London's history, have been virtually eliminated. Undeniably, too, twentieth-century London has been kept infinitely cleaner and healthier than its predecessors. In this connection the Clean Air Act of 1956 deserves special mention for creating smokeless zones and thus putting an end to the fogs which had proved such an inspiration to Charles Dickens's descriptive powers.

Yet for all the new benefits enjoyed by Londoners, the town's *physical* history during this century has shown many signs of continuity with the past. Expansion has continued according to the same centrifugal principles that became evident after the Great Fire, when the City failed to regain its lost numbers. In the nineteenth century, as we have seen, this centrifugal force drew population from the old into the new suburbs; since 1919 it has gained such strength that the bounds of the town have been flung back twice as far as before, and there are now fears of a vacuum in the centre.

It was, moreover, right in line with London's past history that this suburban explosion, and many redevelopments in the heart of town, should have been carried out by private individuals and companies, who have been allowed far more influence than the London County Council on the direction and manner of the town's development, although they are hardly in business to improve the environment. Indeed, the record of modern property developers compares badly with that of the old estates, which often showed concern for the long-term effects of their plans. 'Our London has much that is lovely and gracious . . .' the leader of the London County Council observed in 1943. 'I do not know that any city can rival its parks and gardens, its squares and terraces. But year by year as the nineteenth and twentieth centuries grew more and more absorbed in first gaining and then holding material prosperity, these graces were overlaid and a tide of mean, ugly, unplanned building rose in every London borough and flooded outward over the fields of Middlesex, Surrey, Essex and Kent.' Even after 1947, when the London County Council acquired effective powers to restrict the activity of property developers, it has proved no match for the hundreds of crafty operators who have been able to manipulate the planning laws and make bigger profits than ever. If the shade of the great Dr Barbon could have chosen a period in which to demonstrate his ancient skills to a new generation, he would surely have plumped for the ten years between 1954 and 1964.

THE LONDON COUNTY COUNCIL

The trouble was that the London County Council was conceived and raised in the spirit of *laissez-faire*, and it never really managed to shrug off this inheritance. The Act which set up the Council was produced by a Conservative government as a pre-emptive strike designed to minimize the effects of a reform that was clearly inevitable. For earlier in the 1880s the Liberals had introduced a Bill which revived the seventeenth-century plan of bringing London's administration under the control of an expanded City Corporation. When this scheme lapsed the Conservatives seized their opportunity to create a Council that was initially hardly more formidable than the Metropolitan Board of Works. It possessed no planning or welfare responsibilities whatsoever, while its housing powers, like those of the Board, were confined to slum clearance. The voters did not contain their indifference; even at the first election there was a low poll, returning a majority of 'Progressive' councillors who duly applied themselves to such tasks as bringing London's gas, electricity and water supplies under municipal control.

The work was not glamorous, but then neither were the men who undertook it. When the Moderate (Conservative) Party gained seats at the 1895 London election, Mrs Beatrice Webb, whose socialist principles never quite mastered her patrician instincts, noted that 'the Moderate victories have raised the standard of good looks of the London County Council. Slim aristocrats, well-fed and slightly dissipated-looking frequenters of London drawing rooms and clubs, are, from the scenic point of view, welcome contrasts to the stunted figures of the Labour representatives and the ungraceful corpulence of the Progressive men of business.'

The grey image of the 'gas and water socialists' was in no wise dissipated by their crusading teetotalism or by their inflexible abjuration of all pomp and ceremony. How different they were in this respect from the City rulers, whose enduring privileges they bitterly resented: as late as 1914 the President of the Council and the Lord Mayor engaged in an undignified public scuffle over precedence. Lacking the City's traditions, the Council badly needed panache in order to impress itself on the consciousness of Londoners: the dominant spirit of Puritan self-denial did nothing for public relations. The initial indifference of voters soon hardened into an enduring apathy about the whole process of London government, and the radical impulse evaporated. In 1907 the Moderates won a majority which they were not to lose for another twenty-seven years.

The achievements of the Progressives had been moderate enough in all conscience, but their activities had attracted the deepest suspicions of Lord Salisbury, the Conservative Prime Minister. In 1897 he denounced the London County

Council (the LCC) as 'the place where collectivist and socialistic experiments are tried . . . where a new revolutionary spirit finds its instruments and collects its arms'. A *Punch* cartoon of that year showed the 'Salisbury Frankenstein' addressing the 'Municipal Monster': 'Sorry I ever put you together you great horrid booby! But just you wait a bit. I'll soon take you to pieces again.' And, sure enough, in 1899 the Conservatives applied the principle of 'divide and rule' with Machiavellian cunning. In place of the forty-one almost powerless parish vestries and district boards which had hitherto formed the local structure of the County's administration, they created twenty-eight metropolitan boroughs which were given responsibilities filched from the LCC. The effect was to set up a two-tier system of government which made it even harder for the LCC to put into practice any coherent policy over the entire capital. Two generations later, after London's phenomenal growth had necessitated extending its government to a wider area, the Conservatives, whether by design or no, followed a markedly similar strategy. In replacing the LCC with the Greater London Council with effect from 1965 they enlarged still further the size of the constituent boroughs, which were given so much control over housing and planning within their separate areas that critics of the GLC may be forgiven for wondering precisely what it finds for its myriad employees at County Hall to do. Certainly, as we shall see, it has been conspicuously ineffective in its allotted role of overall planning supervisor.

From the start London government had only a slight influence on the town's physical development. The LCC actually had fewer street schemes to its credit than the much despised Metropolitan Board of Works. Indeed the creation of Kingsway and Aldwych (opened in 1905) remained the sole major twentieth-century public improvement in central London (unless one counts the destruction of Rennie's Waterloo Bridge as an improvement) until the Hyde Park Corner underpass was built in 1962. The Kingsway and Aldwych project, moreover, was carried out in the classic Metropolitan Board of Works vein, the roads being driven through slums and the adjoining sites entrusted to developers. For the most part the buildings attempted an imperial grandeur, the pomposity of which only serves to underline their designers' lack of inspiration.

Unhappily this 'Wrenaissance' style (as some wag

The Greater London Council's area, created in 1965, showing the constituent boroughs. The shaded section, Inner London, corresponds to the former London County Council's area.

christened it) became the accepted mode for large office and shop buildings until after the Second World War, to the virtual exclusion of the modern movement in architecture. In Kingsway only the relatively plain and unadorned Kodak House (1911) pointed the way to the future, although the American Bush House in Aldwych deserves a mention as the first London office building to adopt the open plan system. Elsewhere, Heals (1916) in the Tottenham Court Road, Peter Jones (1935) at Sloane Square, the Express building (1931) in Fleet Street, HMV (1938–9) in Oxford Street, and Barkers (1937) in Kensington High Street were rare exceptions to the rule of a bland and sterile orthodoxy.

TRAMS, TUBES AND BUSES

Kingsway was modern enough in one sense, however, in that its construction had included a subway through to the Embankment, which is now used by motor traffic but was originally built for trams. Since its introduction to the suburbs in the 1870s the tram had proved immensely successful. The relatively light friction of wheels on rails enabled horses to pull twice the load that they could draw on an omnibus, a formula which resulted in considerably lower fares. The very cheapness and popularity of the trams, though, had caused them to be dubbed 'working man's transport' and had inspired a determined campaign to keep central London free of their proletarian taint. The Kingsway subway in fact made possible the first through route by tram between north and south London.

By that time, however, a new form of traction was in use. Profitable though the first trams were, the high cost of keeping horses had encouraged continual experiments with other sources of power. Any number of strange devices appeared in London, the most bizarre being a clockwork tram which was wound up by a steam engine before setting on its way. The eventual solution was the electric tram, which was developed in America during the 1880s although, due to LCC laggardness, it did not run in London until 1901.

It is said that Frank Sprague, the American inventor who made electric traction practical, had been mightily encouraged in his work by being exposed to the suffocating fumes on the steam-powered London underground. Of course electric locomotion presented an ideal answer to this problem. Yet oddly enough the first deep tube, which opened in 1890 between the City and Stockwell (and is now a branch of the Northern line), had been projected without it. Only when tunnelling was nearly complete were plans for a cable train abandoned in favour of electric engines, one of which can be seen in the Science Museum. The tube was privately financed: the LCC had no involvement with public transport beyond an unsuccessful steamboat service and some tramlines, including an experimental system which regularly gave shocks to unwary pedestrians. Due to various technical difficulties the Stockwell line did not make money, and its investors may or may not have drawn solace from the knowledge that the experience gained had paved the way for the success of the next venture.

Even so, the public was understandably cautious about putting up money for another tube, and it needed a team of international financiers to raise the £3·7 million required to build the Central line from Bank to Shepherd's Bush. This line opened in 1900, with an extension to the White City being added five years later in aid of the Anglo-French exhibition being held there. The promoters were nervous about the effect of the tube on buildings above and therefore took the route under roads all the way: in some places (at Notting Hill Gate and Chancery Lane stations for example) the easterly and westerly tracks were placed on top of each other instead of side by side in order not to transgress the narrow bounds of the road overhead. Although property owners along the length of the way still complained about vibrations from the heavy locomotives, the Central line was soon making a handsome profit.

And there the story of London tubes might have rested, but for the intervention of one of the most rugged of all the rugged individuals who have guided London's destiny. Only in its rawest phase could American capitalism have produced a man capable of expressing his business philosophy with the succinctness of Charles Tyson Yerkes. His line, he proclaimed, was to 'buy up old junk, fix it up a little and unload it upon other fellows'. There, in a sentence, is distilled the essential purity of the entrepreneurial spirit. Maybe the sheer economy of style was too much for his compatriots. At any rate, when Yerkes tried his hand at stock-broking and banking they put him in prison; and when he turned his attention to organizing trams and railways in Chicago they came for him with nooses and guns just because the odd financial detail needed sorting out. What could a man do in the circumstances but sell out, and if the shares for which he received twenty million dollars turned out to be valueless, how could he be held responsible for a company no longer under his guiding hand? Still, this career had left the problem of how to spend the money.

Yerkes was by no means at a loss, for his attitude to women was far from Victorian. But nothing seemed to suit his talents so well as arranging the finance for new tubes in London. His penetration of this alien territory began in 1900 when he engaged the confidence of a highly moral Methodist called Perks, secretary to the Metropolitan Railway Company. The Yerkes–Perks alliance, however, was only a beginning. In the five years remaining to him, the quiet evening of his days, Yerkes contrived to form the United

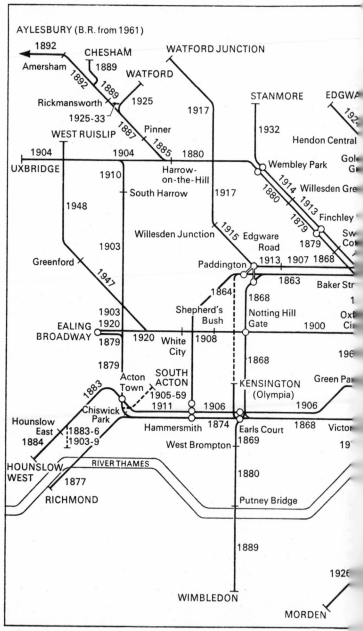

The London Underground system, with dates of the lines' openings.

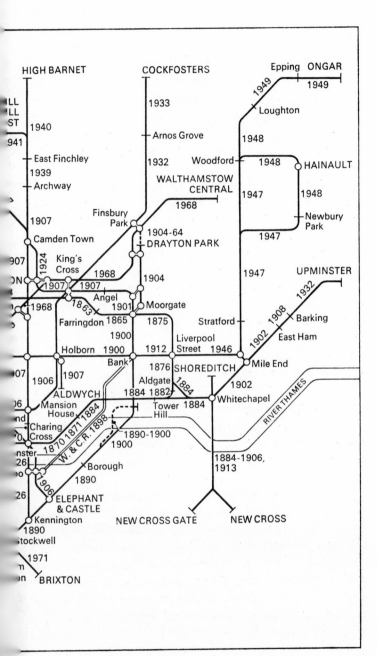

Electric Railways Company, raise millions of pounds through the most artful share issues, scotch a rival scheme for tubes backed by the American banking house of Morgan, run rings round LCC committees, electrify the Metropolitan, and build the Bakerloo, Northern and Piccadilly lines. At the end of 1905 he went on to a better world via the New York Waldorf, just as shareholders were beginning to wonder what they had let themselves in for.

Anyone inclined to underestimate Yerkes's achievement should consider the long-drawn-out saga of the Victoria line, which originated as an anonymous 'Route 8' in a government report of 1946, moved up to a likely looking 'Route C' in another report a few years later, was finally given the go-ahead in 1962 and opened in 1968–9. Thus despite the wonders of modern technology the period of construction alone took as long as the whole gamut of Yerkes's transactions.

As it happened, the speed of Yerkes's operations turned out to have been crucial to London's development. His tubes naturally had a profound effect on the direction of suburban expansion, as can be seen from before-and-after pictures of places like Golders Green. It is doubtful, though, whether even a man of Yerkes's gifts could have raised money for tubes a few years later, when the motor bus began to come into its own.

In fact, petrol-engined buses had run between Kennington and Victoria in 1899, before Yerkes's day, but he was saved by the delay in producing a reliable model. As late as 1905 a tramway manager could show scant respect for the rival conveyance. 'I have no sympathy with the archaic bus – it is an anachronism and is looked on more or less as a fit object for a museum and not for public service.' That was fair comment on the horse-buses which by their very number (in 1900 almost 700 passed the Bank of England every hour) had been largely responsible for the dreadful Victorian traffic jams, but it was tempting fate to make such a remark in the very year that a fleet of moderately efficient motor buses came into service. These early models tended to be handicapped by their drivers, ex-horse-bus men with mechanical leanings which eventually had to be discouraged by locking the engines away from their tender care. But horse-buses were seen no more in London after 1911, and eventually the confident tram was also to fall victim to its despised adversary, although it did not finally go out of service until 1952.

Even Yerkes's tubes were being supported by buses after the First World War when bus routes began to spread out all over the suburbs. The financial link between the two systems dated from 1912 when the United Electric Railways Company shrewdly absorbed London General, the main bus concern and the one which, in 1907, had started the tradition of red buses. In those days, however, anyone could run a bus in London, and passengers suffered from maverick operators who were inclined to abandon a route in mid-journey if they saw promise of more fares in the opposite direction. There were few regrets when all the capital's transport services were brought under monopoly control of a public corporation, the London Passenger Transport Board, in 1933.

LONDON'S AREA QUADRUPLED

Although the London County Council had no control over the Transport Board, it had by this time greatly extended its powers in other fields. The necessities of the First World War set precedents for widespread government action, and afterwards far more effective housing policies prevailed under the driving influence of the 'Homes for Heroes' campaign. Whereas the LCC had originally been obliged to make its housing schemes self-financing – indeed the housing account actually showed a profit before 1914 – now it could recoup nearly all expenditure on houses from the national government. Within a year the LCC had built as many houses as in its entire previous history; and between the wars it established fifteen new estates in the outer suburbs. The largest, with a population by the late 1930s of over 100000 (twice as many as London itself before 1500), was at Becontree, a model of drab civic endeavour plumped down on the Essex flats. These estates, with their two-storey 'cottage' housing, individual gardens and open space, were municipal expressions of the garden suburb ideals first practised at Bedford Park (from 1875) just north of Turnham Green station in Acton, and later, from 1907, at Hampstead Garden suburb, which proved particularly influential. But the old slums often seemed pretty cosy after a couple of years in a place like Becontree where, under LCC auspices, pubs became 'licensed refreshment houses'.

Hampstead Garden suburb was an early sign that there were planners abroad in the land, a manifestation further witnessed by an Act of 1909 which gave councils certain minimal powers to regulate the laying out of the new suburbs. The planners formed their ideas in shocked re-action to the horrors of Victorian industrial slums: in that bright dawn of their movement, utopia itself seemed scarcely more than the product of sensible regulation. After all, one of the apostles of planning confidently explained in 1917, *this* generation 'no longer believe with Karl Marx in the class war . . . we aim at a gradual ordering; we demand intelligent co-operation'. But the planners' theoretical flights still took wing from the secure base of practical impotence. Not until 1932 did the LCC acquire any measure of control over the manner of redevelopment in the centre of town, and even then it was rarely able to enforce its will. Since ownership of land was deemed to include control of its development potential as well, the LCC had to pay compensation when imposing restrictions. So powers to protect historic buildings, for example, were useless without adequate funds. During the 1930s the old aristocratic houses of Mayfair still came tumbling down; and Park Lane, Kensington Square and Berkeley Square had their Georgian façades rudely interrupted by modern blocks of flats.

At least, though, one planning ideal was involuntarily fulfilled: Londoners obtained more space. Whereas in 1918 the metropolis was still contained within a circle of roughly six miles' radius, by 1939 the suburbs stretched out another seven to eleven miles, and further along the main roads and railways. (The Metropolitan railway, indeed, was itself, through a subsidiary company, responsible for building estates beside its lines to Amersham and to Uxbridge, giving that district the name 'Metroland'. In all, the urban area quadrupled between the wars, while its overall population increased only about 10 per cent. By the 1930s most 'Londoners' were living outside the LCC's bounds.

Nowadays the endless stretches of two-storey semi-detached houses are unblushingly condemned by planners as being wasteful of space in their layout, while the many styles of architecture on view, whether neo-Tudor, neo-Jacobean, neo-Queen Anne, neo-Georgian, neo-modern or simply 'Olde World', excite only the freakish fancy. Superior persons may perhaps wonder what private hells of loneliness and repression have been engendered behind those constantly twitching curtains, in streets so racked by petty snobbery and genteel affectation that even bicycling to work could be a social stigma. Nevertheless, the inter-war suburbs brought the possibility of owning a decent house and garden within reach of Londoners who previously could not have dreamt of such a luxury. Three-quarters of the 700 000-odd houses built in outer London between the wars were private builders' speculations, offered for sale at prices which, particularly in the 1930s, were astonishingly cheap even by the standards of salaries then prevailing. It was possible to buy a tiny two-bedroomed house for as little as £345, involving only fifty (new) pence a week mortgage repayments. A schoolmaster on £6·95 a week might afford a four-bedroomed house with a good-sized sitting room and garage at £850, accommodation way beyond the means of his 1970s equivalent.

Between 1921 and 1937 these prices tempted 1·4 million into the outer suburbs. In 1935, Herbert Morrison, leader of the recently returned Labour majority in the LCC, announced that the Council would pay half the cost of any land acquired by local authorities to establish a 'green belt or girdle of open space lands, not necessarily continuous, but as readily accessible from the completely urbanized area of London as practicable'. This was the most far-sighted piece of planning the LCC ever had to its credit, but the old bugbear of compensation prevented the acquisition of more than a few isolated patches, as sellers held out for the full building development value. The pace of building slackened after 1936, but only because the most pressing demand had been temporarily satisfied. Without the intervention of Adolf Hitler, the councils could never have contained suburban growth at the limits reached in 1939. After the Führer's decease, the Town and Country Planning Act of 1947 carried on the good work by establishing a new system of compensation which enabled the councils to make the Green Belt inviolable.

WORLD WAR II AND THE BOMBING OF LONDON

Hitler's war saved the Green Belt; his decision to bomb London may well have saved England. In August 1940 the German Air Force was ordered to eliminate British air power as a preliminary to invasion, and attacked the airfields south of London to such effect that the British air command began to doubt its capacity to continue the struggle. During that month the British, despite successes against bombers, lost twice as many fighters as the Germans, and fighters were England's only remaining defence. The battle only turned decisively against the Luftwaffe after it switched the attack from the airfields on to London at the beginning of September. The reasons for this change of strategy are not clear. Hitler claimed it was an act of reprisal for the British bombing of Berlin. Goering, the Luftwaffe's commander, evidently believed that he could terrorize the civilian population into demanding surrender. All that is certain is that the relief of pressure on the airfields enabled the RAF to fight back with such success in September that, on the 17th, Hitler postponed the projected invasion. So London did not suffer in vain.

All this, of course, is the wisdom of hindsight: Londoners who watched their homes being blasted to pieces had no knowledge of these stategic considerations, and might have been forgiven for finding small comfort in them even if they had. Before the war London had been universally recognized as England's exposed jugular. No great city had ever been subjected to prolonged and massive air attacks and all the best-informed expectations were of total destruction. The Zeppelin raids in the First World War had caused almost 5000 casualties in Britain; military experts predicted that with the vastly increased bombing potential which had been developed since then there would be 600000 dead and twice that number wounded in London within six months of the outbreak of war. At the same time, psychiatrists assured the government that three or four million others would be crazed by fear and panic.

London was to all intents and purposes defenceless, as the policy of evacuating women and children at the beginning of the war tacitly acknowledged. (In fact, as almost a year went by without any bombing nearly all the evacuees returned, preferring like good Londoners to take their chance in the town rather than expose themselves any longer to the rigours of the English countryside.) If the fighters did not stop the bombers – and at night they very rarely did – there was nothing to be done except seek shelter and trust in the blackout. But London could not be hidden – even if when the Crystal Palace burnt down in 1936 there were wild rumours that it had been deliberately set alight in order to remove an obvious direction-finder. On wet moonlit nights the streets showed up with perfect clarity, and at other times flares and incendiaries helped to spotlight the target areas. As for the anti-aircraft barrage, it might have been good for morale, but more Londoners were killed by falling shrapnel than Germans by shells. Luftwaffe pilots threatened by RAF fighters would deliberately fly back into the 'safety' zone of anti-aircraft range.

From 7 September until 3 November 1940 London was attacked every night but one; thereafter, apart from a lull in February 1941, raids were regular until 16 May, when Hitler withdrew the Luftwaffe for service on the Russian front. If the intention had been to stun the population into submission the bombardment proved entirely counter-productive, as, incidentally, did the later Allied air attacks on Berlin and other cities. Far from turning into gibbering neurotic wrecks in line with psychiatric predictions,

Londoners actually began to shed their neuroses. Not only did total strangers risk their lives for one another; they even managed to talk to each other. As long as the bombs fell, all those nice distinctions of class and status which the English are wont to measure so carefully before committing themselves to anything as daring as a 'Good morning' were swept aside. The novelist Elizabeth Bowen has put the matter more imaginatively: 'There was a diffused gallantry in the atmosphere, an unmarriedness: it came to be rumoured about the country, among the self-banished, the uneasy, the put-upon and the safe, that everybody in London was in love – which was true, if not in the sense the country meant.'

The only sign of a crack in morale was after the earliest raids, the effects of which appeared to justify the gloomy pre-war forecasts. The whole of dockland was set ablaze and acres of slum housing pulverized. In the first ten hours of attack on 7/8 September 1000 were killed, and many times that number injured. A particularly appalling tragedy occurred in West Ham on the night of 9 September. Four hundred and fifty of those rendered homeless on the previous nights had been shepherded into a school right in the middle of the target area. Buses to remove them were promised but failed to turn up for twenty-four hours or so due to administrative blunders. When they finally did arrive the sirens were sounding warning of another raid and the evacuation was further postponed. The delay was fatal: the school was razed and everyone in it perished.

Ugly rumours permeated the unscathed clubs of Mayfair. 'Everybody is worried about the feeling in the East End', recorded Harold Nicolson in his diary. 'There is much bitterness. It is said that the king and queen were booed when they visited the destroyed areas.' Possibly if the Germans had continued to attack dockland exclusively they might have fanned this resentment into a dangerous revolt against the government. But on 13 September the social bonds were tightened when Buckingham Palace was bombed and the king and queen only narrowly escaped. Thereafter, although the East End and the City continued to bear the brunt of the attack, there was at least some community of suffering. Revolutionary sentiment was at a discount when bombs dropped on the Café de Paris in full swing as well as on the slums of Stepney.

The spirit affected was one of plucky nonchalance – 'that 'Itler'll get 'imself disliked if 'e goes on like this'. Most Londoners never bothered to seek shelter. A few (about 4 per cent) crowded into the tubes, even sleeping between the rails after the current was turned off at 10.30, a resting place well designed to encourage early rising as the trains started up again at dawn. In fact even the tubes were not necessarily safe: over 100 were killed when Bank station was hit, and at Balham shelterers were drowned by a burst water main.

Altogether about 20000 died and another 25000 were hurt in the London blitz between September 1940 and May 1941. Such figures were terrible enough, but infinitely fewer than pre-war projections. The deaths worked out at about one for every ton of explosive dropped, instead of the predicted sixteen fatalities for this amount. Again, though, hindsight diminishes the ordeal. In May 1941 it must have seemed likely that the bombing would go on until London was entirely flattened. The April raids had included the heaviest yet experienced, and the Germans were developing far more destructive bombs than they dropped at the beginning of the blitz. Who was to know that when the 'all clear' sounded on 16 May London's trial was over until the rocket attacks of 1944–5? It is the absence of any reasonable grounds for hope which makes the good-humoured endurance of Londoners so remarkable.

There is a photograph of St Paul's rising unscathed above the smoke and fire which movingly symbolizes the town's indestructible spirit. Anyone in search of a miracle could do worse than ponder the survival of St Paul's. Nearly all buildings around the cathedral were annihilated. On 12 September 1940 a bomb landed near the south-west tower and penetrated to a depth of twenty-seven feet without exploding. On 16 April 1941 a large landmine, powerful enough of itself to wreck the cathedral completely, came to rest a few feet from the north-east end of the cathedral but again did not go off. When the bomb-disposal experts were working on it a fire engine driven fast between Cheapside and Cannon Street set the magnetic fuse ticking . . . for a while.

But the escape which made the greatest impression on the members of the St Paul's Watch, who protected the building throughout the blitz, came during the Great Fire of 29 December when an incendiary bomb lodged in the dome. It thus threatened the cathedral at its most combustible point, since there is a complex of original wooden beams between the outer dome and its smaller counterpart seen from within the church. As the incendiary was out of reach the fire-watchers could only await the conflagration which would inevitably follow when it dropped through the melting lead. Suddenly, for no apparent reason, the bomb fell outwards on to the Stone Gallery where it was easily put out. After which it seems anti-climactic to mention that St Paul's *did* receive two direct hits, one which lifted off some of the choir roof and the other which exploded inside the north transept, blowing the walls six inches and more out of alignment. But the great church did not fall. Just what it meant to Londoners was movingly expressed by a woman from Bethnal Green who recorded her memories of 29 December 1940 thus: 'I went up on the roof with some of the firemen, to look at the City. And I've always remembered how I was choked, I think I was crying a little. I could see St Paul's standing there, and the fire all around, and I just said: "Please God, don't let it go." I couldn't help it, I felt that if St Paul's had gone, something would have gone from us. But it stood in defiance, it did. And when the boys were coming back, the firemen said: "It's bad, but, oh, the old church stood it." Lovely, that was.'

PLANNING HOPES UNREALIZED

So Wren's cathedral proved more fortunate than its predecessor in the Great Fire of 1666. Within the City 225 acres were devastated by the blitz compared with 437 acres destroyed three centuries previously. But of course the damage covered an infinitely wider area than the City: much of Stepney, Poplar and Bermondsey had been laid waste, and the total reconstruction required was certainly more than that after the Fire. Moreover the government seemed far better equipped to seize the opportunity presented, for at last the planners had come into their own.

An Act of 1944 had given local authorities the right compulsorily to purchase blitzed areas, and the City had acquired 115 acres, including much of the present Barbican site, under this law. (To the City's chagrin it had to accept LCC participation in the planning of this area, but the resulting scheme showed considerable imagination. While the southern part of the Barbican was given up to commerce, the northern was reserved for residential use. The City, where numbers had declined more sharply than anywhere else, thus became the only part of central London where this population trend was reversed during the twentieth century.) Besides the right of compulsory purchase the LCC and the boroughs were also given comprehensive powers of control over all private redevelopment in their areas; and for good measure the Labour government added a 100-per-cent tax on all developers' profits.

It seemed, in fact, as though the LCC would be in firm control of the future planning not just of the blitzed parts but of London as a whole. And the planners were prepared for the challenge. Two reports produced in 1943-4 by Professor Patrick Abercrombie, an acknowledged guru of early twentieth-century planning, had laid down firm guidelines for the future of the capital. Away with dirty polluting industries – commerce too for that matter – from residential districts; let a further million leave inner London that there might be more space for housing and for parks; develop new towns outside the Green Belt to absorb these emigrants. The crisp, confident prescriptions left no room for uncertainty.

Yet more than thirty years later, when many of Abercrombie's objectives have been achieved, the ungrateful Londoners do not, apparently, appreciate the results. In fact most of them (if a 1976 poll is to be believed) want to leave. Moreover, the physical appearance of the town bears few traces of a master guiding hand. One may like or loathe the individual tower blocks that have sprouted up since the 1950s, but not even the greatest enthusiast could claim that their positioning betrays any predominant influence. Compare the vista presented by the modern city with Canaletto's eighteenth-century view of Wren's steeples and the failure of planning becomes positively glaring.

What on earth went wrong? The planners might claim that they have not, after all, had sufficient powers. Inevitably there has been a lack of consistency in the attitudes of different governments towards developers. After the war the Labour government strictly limited all redevelopment to work on bombed sites and government offices. Then in the early fifties the returning Tories, committed to 'setting the people free', made an early start with property developers. Labour building restrictions were removed (1954) and Mr Macmillan, in abandoning the development tax (1953), allowed himself a little homily on the virtues of private enterprise. 'The people whom the government must help', he opined, 'are those who do things: the developers, the people who create wealth, whether humble or exalted.' Still, however, the LCC retained its formidable powers of control. All redevelopment was conditional on Council permission, and compulsory purchase remained as a means of dealing with landowners who obstructed its schemes. But in the event all these weapons proved insufficient. Though the LCC had all power so that it could move mountains, and had not money, it was nothing.

In the post-war years, as before, the unchallengeable first priority was housing, and in this field the LCC could boast impressive achievements, architectural and social, not least in bombed-out Stepney and Poplar. Only exceptionally could the Council afford to undertake other kinds of building, such as the Royal Festival Hall erected on the south bank for the Festival of Britain in 1951. The adjoining Queen Elizabeth Hall and Purcell Room did not open until 1968, and the National Theatre (largely government-financed) not until 1976, while the huge Greater London Council site to the west of the Festival Hall is still vacant in the late seventies.

But the Council's committal of its resources to housing does not explain why the authorities failed to keep a tighter rein on private development. The approach of planning departments during the 1950s and 1960s suggested that they still subscribed to the notion that a man's land was his to use as he would. The law now stated otherwise, but the *laissez-faire* tradition died hard. There was also a feeling that the post-war reconstruction of London could not be indefinitely postponed by planning wrangles. And of course private developers were only too willing to make a contribution.

THE GOLDEN YEARS FOR PROPERTY DEVELOPERS (1954–64)

Many property men had had a good war, picking up prime sites at ridiculously cheap prices. The story goes that one practitioner used to ring up his agents with words of encouragement after heavy raids – 'Did you hear the bombs last night? There must be some bargains around this morning.' And it was not just the war which had brought land on to the market, to be snapped up by budding Barbons. The old London estate owners – the Bedfords, Portmans, Portlands and their like – were being forced to sell by crippling death duties. In 1953, on the death of the second Duke of Westminster, the Grosvenors had to pay £20 million, a tax bill they were able to meet through having sold their Pimlico domain three years previously. Even so, the Grosvenors still possess far more London property than any other private family, with ninety acres in Mayfair and twice that amount in Belgravia. Their Mayfair holding includes the site of the United States Embassy (1958–61), which the Americans tried to buy in the early 1950s. The Duke of Westminster showed himself ready to deal, but on one condition: the return of 12000 Grosvenor acres in East Florida 'confiscated by the American nation at the time of the war of independence'. Since this land appeared to include Cape Kennedy, negotiations broke down.

Generally, though, there was no shortage of property for developers to buy after the war; no shortage either, once controls had been removed, of reward for their efforts.

When Harold Samuel bought a property company called Land Securities in 1943, the previous annual report had stated somewhat forlornly that 'the only real estate of the company now comprises three houses in Kensington, two of which, the directors regret to state, are unoccupied'. Twenty-five years later the assets of Land Securities amounted to £28 million. Another company, Oldham Estates, possessed property valued at £22 328 in 1959, when it was taken over by Harry Hyams, and more than £46 million in 1967.

Extraordinarily, so far from attempting to enter such a profitable field for themselves, the local authorities, government and even private landlords rushed to put more business the developers' way. All five of the great office blocks flanking London Wall to the east of the Museum of London were built by property men on land leased from the City – and the profits ranged from £1·4 to £2·9 million per building. The government likewise called upon developers to build offices. And though the Cadogan estate erected the Carlton Towers Hotel off Sloane Street, the old landowners were usually too conservative to exploit the potential of their depleted lands without assistance. One developer, Max Rayne, was able to specialize in leading estates towards the modern Eldorado. In 1958 he built Eastbourne Terrace by Paddington station for the Church of England, pocketing a cool £2·9 million (half the profit) on a project in which he personally invested a mere £1000. Rayne also put his expensive services at the disposal of the Portman estate.

Almost any development paid in the 1950s and 1960s, but none so well as tall office blocks. One would hardly imagine, to look at London's skyline, that the 1939 London Building Act had limited the heights of buildings to 100 feet, or eighty feet where the ground area exceeded 10 000 square feet – 'unless the Council otherwise consent'. Clearly there has been a whole lot of consenting. Indeed, in the 1950s and 1960s the LCC's own housing policies hardly strengthened its ability to refuse. For this was the age of the tower block council building, extolled by planners of the day as 'vertical streets' that made possible open space at ground level. This particular vogue was already under attack when a 'vertical street' called Ronan Point in the East End made a sudden shift to the horizontal, killing several of its inmates in the process. After that the fashion in council estates changed to lower groupings of buildings, with emphasis on the separateness of each house. Lillington Gardens estate (1972), off the Vauxhall Bridge Road, is an outstanding example of this new genre.

In 1960 the government itself had contributed towards the general acceptance of high buildings by allowing Basil Spence to design a tower block at Knightsbridge barracks (although they were not in fact erected until 1967–70). This was a breach of a cardinal principal, also defied at that time by the Hilton Hotel (1962), that no skyscrapers should overlook the parks.

But it was the LCC's inability to afford land for road schemes which really put the planners in the developers' pockets. In such instances there was a more or less straight deal between the two interests. The essence of the bargain was that the developers bought up the land required for the new roads and gave it to the LCC; in return the Council proved remarkably amenable with planning permission on any adjoining land owned or controlled by their benefactor. This is what happened in the most notorious case of all, the building of Centre Point at the intersection of Tottenham Court Road and Oxford Street. In the late 1950s the LCC found their plan for a huge roundabout there being thwarted by the Pearlmans, directors of the Ve-ri-best Manufacturing Company (in fact a property concern) which owned the land that was required. The Pearlmans laughed at the LCC offer of £55000, the highest that the Council was em- powered to make, and successfully parried attempts to gain possession of the land by compulsion. Just when all seemed lost for the LCC, help arrived from the generous hands of Harry Hyams Esq., the doyen of developers, who proceeded to buy out the Pearlmans for half a million and to collect several adjacent properties, eventually handing over £1·5 million worth of land to the Council. He then rented back the entire area, including some extra land that had been bought by the LCC, on a 150-year lease at the more than reasonable rent of £18 500 per annum. Part of this plot was reserved for the traffic scheme, but Hyams received what he most prized, namely permission to erect a thirty-five- storey office block.

After these negotiations the economics were simple: construction costs amounted to £3·5 million, including interest on borrowed money; the finished building was worth about £17 million by 1968; and the net profit at that date was over £11 million. Even that did not satisfy Hyams: the building remained empty for years while he waited for rents to rise with inflation and establish a still higher capital value. But the best bit comes last. The GLC never built the roundabout due to the introduction of a one-way traffic system.

A broadly similar 'exchange' of planning permission and developers' cash for road schemes was responsible for several other tower blocks, including the Euston Centre (where the LCC received £2 million worth of land and Joe Levy's company, Stock Conversion and Investment Trust, made an estimated £22 million development profit), Stag Place in Victoria and Camden Towers in Notting Hill Gate. The Bowater building in Knightsbridge, though less tall, belongs to the same category.

The acknowledged master of this type of development is the architect Richard Seifert, a man who knows every planning regulation inside out and who has again and again squeezed every last cubic foot of permitted space out of the LCC and the GLC. 'We shall be glad to discuss any amendments,' he decently informed the Council when sending in the planning application for Centre Point, 'but it is most important that the bulk of the building should not be reduced.' It is Seifert's way with planners, no less than his architectural talents, which has given him more influence over the London skyline than any man since Wren. Besides Centre Point (completed in 1967), he has been responsible for the circular Space House (1968) in Kingsway; the Drapers Gardens tower (1965) in Throgmorton Avenue; the Park Tower Hotel in Knightsbridge (1972); London's tallest building, the streamlined 638-foot National Westminster tower (under construction 1977) in Bishopsgate, and many others.

Seifert's work for developers has laid him open to charges of creating commercial packages rather than buildings to delight the eye, although there is no reason why the two should be incompatible. It may safely be assumed, though, that developers are unlikely to allow their concern for appearances to override their hopes of profit. Mr Charles Clore, for example, has said that he does not believe in great architectural triumphs which end up in bankruptcy, and the design of the Hilton Hotel shows him to be a man of his word. Perhaps it is not coincidence that some of London's more interesting post-war buildings have been commissioned by their eventual occupiers rather than put up as speculations by developers. These include: Thorn House (1959) in Upper St Martin's Lane; British Leyland – formerly Castrol – House in the Marylebone Road; New Zealand House (1963) at the corner of Haymarket and Pall

Mall; Vickers House (1963) on Millbank; the *Economist*'s offices (1964) in St James's Street; the Post Office Tower (1965) in Cleveland Street, the Commercial Union and P & O buildings (1969) off Leadenhall Street; and the Heart of Oak Building Society's head office (1970) opposite St Pancras Church in the Euston Road. Shell's headquarters (1962) on the south bank must be counted as an exception which proves the rule.

THE DEVELOPERS ATTACKED: PLANNING PARALYSIS

By 1963 it was beginning to dawn on Londoners that the sky-scrapers, though hardly worthy of the name by New York standards, were profoundly changing the aspect of the town. Wren's St Paul's had always been the tallest building in London before the Hilton Hotel rose up between 1961 and 1963, but thereafter it was eclipsed by another tower almost every year. Such a transformation was bound to provoke opposition, which was only intensified by rumours of the developers' mammoth profits. All over London residents' associations, preservation societies and other groups sprang up to defend their inheritance. At the same time the property men, lured on by avarice, began to entertain wilder and wilder notions. No landmark was too famous to be spared the peril of their attention. During the 1960s there were schemes abroad which contemplated the demolition of St Pancras station, the Foreign Office in Whitehall, Tower Bridge, and even the Houses of Parliament.

As the conflict between the conservationists and developers waxed ever fiercer, the Greater London Council and the boroughs, which shared responsibility for giving planning permissions, were caught in the cross-fire. It was an invidious position and the departments concerned sought refuge in a reassessment of their functions, enshrining the results of these cogitations in a brand-new piece of jargon. 'Social planning', as it is called, involves an elaborate parade of caution designed to neutralize objections by deferring decisions until every interest has been consulted and every option considered. So the number of planners multiplied even as their confidence decreased. Whereas Professor Abercrombie had felt able to prepare his prescriptions for London's future in a year with a mere nine assistants, a GLC team of hundreds laboured four years (1965-9) to produce its report on the same subject. After that their conclusions were thrown open to public enquiry (1969-73); then the Department of the Environment considered the enquiry for three more years; and finally, in 1976, the 'modified plan' was published – against a background of public indifference.

Of course no amount of attention to detail can ever hope to satisfy every interest in such a vastly complex organism as London. A new factory will please some by creating employment, antagonize others by spoiling the environment. Better roads will put house prices up in some areas and depress them elsewhere – and so on. Far from speaking in a voice like thunder, *vox populi* emits a thousand contradictory crackles. 'Social planning', in fact, can all too easily mean paralysis and stagnation, as has been demonstrated at Piccadilly Circus and Covent Garden.

The future of Piccadilly Circus was almost settled without either public involvement or knowledge in 1959 when the LCC actually approved a project presented by the developer Jack Cotton, subject only to final confirmation when some trifling technicality about parking had been sorted out. Cotton, however, suffered from the fatal handicap of being proud of his work, and insisted on showing off his plans at a press conference before the final go-ahead had been given.

His model provoked such universal horror that the Minister of Housing was obliged to intervene and veto the scheme. Thereafter the LCC and its successor, the Greater London Council, toyed with a series of ideas before shovelling responsibility for the circus on to Westminster City Council. In 1972, just when the tide was running the conservationists' way, Westminster produced plans for a joint project with developers that scored the distinction of arousing even greater public hostility than had Cotton. Since that traumatic experience Westminster has played it safe, tentatively suggesting various options and gauging public reaction. Now the circus is to be renovated rather than rebuilt.

Public participation has also undermined the planners' original ideas at Covent Garden. In anticipation of the market's removal to Nine Elms in 1974 the Greater London Council produced an extensive scheme of reconstruction that appeared to many as a threat to the area's special, somewhat bohemian, character. The proposals were duly savaged by local community groups and the national press alike, so in 1976 the GLC published another plan which in effect abandoned ideas of comprehensive redevelopment in favour of piecemeal action, with emphasis on preserving Covent Garden's flavour through policies of gradual rehabilitation rather than wholesale destruction.

At least, it might be urged, disaster has been avoided at Piccadilly and Covent Garden, and the victories of local pressure groups over government bureaucrats are certainly in the individualist London tradition. If social planning means paralysis, would that it had caught on earlier anyone looking around London can find places where it might have been applied with advantage. At Elephant and Castle, for instance, the LCC built a shopping precinct of such ghastliness that the popularity of the nearby markets of Walworth and the New Kent Road noticeably increased.

Yet planners do, after all, have an immense potential for good as well as for bad, as is shown by the west end of Victoria Street, where buildings have recently been demolished to provide a splendid prospect of the Roman Catholic Westminster Cathedral, which was built between 1895 and 1903 in the architect Bentley's mixture of Byzantine and Italianate styles, but which has only now been properly exposed to public view. Moreover, moving east from the cathedral, the new south side of Victoria Street, with its broken skyline and distinct design up to and including the Army and Navy Stores, presents a lively façade, the more especially in contrast to the dull slabs opposite. Such achievements get ignored in the universal zest for criticism. The public has lost trust in the planning departments to such an extent that foiling their schemes has come to be regarded as almost an end in itself.

Nothing better illustrates the manner in which the crazily rational world of planning ideals ran foul of the muddled and divided aspirations of millions of Londoners than the controversy over new roads. Driving roads through the hearts of towns has a natural appeal to the more megalomaniac planning intelligence: it is enormously expensive, highly destructive work that can nearly always be justified according to some economic argument or other. Abercrombie's report set the post-war pace. This being the 'age of mobility', London must possess speedy routes to and from the town centre as well as bypasses for through traffic. To that end Abercrombie proposed a system of no less than five ring roads, to be linked by ten radial routes. Mercifully, lack of money prevented this scheme being carried out, but as the traffic snarl-ups worsened in the 1950s the planners returned to the attack. By the time that the GLC's development plan was published (1969) they were advocating three ringway systems. True, these roads would cost £2000 million and destroy 30000 homes, but the convenience, the increased traffic flow, the economic benefits – they would be quite something.

The 30000 threatened, and many others, were simply not good enough economists to see it that way, and pressure against the road schemes mounted. When Westway, connecting the Marylebone Road with the White City, opened in 1969, the local residents marched down it to demonstrate their hostility. The implications were not lost on GLC politicians. The Labour majority on the Council, having extolled the benefits of a 'new and efficient system of roads' in 1967 had concluded by 1973 that the whole ringways idea was a 'reckless and irrelevant Tory plan'. In 1976 the scheme was finally abandoned; 'at last we can say "good riddance" to the last of these outdated and destructive roads,' proclaimed the GLC official concerned. Meanwhile, through the relatively simple means of one-way streets and parking restrictions, the average speed of peak-hour traffic in central London had risen from 8 mph in 1959 to 14 mph in 1976.

INNER LONDON IN DECLINE?

As far as inner London as a whole is concerned, it has been the fulfilment rather than the failure of planning strategies that has created the most intractable problems. In 1943 Professor Abercrombie's report recommended reducing inner London's population by a further million; between 1951 and 1976 the number living there decreased by 850000. Abercrombie laid down that industry should leave the centre of town, and since 1960 over a third of the manufacturing jobs there have duly been lost. Yet today's experts do not rejoice at these figures. By 1975–6 inner London, for so long the butt of the rest of the country's envy, actually had an unemployment rate above the national average.

Of course Abercrombie's ambition of removing population and manufacturing from the centre of London has been achieved because it was consistent with trends that had already been long established. We have noted how industry was gravitating to the edge of the City in the sixteenth and seventeenth centuries. As the town expanded it repeatedly overtook old manufacturing centres and established others on the new periphery. In the 1920s and 1930s this process had brought factories to the main routes leading out of London, particularly up the Lea Valley in Hertfordshire and on the west side of town. A jaunt down the Great West Road (the A4) reveals a succession of factories from this period, such as the Gillette, Firestone and Coty buildings. But the most notable example of jazz-age design is the Hoover building (1937) near Perivale station on Western Avenue (the A40).

If factories were gravitating towards the outskirts anyway, was it really wise to reinforce this tendency? Abercrombie belonged to the generation of planners to whom the word 'industry' was synonymous with grime, pollution and squalor, but in fact London's industries – many of them, like furniture-making, printing, light engineering and clothing with traditions stretching back hundreds of years – are not environmentally disastrous. Although the capital has remained the country's greatest manufacturing centre, the scale of operation is still generally small. Of course the convenience of river transport for heavy and bulky materials has attracted large plant to the banks of the Thames, but the oil refineries, sugar refineries, paper factories and the like are mostly well away from the centre of town, where a colossus like Battersea Power Station is very much an exception. Ship-building, which had once flourished

The flight from the centre: GLC boroughs (created 1965)

Population in thousands and percentage change from 1951

INNER LONDON (former LCC area)	1951	1961	1971	1976
Camden	258	246 (−5)	207 (−20)	190 (−26)
Greenwich	236	230 (−3)	218 (−8)	209 (−11)
Hackney	265	258 (−3)	220 (−17)	198 (−25)
Hammersmith	241	222 (−8)	187 (−22)	166 (−31)
Islington	271	261 (−4)	202 (−25)	171 (−37)
Kensington and Chelsea	219	219 (−)	188 (−14)	160 (−27)
Lambeth	347	342 (−2)	308 (−11)	287 (−17)
Lewisham	303	291 (−4)	268 (−12)	241 (−20)
Southwark	338	313 (−7)	262 (−22)	228 (−33)
Tower Hamlets	231	206 (−11)	166 (−28)	146 (−37)
Wandsworth	331	335 (+1)	302 (−9)	283 (−15)
Westminster	300	272 (−9)	240 (−20)	215 (−28)
City of London	5	5	4 (−20)	7 (+40)
	3345	3200 (−4)	2772 (−17)	2501 (−25)
OUTER LONDON				
Barking	189	177 (−6)	161 (−15)	154 (−19)
Barnet	320	318 (−1)	307 (−4)	299 (−7)
Bexley	205	210 (+2)	217 (+6)	215 (+5)
Brent	311	296 (+5)	281 (−10)	258 (−17)
Bromley	268	293 (+9)	305 (+14)	297 (+11)
Croydon	310	324 (+5)	334 (+8)	329 (+6)
Ealing	311	302 (+3)	301 (−3)	298 (−4)
Enfield	288	274 (−5)	268 (−7)	261 (−9)
Haringey	277	259 (−6)	240 (−13)	227 (−18)
Harrow	219	209 (−5)	203 (−7)	201 (−8)
Havering	192	246 (+28)	248 (+29)	238 (+24)
Hillingdon	210	228 (+9)	235 (+12)	230 (+10)
Hounslow	211	209 (−1)	207 (−2)	200 (−5)

Kingston upon Thames	147	146 (−1)	141 (−4)	136 (−7)
Merton	200	189 (−5)	177 (−11)	170 (−15)
Newham	294	265 (−10)	237 (−19)	229 (−22)
Redbridge	257	250 (−3)	240 (−7)	231 (−10)
Richmond upon Thames	188	181 (−4)	175 (−7)	166 (−12)
Sutton	176	169 (−4)	169 (−4)	167 (−5)
Waltham Forest	275	249 (−9)	235 (−15)	223 (−19)
	4848	4794 (−1)	4681 (−4)	4529 (−7)
TOTAL FOR GLC	8193	7994 (−2)	7453 (−9)	7030 (−14)

SOURCE: Office of Population Census and Surveys.

GLC boroughs are larger than the old LCC boroughs, and are not comparable.

in London, withered away in the late nineteenth century.

For years the decline of manufacturing in the capital was offset by the increase in the number of white-collar jobs. From the late nineteenth-century Mayfair houses were being transformed into offices; and the appearance of tower blocks dedicated to business might be seen as the latest stage in the same movement. Yet although services such as banking and insurance, the City's specialities, are flourishing, and government employees steadily multiply, the prestige blocks in the West End are deceptive. From the mid-sixties the number of office jobs in central London began to fall off, for the authorities have encouraged businesses, no less than industry, to move out. But it is odd to see government posters extolling the delights of working in the country when London's unemployment rate is higher than the national figure.

So there is scope for gloom about London's future. The town has been trebly renowned, as a commercial, financial and political capital. Now the port lies far downstream, the Common Market could undermine the City's economic supremacy, and even its political status is threatened by devolution. At least geography still favours London: it is now the point of interchange for air travellers between continents, as once it was a natural capital of sea commerce. But the town's reputation undoubtedly owes more to past glories than to present performance. Perhaps that is partly what makes it such a delightful place in which to live; and perhaps that is why overseas tourists made nearly ten million visits there in 1977.

It would be rash to end on a note of pessimism. Every generation has produced its prophets of London's eclipse, and London has always heaped the debris of its prosperity high on their bones. William Caxton (1422–91), who in many ways exemplified all those qualities of energy, initiative and enterprise which brought such wealth to the City, was not at all sanguine about London's future. A member of the Mercers' Company, he was a successful merchant in the Low Countries, where he studied the new art of printing before returning to set up the first English press at Westminster. In a preface to one of the books which he printed he expressed his love of London, regarding himself as duty-bound to serve the City as 'my mother of whom I have received my nourriture and living. And [I] shall pray for the good prosperity and policy of the same during my life, for as me seemeth it is of great need by cause I have known it in my young age much more wealthy, prosperous and richer than it is at this day. And the cause is that there is almost none that intendeth to the common weal but only every man for his singular profit.' Those words, written nearly 500 years ago, with London on the brink of its golden

age, express sentiments often heard today. May our jere-
miads seem as misconceived at the end of the twenty-fifth
century.

Aeons hence, no doubt, nature will have her way with
the miles of brick, stone and tarmac. At the end of the
nineteenth century the naturalist W. H. Hudson, watching
an old woman collecting twigs in Kensington Gardens,
was inspired to a memorable passage: 'It was as if she had
shown me a vision of some far time, after this London,
after the dust of her people . . . had been blown about by
the winds of many centuries – a vision of old trees growing
again on this desolate spot as in past ages, oak and elm, and
beech and chestnut, the happy green homes of squirrel and
bird and bee.' Hudson gloried in his vision: 'it was very
sweet to see London beautified and made healthy at last!
And I thought, quoting Hafiz, that after a thousand years my
bones would be filled with gladness, and, uprising, dance
upon the sepulchre.' But will there not be legions of other
spirits forlorn and desolate in that arboreal paradise, true
Londoners like Charles Lamb who never imagined, even
under the influence of a purple patch, 'that health, and rest,
and innocent occupation, interchange of converse sweet,
and recreative study, can make the country anything better
than altogether odious and detestable!'

Appendix 1 : The growth of London's population (figures in thousands)

Date	City[1]	Rest of London	Total London	England and Wales	London as percentage of England and Wales	Next largest UK towns		Other large towns	
c. 200	20		20	1000	2	York	20	Rome	800
c. 1100	15	15	15	1500	1	York	9	Constantinople	700
						Lincoln	4	Cordoba	100
						Oxford	4		
						Norwich	4		
c. 1400	45	?[2]	45	2250	2	York	11	Venice	100
						Bristol	9	Milan	100
						Norwich	7	Naples	100
						Plymouth	7	Paris	80
						Coventry	7	Florence	60

c. 1500	75	?²	3000	2·5	York	20	Naples	230
					Norwich	15	Venice	150
					Bristol	15	Paris	100
							Milan	100
							Lisbon	100
c. 1600	186	·34	4500	5	Edinburgh	35	Naples	300
					Norwich	20	Paris	200
					York	20	Milan	200
							Venice	150
							Amsterdam	100
c. 1700	208	367	6000	9·6	Edinburgh	80	Paris	500
					Bristol	30	Tokyo	500
					Norwich	29	Naples	320
							Amsterdam	150
							Rome	150

Date	City[1] London	Rest of London	Total London	England and Wales	London as percentage of England and Wales	Next largest UK towns	Other large towns
1801	128	831[3]	959[3] (1117)[4]	8890	10·8 (12·6)	Edinburgh 83 · Liverpool 82 · Manchester 75 · Birmingham 71	Tokyo 800 · Constantinople 600 · Paris 547 · Naples 427 · Shanghai 300
1851	128	2235[3]	2363[3] (2685)[4]	17983	13·1 (14·9)	Liverpool 376 · Glasgow 357 · Manchester 338 · Birmingham 233	Tokyo 1200 · Paris 1053 · New York 696 · St Petersburg 485 · Naples 449 · Vienna 444
1901	27	4398[3]	4425[3] (6586)[4]	32612	13·6 (20·2)	Glasgow 776 · Liverpool 704 · Manchester 645 · Birmingham 523	New York 3437 · Paris 2714 · Berlin 1889 · Chicago 1699 · Vienna 1675 · Tokyo 1600

1951	5	8188[4]	8193[4]	43758	18·7	Birmingham	1113	New York	7900
						Glasgow	1090	Tokyo	5425
						Liverpool	789	Shanghai	5500
						Manchester	703	Moscow	4700
								Chicago	3630
								Paris	2810
1976	7	7020[4]	7027[4]	49184	14·3	Birmingham	1062	Shanghai	10820 (1970)
						Glasgow	856	Tokyo	8640 (1975)
						Leeds	744	Mexico	8592 (1975)
						Sheffield	555	New York	7647 (1973)
						Liverpool	542	Peking	7570 (1970)
						Manchester	496	Rome	2868 (1975)
								Paris	2290 (1975)

SOURCES: R. Mols, *Introduction à la démographie historique des villes d'Europe du xiv au xviii siècle* (1954–6)

R. R. Palmer, *Atlas of World History* (1957)

B. R. Mitchell, *European Historical Statistics 1750–1970* (1975)

B. R. Mitchell and P. Deane, *Abstract of British Historical Statistics* (1962)

Demographic Yearbook 1976 (UN, 1976)

The figures given in this table should be treated with caution. There are no reliable population statistics for periods before the nineteenth century. The most that can be said for the estimates presented here is that they are the guesses of distinguished scholars. But it would be easy to find very different figures in the work of equally distinguished scholars – for example, 45 000 for the population of Roman London. And some scholars are so distinguished that they refuse to guess at all.

The first census in England was in 1801. Thereafter the problem is only one of definition: exactly what constituted 'London' at any particular time? The footnotes define the relevant limits. Where possible, figures for other towns refer to areas that are comparable to the contemporary London definition.

[1] Includes whole area within the bars established 1222.

[2] There was certainly some population beyond the bars at this time – royal officials and servants, the monks at Westminster, the lawyers in the Inns, the bishops' households in their palaces along the river – but the total cannot have been great.

[3] Area of LCC (established 1889). See map on page 296 and population table on pages 258–9 for individual boroughs.

[4] Area of GLC (established 1965). See map on page 296 and population table on pages 326–7 for individual boroughs.

Appendix 2 : Some notable surviving works

Asterisks indicate that the original buildings have been mainly or wholly replaced. Italicized figures refer to pages in this book.

NORMANS (1066–1154)

William I (1066–87)	The White Tower (1077–97), *74*
William II (1087–110)	Westminster Hall (1907–9)*, *101*
	St Mary-le-Bow crypt, *90*
Henry I (1100–35)	St Bartholomew the Great (from 1123), *94*
Stephen (1135–54)	Crypt of St John's Priory, Clerkenwell (*c.* 1140–80), *97–8*

ANGEVINS, or PLANTAGENETS (1154–1399)

Henry II (1154–89)	Temple Church (1160–85 and later), *97–8*
Richard I (1189–99)	Longchamp's Tower defences (1191)*, *78*
John (1199–1216)	St Helen's Bishopsgate (1205–15), *92*
Henry III (1216–72)	Further Tower defences (from 1240), *109*
	Chancel, transepts and part of nave of Westminster Abbey (1245–69), *102*
	Chancel and north transept of Southwark Cathedral (late thirteenth century), *94*

Edward I (1272–1307)	Further Tower defences, *111*
Edward II (1307–27)	
Edward III (1327–77)	Jewel Tower, Westminster (1364–6)
	Charterhouse founded (1371), *91*
Richard II (1377–99)	Continuation of Westminster Abbey nave (from 1375), *102*
	Hammerbeam roof of Westminster Hall (1394–1401), *115*
	St Ethelburga, Bishopsgate, *90*

LANCASTRIANS (1399–1461)

Henry IV (1399–1413)	The Guildhall (1411–39), *121–2*
Henry V (1413–22)	
Henry VI (1422–61)	Lollards Tower, Lambeth Palace (1435)

YORKISTS (1461–1485)

Edward IV (1461–83)	Crosby Hall (1460–70), *130*
	City Wall rebuilt (1476–7)★
Edward V (1483)	
Richard III (1483–5)	

TUDORS (1485–1603)

Henry VII (1485–1509)	Old Hall, Lincoln's Inn (1490–2)
	Lambeth Palace gatehouse (1495)
	Chapel in Westminster Abbey (1503–12), *102*
	St Margaret Westminster (1504–23), *13*
	Gatehouse of St John's Priory, Clerkenwell (1504), *97*
Henry VIII (1509–47)	Lincoln's Inn gatehouse (1518)
	St Peter ad Vincula in the Tower (1520), *15*

James II (1685–8)   Royal Hospital, Chelsea (1682–9), *210*
William III and Mary II   Kensington Palace (1689–95), *204*
  (1689–1702)   Kensington Square (*c.* 1700), *204*
Anne (1702–14)   1 and 2 Laurence Pountney Hill
        (1703), *199*
        Queen Anne's Gate (1704)
        St John's Smith Square (1713–14),
        229

HANOVERIANS (1714: to present; called Windsors after 1917)

George I (1714–27)   The Hawksmoor churches (1711–31),
        229
        Hanover Square (from 1715)★, *220*
        Cavendish Square (from 1717)★
        Burlington House (1717–20), *214–15*
        St Martin-in-the-Fields (1722–6), *229*
        Grosvenor Square (from 1725)★, *217*
George II (1727–60)   St Bartholomew's Hospital (from
        1730)
        Berkeley Square (from 1738)★, *221*
        Mansion House (1739–53), *200*
        Horse Guards (1750–60), *215*
        Marylebone Road, Euston Road
        (1756–7), *221*
        Spencer House (1756–60), *215*
George III (1760–1820;   Portman Square (from 1761)★, *221*
  Prince Regent after   Bedford Square (from 1775), *222*
  1811)   Portland Place (from 1775)★, *216*
        Somerset House (from 1776), *215*
        Bank of England (from 1788)★,
        248–9
        Fitzroy Square (from *c.* 1790), *216*
        Baker Street (from *c.* 1790)
        Russell Square (from 1800), *253*
        The Docks (the first opened 1802),
        237
        Dulwich Art Gallery (1811–14), *249*

	Lines (1900–5), *302*
	Harrods (1901–5), *286*
	Kingsway (opened 1905), *295*
	Ritz Hotel (1906)
	Selfridges (1908), *286*
George V (1910–35)	Admiralty Arch (1911)
	Australia House (1912–18)
	East front of Buckingham Palace remodelled (1913), *247–8*
	London University Senate House (from 1932), *268*
Edward VIII (1936)	
George VI (1936–52)	Hoover Building, Perivale (1937), *325*
	Royal Festival Hall (1951), *314*
Elizabeth II (1952–)	New Zealand House (1960–3), *319*
	Hilton Hotel (1961–3), *317*
	Vickers Building (1963), *320*
	Centre Point (1963–7), *317*
	Barbican (from 1963), *312*
	Economist Building (1964), *320*
	GPO Tower (1965), *320*
	World Trade Centre, St Katherine's Dock (1965), *240*
	Knightsbridge Barracks (1967–70), *317*
	Space House off Kingsway (1968), *319*
	Commercial Union building (1968–9), *320*
	Victoria Line (opened 1969), *302*
	Lillington Gardens Housing Estate (from 1968), *317*
	Heart of Oak House (1970), *320*
	National Theatre (opened 1976), *314*
	National Westminster Tower (under construction 1977), *319*

Select bibliography

The literature on London's history is vast, as anyone may verify by visiting the Reading Room of the Guildhall Library in the City. The following list simply comprehends books from which so much material has been drawn that it would be ungracious not to acknowledge the debt.

Baker, T. *Medieval London*. Cassell, 1970

Barker, T. C. and Robbins, M. *A History of London Transport*. 2 vols, Allen & Unwin, 1963 and 1974

Bebbington, G. *London Street Names*. Batsford, 1972

Bell, W. G. *The Great Fire of London in 1666*. Lane, 1951

——. *The Great Plague in London in 1665*. Bodley, 1951

Bird, R. *The Turbulent London of Richard II*. Longmans Green, 1951

Booker, C. and Green, C. Lycett. *Goodbye London*. Fontana, 1973

Brett-James, N. *The Growth of Stuart London*. Allen & Unwin, 1935

Brooke, C. and Keir, G. *London 800–1216: The Shaping of a City*. Secker & Warburg, 1975

Clayton, R. ed. *The Geography of Greater London*. George Philip & Son, 1964

Cobb, G. *London City Churches*. Batsford, 1977

Davis, T. *John Nash*. David & Charles, 1973

Fitzgibbon, C. *The Blitz*. Macdonald, 1970

George, D. *London Life in the Eighteenth Century*. Penguin, 1966

Jackson, A. A. *Semi-detached London*. Allen & Unwin, 1973

Jenkins, S. *Landlords to London*. Constable, 1975

Kent, W. ed. *An Encyclopedia of London*. Dent, 1970

Marriott, O. *The Property Boom*. Pan, 1967

Merrifield, R. *The Roman City of London*. Ernest Benn, 1965

——. *Roman London*. Cassell, 1969

Mitchell, R. J. and Leys, M. D. A. *A History of London Life.* Longmans Green, 1958

Olsen, D. J. *The Growth of Victorian London.* Batsford, 1976

Pevsner, N. *The Buildings of England: London I and London II.* Penguin, 1973 and 1952

Piper, D. *The Companion Guide to London.* Collins, 1974

Reddaway, R. F. *The Rebuilding of London After the Great Fire.* Cape, 1940

Roth, C. *A History of the Jews in England.* Oxford, 1941.

Rude, G. *Hanoverian London 1714–1808.* Secker & Warburg, 1971

Seaman, L. C. B. *Life in Victorian London.* Batsford, 1973

Sheppard, F. *London 1808–1870: The Infernal Wen.* Secker & Warburg, 1971

Stenton, F. M. *Norman London.* Historical Association, 1934

Summerson, J. *Georgian London.* Barrie and Jenkins, 1962

Thrupp. S. L. *The Merchant Class of Medieval London.* Chicago, 1948

Tout, T. F. *Beginnings of a Modern Capital: London and Westminster in the Fourteenth Century.* Proceedings of the British Academy, vol. xi, 1933

Unwin, G. *The Gilds and Companies of London,* Methuen, 1908.

Wheeler, R. E. M. *London and the Saxons.* London Museum Catalogue No. 6, 1935

——. *London and the Vikings.* London Museum Catalogue No. 1, 1927

Whinney, M. *Wren.* Thames & Hudson, 1971

Wilcox, D. London: *The Heartless City.* Thames Television, 1977

Williams, G. A. *Medieval London: From Commune to Capital.* Athlone Press, 1963

Index